Mao Zedong and China IN THE
TWENTIETH-CENTURY WORLD

D1384213

Asia-Pacific: Culture, Politics, and Society

EDITORS: Rey Chow, Michael Dutton, H. D. Harootunian, and Rosalind Morris

Mao Zedong and China IN THE
TWENTIETH-CENTURY WORLD

A
Concise
History

Rebecca E. Karl

DUKE UNIVERSITY PRESS   DURHAM AND LONDON   2010

© 2010 Duke University Press

All rights reserved

Printed in the United States of America on acid-free paper ♾

Designed by Heather Hensley

Typeset in Warnock Pro by Keystone Typesetting, Inc.

Library of Congress Cataloging-in-Publication Data appear
on the last printed page of this book.

TO MY NEPHEW, CHRISTOPHER,

AND MY NIECES, TEPI, CHANNA, SOPHIA, AND NORA:

with love and in hope.

Contents

Preface and Acknowledgements

Say "Mao Zedong" in China or among China scholars anywhere and there is a ready-made argument. The disputes over Jung Chang's and Jon Halliday's recently published *Mao: The Unknown Story* provide just one example. According to many reviewers of that book, the story therein told is unknown because Chang and Halliday substantially fabricated or exaggerated it into existence. According to others, Chang and Halliday have finally exposed Mao in all his naked cruelty to a hitherto credulous world. Whichever side one takes—and there are more than these two alone—the polemic gets polarized, the rhetoric heated, and the arguments intolerant. In China, it is even worse. Attempts to reassess portions of the Mao period—particularly by taking the Cultural Revolution (1966–76) seriously—bring accusations of desires to bring Maoism back to life, of wishing to negate the post-Mao Dengist reforms and return the country to poverty and global irrelevance, and of being anti-Chinese.

As Mao Zedong and his legacy for China are fought over by scholars and laypeople alike, certain parts of Maoism are now detached from their revolutionary meaning and historical context and reborn as fundamentalist capitalist tenets. Business schools routinely teach about "guerilla marketing," a strategy supposedly derived from Mao's theorization of "protracted war." Mao as kitsch and commodity floods the consumer market, available on eBay or at any roadside stand in Chinese tourist spots. As the scholar Michael Dutton wrote of this phenomenon in 1998, "Mao sells, but what he sells today is the very new idea of everything being for sale" (*Streetlife China*).

The current text joins the scholarly fray implicitly and becomes yet another commodity on the market, yet it engages neither the academic nor the market realm explicitly. But, it engages both implicitly. In the case of the scholarly fray, what can be said of the current effort is that the book takes Mao Zedong and his era—in Chinese and in global terms—quite seriously. It takes socialism in China and the world as integral to the history of the twentieth century. It construes Mao and Maoism as central to the history of Chinese and global socialism, as well as central to the history of revolution and modernity in the last century. Even this mildest of approaches to the subject lands the text in fraught politics. Some would like to understand those politics in terms of *today's* uncompromising opposition between "freedom" and "tyranny." In the absurd "good vs. evil" passing for political analysis in some quarters these days, taking Mao and socialism seriously puts one, by taint of conflated ideological association, on the side of "evil" and "tyranny." This text, then, could be taken as an extended argument against such simplistic reductions.

As for the book as a commodity, the market will decide. I have written the text as accessibly as possible without sacrificing complexity. While Mao's life is the chronological frame of the narrative, twentieth-century Chinese and world history are what makes Mao possible. Discussing Mao without Chinese and world history is quite impossible, just as discussing modern Chinese history without Mao is also quite impossible. The book makes every effort to make Mao and China reflect on one another in complex ways.

This text attempts to reattach Mao to a historical moment of crisis demanding critique and action. It tries to understand how, out of the multiple catastrophes of the early twentieth century (Chinese and global), Mao dared to propose and activate a revolutionary project calling every convention into question so as to remake the world. Recalling Mao's challenge is to recall a time when many things seemed possible; it is to remember possibility against the pressure to concede to the world as it now appears. In this sense, I am less concerned in the text about whether Mao individually wrote or thought all the things attributed to him and more concerned with Mao as a figure in Chinese and global history: as a maker of revolution. This is not a biography but rather a history on the model of Georg Lukács's consideration of Lenin in the 1920s.

For many of the formulations and approaches in this book, I am grateful to two sets of intrepid and intelligent undergraduate students at New York University: those in my inaugural "Mao and the Chinese Revolution" class of Fall 2005, assisted by the PHD student and tireless graduate labor organizer (GSOC), Maggie Clinton; and those of the Fall 2006 version of that course, ably assisted by the PHD students Feng Miao and He Xiang. In Fall 2005, in addition to learning about Mao, students were forced to confront politics in their everyday lives, as we faced the stand-off between the graduate student union and the NYU administration. It was a marvelous lesson in politics in action, although also a dispiriting lesson about strong-arm domination in reality.

The students in these two classes allowed me—with significant challenge —to introduce Mao and his revolutionary philosophy in terms a politically engaged, yet slightly confused, younger generation might understand. They allowed me to discuss Mao in ways relevant to today's world, without conflating today's problems with Mao's. Most important, they permitted me to engage them in a theoretical and historical sophistication sufficient to forestall simplistic reductions. Together, we strove to restore complexity and philosophy to historical inquiry and contemporary critique. The most industrious of these students—Eliot Ayer, Jessica Perlman, Margaret Hsu, Andrew Ongchin, Max Kubicki, Mark McConaghy, Sylwia Weiwora, Andrew Samuel, Riazul Islam, Kaitlin Collins, Megan Smith, and Destin Hodges, among others—learned to grapple with the philosophical problems of revolutionary thought and practice, while working through the politics and historical problems Mao faced as a committed Marxist revolutionary and a Chinese living in the twentieth-century world. They demonstrated great ability to resist the conflation of the past with the present, while also recognizing how the past can potentially exist in the present as a principle of historical transformation. In this, they proved both wise and adept. I am grateful to them for taking me seriously and allowing me to learn from their questions and confusions.

One motivation for writing this book was personal. It is dedicated to my nephew, Christopher, and my nieces, Tepi, Channa, Sophia, and Nora, who face so many challenges, in part as legacies of the historical moment discussed here. The world they and their generation will inherit is much poorer for what has been called the project of *disutopia*, which is "not just the temporary absence of Utopia, but the political celebration of the end of social dreams."(Žižek, *Repeating Lenin*, 9). This book introduces a historical moment, when fundamental global transformation could be thought. It is a moment I admire. Yet, I harbor no illusion that the specific projects toward which Mao Zedong worked are appropriate or even sufficient for today or for his world. I am optimistic, though, something of his philosophy, passion, and historical method can be retrieved for a rethinking of our present.

I also want to thank others, without whom this would have been a less enjoyable project. Deborah Karl gave me good advice; after all these years, I should just learn to listen to her. I am grateful to my initial readers, on whom I relied to tell me what required elaboration and what was *just too much*. Joanne Filley read with humor and sympathy the early chapters. F. David Bell read the entire text with a critical and knowing eye toward my tendency to excess. My mother, Dolores Karl, removed many writing infelicities, while also reading carefully for coherence and accessibility. However much I've depended on them, everyone mentioned above and below is absolved of responsibility for what remains.

Several of my graduate students and colleagues assisted in crucial ways. He Xiang taught me what I know of Mao's poetic practice. Zhu Qian traveled with me to China in May 2007, recorded the interviews there, and transcribed them for me. Her good humor, intelligence, and enthusiasm for food made the trip a joy and a learning experience. I thank Harry and Kristin for their house and the isolation I needed to finish writing. And I am grateful to Maggie Clinton for finding books in China for me; sharing my monastic retreat; and enduring weird cats and bold mice as I worked through the final chapters.

I want to express gratitude to Professor Wang Hui at Tsinghua University for sharing his time and insight with me; to Sabu Kohso in New York for years of political camaraderie, and wonderful perspicacity on things near and far; and to Wu Hongsen, the best friend a person can have. I am deeply sorry that Mr. Wang Yuanhua, one of the most extraordinary people I have had the good fortune to know, died before this book could be published. While he would never have agreed with me on many things in it, we would have enjoyed a good-natured argument about them, followed by lunch and great conversation about a number of other things. His passing truly marks the passing of an era. I will miss him and his energy.

Finally, thanks to my editor, Reynolds Smith, who got this book peer-reviewed and into production quickly. To the readers, particularly Wang Ban, I am grateful for the suggestions and encouragement. And to those at Duke University Press involved in the production of the book, especially Mark Mastromarino, I am grateful for the hard work and creative energy invested.

1 China in the World in Mao's Youth

Mao Zedong was born on December 26, 1893, in China's south-central Hunan Province, in a small village called Shaoshan. Located in a fertile rice-growing valley at the foot of Mount Hengshan, the village is about eighty-one miles southwest from the provincial capital, Changsha. Although Mao's birthplace was a quiet rural backwater, the political and social situation in China at the beginning of the twentieth century was becoming increasingly fraught.

Free Trade, Opium, Tea, and Silver

At the time of Mao's birth, China was ruled by its last imperial dynasty, the Qing. The Manchus who founded the Qing had swept into China in the seventeenth century from their base in Manchuria to overrun the native Han-Chinese Ming Dynasty. Initially a robust dynasty, the Qing had entered a long decline by the early 1800s as the empire was repeatedly assaulted by aggressive foreign powers (led by the British) who were attempting to force China into free trade agreements the Qing resisted.

The assault on China's territorial integrity and political sovereignty began in the mid-nineteenth century with the infamous Opium Wars. These conflicts were fought between China and Britain, primarily. Trade between those two countries had thrived in the eighteenth century. By the early nineteenth century, however, the British could find nothing that the Chinese wished to purchase from them in large enough quantities to offset the increasing British demand for Chinese tea. With the South American wars of independence against Spain closing the silver mines and provoking a global silver crisis, the British were desperate to find an alternative mode of payment for their burgeoning tea-drinking habit. They hit upon opium. Highly addictive and easily grown by the British in their newly secured nearby Indian colonies, opium began to be imported to China by British merchants in great quantities as a substitute for silver. The Dao Guang Emperor attempted to enforce a ban on the opium trade as the drug devastation spread like wildfire through his empire. Queen Victoria, incensed at the trampling of British trade prerogatives, declared war against the Qing to enforce Britain's right to "free trade."

The Chinese were no match for the powerful British navy, which decimated their coastal forts. The Qing armies had never encountered the technology possessed by the British troops. They suffered one defeat after another. Finally, in 1842, the Chinese were forced to sign a humiliating settlement, known as the Treaty of Nanjing. The treaty was weighted entirely in favor of the British. One key concession was "extraterritoriality," which meant that British citizens on Chinese soil would be subjected to British, not Chinese, law. In addition, trade would no longer be restricted by Qing imperial custom. Five ports were opened for foreign trade—Canton, Shanghai, Fuzhou, Ningbo, and Xiamen (Amoy)—while Hong Kong was ceded to the British as a foothold on the Chinese coast. In subsequent decades, with the strengthening of the British colonial grip in India and Southeast Asia, the volume of opium grown increased quickly and imports of opium more than doubled.

Most destructively, the Nanjing Treaty established the principle of "most favored nation." This clause provided that any commercial or other rights wrested from the Chinese by other countries would automatically be granted to Britain. Two years later, the Qing was forced at gunpoint to sign new treaties with France and the United States; these were followed by treaties with Prussia, Italy, Russia, and other European nations. This marks the beginning of what the Chinese later would call the "century of humiliation," a century Mao is credited with ending by the founding of a strong and sovereign China in 1949.

A Crumbling Society and Defeat by Japan

The fallout from the Opium Wars played a crucial part in the decline of the imperial grip on China, which for centuries had been administered through a thinly spread network of well-educated bureaucrats. As the authority of the central government weakened, the sway of local power holders increased. A series of huge mid-century peasant rebellions—in part set off because of the Opium War disruptions—then forced the emperor to cede even more power to local officials, so that they could defeat the uprisings in their midst. The most famous of these uprisings—the Taipings—lasted for fourteen long years, before the Qing state could muster the force finally to suppress it.

Meanwhile, the spread of European and American commercial and religious settlements, initially restricted to the coastal areas, had reached, by Mao's childhood in the 1890s, the hinterlands of Hunan and beyond. The presence of foreigners, with their capitalist and Christian priorities, was insidiously destructive of the established order. Peasant handicraft production was squeezed; railroads were built where no transport systems had existed, thus rerouting familiar trade patterns; and missionary stations were set up with educational and hospital facilities that often created violent tension with local populations, whose suspicions about alien practices were often fueled by the contempt in which missionaries held local "heathen" society.

China's weakness attracted the predatory attention of the rising Japanese —a people who long had been regarded by the Chinese as the "dwarves of the East," or as pesky pirates operating lawlessly near China's coasts. China was completely demoralized when the Japanese convincingly defeated their forces in a dispute over the Korean monarchy. In the process, Japan destroyed the Qing government's new navy, which was supposed to be the strongest fleet in Asia and which had been built under the supervision of French and British naval assistants. The 1895 treaty—signed at Shimoneseki—ended the short war. China was forced to cede Taiwan to Japan; to provide huge indemnity payments to Japan; and to grant Japan manufacturing rights in China's open ports.

After China's defeat at the hands of the Japanese, the Qing dynasty entered its final death throes. Failure to confront these previously weak neighbors made the educated and commercial classes of China seriously question the dynastic state's ability to safeguard China from outside assault. An attempt made in 1898 by educated elites to force the dynasty to reform its practices failed miserably. These two failures, combined with far-reaching social trouble brewing within China, led to a serious weakening of the state.

The special privileges enjoyed by colonial foreigners (British, French, Germans, Americans, and after 1895, Japanese) and native holders of local power soon provoked endemic rural violence, culminating in the Boxer Rebellion of 1899–1901. This uprising was initiated by members of a secret Chinese martial arts group known as the "Righteous Harmonious Fists" or, as many non-Chinese called them, the "Boxers." Targeted initially at missionaries and their native converts, whose presence was deemed disruptive of local social order, the Boxer rebellion soon grew into an all-purpose anti-foreign and anti-Christian uprising. The rebels seized Beijing, executing scores of foreigners and thousands of Chinese Christian converts. The Qing joined the rebels, in a bid to regain some popular credibility. This triggered an invasion by a combined force of eight foreign nations, which in its turn massacred any Chinese suspected of sympathizing with the Boxers. The Qing court abandoned the capital, and Beijing became a bloodbath. In the ensuing punitive settlement forced upon the Qing by the allied powers (led by Britain, the United States, Prussia, and Japan), the dynasty staved off final demise, but only by effectively giving away the country to its foreign creditors.

Through the turbulent years at the beginning of the twentieth century, many rival contenders to state power emerged. Hunan Province, Mao's home region, was a hotbed of all kinds of anti-dynastic activity. However, it took some time for Mao to become aware of what was happening around him.

Mao at home in Hunan

Mao's parents had seven children (five sons and two daughters) but only three survived, all boys. Mao Zedong was the eldest; Zemin, the middle brother, and Zetan, the youngest, soon followed. All three brothers remained close through childhood. Growing up on his father's farm, in a spacious courtyard house surrounded by hills, terraced paddy fields, and ponds, Mao enjoyed the extraordinary luxury of having his own bedroom, even after his brothers were born. He worked on his father's farm from the age of six, and even when he began to attend the village school, and later a nearby higher primary school, he continued to work in the early mornings and evenings. His experience as a working peasant was limited to this childhood period, even though he later vividly recalled carrying buckets of manure from collection pits to the paddy fields for fertilizer.

Mao's father, Mao Rensheng, was a relatively wealthy but poorly educated peasant. Mao remembered him as authoritarian and unpleasant, and unsympathetic to his son's desire for a good education. According to Edgar Snow, who based his biography of Mao on interviews with him in the late 1930s, Mao attributed his father's disposition to his stint in the Qing dynasty's army.[1] After leaving the army, he became highly preoccupied with accumulating wealth. Through dint of luck, labor, and parsimony, by 1893 he had become one of the richest of the 300 families of Mao's natal village, Shaoshan. He owned about 2.5 acres of land—later acquiring another acre or so—which produced around 133 pounds of rice, of which about two-thirds was consumed by the family, leaving one-third as surplus for the market. With two hired laborers to assist on the farm, Mao's father soon began a grain transport and selling business, and set himself up as a middleman for urban markets. The middleman merchant was a feature of the rural areas, and would later be defined by the Marxist Mao as "parasitic," and thus a target for revolutionary overthrow.

In contrast to his near-contempt for his father, Mao loved and revered his mother, née Wen Qimei. A hardworking woman who died young (at the age of fifty-three), she was reputedly selfless in her sacrifice for her sons and family. Born just beyond the mountains from Shaoshan, she and her husband actually spoke different dialects of Chinese; nevertheless, family discussions, in which she participated fully, were reputedly always vigorous and spirited. Mao's emotionally charged funeral oration for her, delivered on October 8, 1919, highlighted his mother's steadfastness, her adherence to the traditional virtues, her cleanliness and sense of order, her charity, and most important, her hatred for injustice of any sort. Indeed, Mao credited his mother for being adept at analysis, a skill that she used in supporting his side in his stormy relationship with his father.[2] A devout Buddhist, his mother clearly imparted to Mao a distinctive ethical stance. This was not a reverence for religion, which Mao eventually labeled as "superstition" and pledged to stamp out; rather, it was a desire to correct the problems of his world through action. His mother's love and affection were a touchstone for Mao throughout his life.

Mao's early education at the local school was presided over by an old-style scholar, whose interest in world and dynastic affairs was apparently minimal and whose mode of teaching relied on the age-old method of rote memorization of the Confucian classics. In an oft-told story, Mao narrates that after a particularly harsh lesson, he ran away from school and home. His worried family found him only after he had wandered alone without food for three days. Upon his return home, Mao claims, his father's disposition towards him moderated, at least temporarily, as did the teacher's. According to Mao, in a clearly apocryphal attachment of significance to a childhood prank, this episode indelibly taught him the value and utility of rebellion.[3]

As the eldest son and only literate one in the family, Mao was soon put to work at bookkeeping for his father's business, a task that required writing ability as well as facility with an abacus. By this point, the business included not only farming activities and grain transport, but also the mortgages that Mao's father had bought on other people's land, part of the usurious rural credit and petty landlord system that Mao later learned to despise. It is during this period the disciplinarian side of his father flourished, and confrontations over Mao's continued education became endemic. Mao recalls that for these several years he was often beaten as well as deprived of meat and eggs in his diet. In subsequent years—after learning the Marxist analytical method—Mao often referred to his father as "the Ruling Power" that he, his mother, and assorted laborers always tried to overthrow in an ever-shifting dialectic of family relations.

Meanwhile, at school, Mao had become acquainted with the Confucian texts, which he found dry and boring. He nevertheless learned to cite them from memory, sometimes hurling Confucian sayings at his father during their arguments. He soon became attracted to the old novels of China, including the popular stories of rebellion, knights-errant, mythology, and romance. His lifelong love of books, and in particular of classical tales and legends, clearly stemmed from his voracious reading as a youngster. In his subsequent theoretical, philosophical, and historical writings, Mao never ceased to illustrate his political and social lessons with the folksy and earthy color derived from these popular yarns.

It was only after leaving the stifling atmosphere of the traditional-style school that Mao seems to have discovered the roiling debates over dynastic and republican politics then animating the urban scene all over China. He began reading political articles published in journals smuggled in from the coast. These primarily featured members of a reformist monarchical faction, led by Liang Qichao and Kang Youwei, and a revolutionary republican faction, led by Sun Yatsen, all of whom were exiles in Japan. In addition to these factions based abroad, there were various conservative defenders of the dynasty, as well as local activists, who advocated regional autonomy in China, with calls for Hunanese independence leading the way. Mao subsequently commented that he found all these issues very exciting—except for the dynastic defense—but that he couldn't tell any of them apart at the time.

Right before the fall of the Qing dynasty in late 1911, the social and political situations became even more chaotic. Famines were endemic, in part stemming from poor weather but also in part because merchants like Mao's father shipped rice from rural areas into the cities for enormous profit. Peasants rebelled in frustration and were ruthlessly suppressed by local forces of order. These local rebellions, in Mao's later recounting, were of great significance to the development of his political consciousness: he particularly remembered having to pass the severed heads of executed rebels stuck on top of stakes in public places that served as a warning to would-be troublemakers. And yet, he was not a wholehearted sympathizer of the peasants: while he condemned people like his father for their rapaciousness, he did not support violent seizures of other people's property.

Mao leaves home

In 1909, at the age of sixteen, Mao convinced his father to pay for him to go to the district city of Xiangtan, a busy trading center on the Xiang River around twenty-five miles away from Shaoshan. There he enrolled in a new-style school, whose curriculum was not defined by the Confucian classics, but rather included natural sciences and what was called at the time "Western learning." One of the teachers had even studied in Japan and had completely different ideas about learning from those of the old-style Confucianists. In this context Mao was more systematically introduced to the anti-dynastic thought of the time. He was also exposed to a worldly milieu, in which China was conceived as part of the larger global historical moment, which included the contemporary situations of Japan and Russia after Japan's surprise victory in the Russo-Japanese War of 1904–5; the colonizations of neighboring countries such as Vietnam (French), Korea (Japanese), Burma (British), and the Philippines (American); as well as knowledge of the American and French Revolutions. He also encountered the biographies of past European and American political and intellectual leaders, such as Napoleon, Catherine the Great, Peter the Great, Rousseau, Montesquieu, and Lincoln, even as he continued to be fascinated by the rebels and heroes of Chinese history.

On the eve of the establishment of the Republic in 1912, nothing in Mao's thought or action indicated the revolutionary he was to become. His politics—vague, at best—were mostly informed by his personal opposition to his father rather than by any intellectual analysis of China's ills. By the same token, his readings in classics had not attracted him to the ideal of a Confucian gentleman as a personal or social role model. And, while his interest in the anti-dynastic and anti-Confucian debates of the time, as well as his spotty introduction to Western thought, had given him an inchoate sense of socio-political excitement, none of this had developed into any sort of firm ideology. In this sense, contrary to what some interpreters have claimed, Mao's early views did not indicate the political theorist that he was later to become.

In other ways, Mao changed little. His personal habits were ingrained early and never faded, no matter how high and mighty he later became. He was contemptuous of flush toilets and toothbrushes (washing his mouth with tea leaves), and he habitually burped and broke wind loudly. He always wore shabby, patched clothes, with complete disregard for outward appearance. Mao held on to his rural habits throughout his life, often regarding his more cosmopolitan and "modern" associates with suspicion and disdain. Some time after he left the close provincial community of his childhood, he came to articulate his rural personal habits as an expression of political purity.

2 From Liberal to Communist, 1912–1921

The 1911 Revolution and Aftermath

Just a few months before the October revolution that overthrew the Qing dynasty, Mao moved from Xiangtan to Hunan's provincial capital, Changsha. He was one of the first in his school to support the revolution by cutting the long tail of hair—the queue—that all boys and men wore. For 260 years, this had been an enforced sartorial symbol of fealty to the Manchu Qing; removing it was subject to the death penalty. When the 1911 ("xinhai") revolution broke out, Mao joined the local revolutionary army and served as a soldier in Hunan, although he saw no action. With the first salary of his life, he paid others to haul water for him (probably because he had endured enough hauling of buckets on his father's farm), bought food, and used the remaining money to purchase a variety of journals and newspapers. Through this new practice of daily newspaper reading, Mao avidly followed the fortunes of the revolutionary armies around the country. He later claimed that it was also at this time that he first encountered the concept of "socialism," although if so, it did not leave any immediate impression.

A few months of soldiering was plenty at this point for Mao. Believing the revolution to have been successfully completed after the emperor's abdication in February 1912 and the ascension to power of General Yuan Shikai, Mao went back to school to broaden his education. It took him several tries to find an appropriate venue. A short stint at a vocational school for soap making was followed by several other ill-fated educational attempts—a commercial school whose curriculum was in English and thus inaccessible to Mao; a law school whose regulations were objectionable; and so on—and then a period of self-study at the recently established Hunan Provincial Library. There Mao first read Adam Smith's *Wealth of Nations*, Charles Darwin's *On the Origin of Species*, and Herbert Spencer's *Principles of Sociology*, among other translated books of European philosophy. He also consulted the first world maps he'd ever seen and made a systematic study of ancient Greece, and the modern histories of England, Russia, the United States, and France.

By 1913 Mao found his educational home. He entered the Fourth Provincial Normal School—soon merged with and renamed the First Provincial Normal School—a teacher training institution at the secondary level, from which he graduated in 1918. "First Normal" had a profound influence on Mao's subsequent intellectual and political formation. Indeed, the New People's Study Society, a student organization that Mao led, produced many future members of the Chinese Communist Party: friendships formed here thus were of crucial personal and political significance. It was at First Normal that Mao began his formal guided study of Western philosophy, of politics and society, and of China's place in the twentieth-century world. Not yet exposed to Marxism, Mao became an idealist liberal, convinced that if individuals cultivated themselves, an unjust and imperfectly governed society could be transformed into an ideal political community presided over by intelligent and upright leaders.

There were several teachers at First Normal who left an indelible impression upon Mao—but this was not always positive. The most negative impression was ingrained by the school's four physical education teachers. Physical education had only recently become incorporated into schools in China. In the long history of China's scholarly tradition, aesthetic refinement and mental activity were always posed as the polar opposites to physical strength and manual labor. Physical exertion, from this point of view, was inappropriate to the scholar and contrary to the proper cultivation of the mind. The physical ideal of a learned man included extreme pallor, lack of musculature, long pinkie nails, flowing gowns that impeded movement, languid activity. For refined, elite women, the ideal was even more extreme, including as it did, alabaster-white skin, three-inch bound feet, corpulence, and no activity except embroidery and weaving.

By the early twentieth century, ideas about the relationship between mental and manual exercise began changing; they were now seen as mutually reinforcing rather than mutually opposed. Ideas about the status of women in the family and society were also in flux: the ideal of the dependent, illiterate woman, skilled only at self-adornment and crippled by bound feet became a target of nationalist, feminist, and reformist repudiation. Indeed, as one part of the fermenting "new culture" intellectual movement of the time—which rejected all aspects of what was named Chinese "tradition"—promotion of male and female physical strength became a touchstone for many forward-looking thinkers and intellectuals. A robust figure was now promoted as an outward manifestation of the rejection of Confucian values, mores, and obedient behaviors. Rather than submit to what were increasingly understood as feminine norms that produced physically and mentally weak people, men and women of China were exhorted to reject old ideas and values by cultivating their minds and their bodies in ways appropriate to the demands of the new world. A new dynamic and "masculine" connection between a healthy mind and a healthy body was born.

These ideas about the centrality of cultivating physical strength to any adequate definition of a modern citizen—male or female—were mostly imported from Japan, which in turn had learned from Germany. In China, as in Japan, the physical education emphasis in new-style schools was on military drills, parade-ground formations, and other regimented activities. According to Mao, this emphasis, rather than inspiring a love of physical activity, merely inspired hatred and resentment of such pursuits, precisely the opposite of what a modern republic required.

In his first published essay, Mao wrote passionately on the importance of physical education. Printed in April 1917 in *New Youth*, the premier "new culture" journal of the time, Mao's "A Study of Physical Education" makes an explicit link between the individual body and the body politic of the nation. The opening lines read: "Our nation is wanting in strength; the military spirit has not been encouraged. The physical condition of our people deteriorates daily." Later in the essay, Mao wrote, "Civilize the mind and make savage the body." In a rhetorical move that was to become characteristic of much of his writing, Mao calls for the ideal unity of contradictory opposites, here of "civilization" and "savagery" in the bodies of all.[1]

The declarative boldness and structure of this essay show glimpses of what was to become Mao's quintessential mode of public address: from the direct posing of the problem, to the uncompromising statement of the solution. In this particular case, Mao's prescribed remedy for the stated problem—weak bodies = weak nation—was for individuals to do squat exercises and swim themselves into good health, if possible in the nude but if not in the nude, then in thin loose clothing.

Thus, at this point, Mao's solution to China's problems was premised not on socio-structural, but individual, personal, transformation. And yet, it was also here that Mao began to pay particular attention to the everyday practices that could be revolutionized to produce larger social change. Taking his own advice, Mao cultivated a lifelong passion for swimming, for long explorative hikes into the countryside, and for physical activity in general. In subsequent years of revolutionary rigor in the far northwest desert regions, where the Communist vanguard lived in caves, Mao was singularly unsympathetic to the politically radical but effete intellectuals from urban areas who chafed at the harsh conditions under which they found themselves. Personal practice was to become thoroughly political.

Philosophy and Friendship at First Normal

Mao's hatred for the physical education teachers was balanced out by his admiration for his favorite teacher at First Normal, Yang Changji. Yang had studied in Europe, where he had taken a philosophy degree at Edinburgh University and another in Germany with a focus on Immanuel Kant. Yang taught philosophy and ethics not as timeless and abstract norms, but rather as historical systems of transformative social change. Because of his upright personal demeanor, Yang was dubbed the "Confucius of First Normal" by Mao and his best friend Xiao Yu.

Teacher Yang introduced Mao to the Western philosophical framework that was to be the foundation for his later study of Marxism and his general worldview. Mao's marginal notes on his translated copy of the German philosopher Friedrich Paulsen's *A System of Ethics* demonstrate his lively engagement with the unfamiliar terms and ideas. While these notes do not show unique brilliance, they do provide evidence that Mao was serious about working through the new problems Western philosophy posed to his thinking. Yang also encouraged Mao to meet with such important figures as the Japanese pan-Asianist, Miyazaki Tōten, who was invited to First Normal to lecture. It was hence through Teacher Yang that Mao not only broadened his intellectual horizons, but also his social connections and sense of being a man in a wider world. For even though Mao was now in his early twenties, he had never left Hunan and was still quite provincial in outlook.

In addition to his studies, Mao's friendships with Xiao Yu and another classmate, Cai Hesen, were also of enormous importance. During the First Normal years, Xiao, Cai, and Mao became inseparable, taking classes with Teacher Yang; reading the latest "new culture" journals from Beijing and Shanghai; debating intellectual, political, and cultural issues of common concern; and learning to understand the world of which China was such an important and yet subjugated part. The correspondence between Mao and Xiao provides many of our glimpses into Mao's early years (even though the two were to have an acrimonious political falling out in the 1920s). Aside from their letter writing, Mao and Xiao embarked on long exploratory travels in Hunan Province during summer vacations, traipsing through the countryside pretending to be beggars. These travels tempered Mao's body and taught him about the material poverty and resources of will of his fellow Chinese.

Cai Hesen was personally and politically allied with Mao throughout his short life. Cai journeyed to France after graduation in 1918 on an anarchist-inspired work-study program based in Montargis, where he became a Marxist and Communist Party member. Cai stimulated in Mao an interest in the relationship between theory and practice. Indeed, it is said by most scholars that Cai's letters to Mao from France advocating the founding of a Chinese Communist Party were very influential in Mao's turn to Marxism. Cai's execution in 1931 by the Nationalists (GMD) cut his life short. Despite this, he is recognized as an important early figure in Chinese Communism and as a major contributor to Mao's early political education.

Mao's First Sojourn in Beijing

In 1918, after graduation, Mao was at loose ends. Teacher Yang was invited to be a professor of philosophy at Beijing University, known as "Beida," the oldest modern institution of learning in China. Yang proposed that Mao accompany him there, and Mao accepted with great enthusiasm.

A few months later, Mao arrived in Beijing where he knew nobody apart from his teacher. He was not only an outsider, but he looked so different from the sophisticated Beijing folk at the university that he later claimed he felt almost alien. Most university students hailed from the privileged urban classes; they dressed neatly with an attempt at style, and they adopted what Mao would call affected manners. In his patched and faded peasant clothing—dyed blue to resist staining—with his toned and tempered body, relatively tall for a Chinese but with crude habits, Mao was no typical university student.

Teacher Yang—now Professor Yang—found Mao a job as a clerical worker at the Beijing University library. Mao's responsibility was to log everyone in and out. He came to know all the big-name professors and renowned scholars, as well as, more meaningfully to him, the editors of his favorite journal, *New Youth*, in which he had published his essay on physical education. At the center of activity and yet also on the outside looking in, Mao joined some reading groups sponsored by Li Dazhao and Chen Duxiu, editors of *New Youth* and famous professors. He tried to make an impression on those he so admired. Apparently, at this point, the only person he made a really deep impression on was Professor Yang's daughter, Yang Kaihui, who later became his first wife and mother of several of his children.

It was in the context of the reading groups that Mao first became acquainted with Marxism as an analytical method, revolutionary strategy, and critique of the capitalist-imperialist world. Often filtered through anarchist language and concepts, Marxism at this time in China was neither rigorously understood nor systematically translated. Yet, the 1917 revolution in Russia that toppled the tsar and brought Lenin and the Russian Communist Party to power had greatly impressed Li Dazhao. Li wrote a long essay for *New Youth* in 1918 extolling the Bolsheviks as true revolutionaries in comparison to China's anemic Republican Revolutionaries of 1911. Li, along with Chen Duxiu, also translated Marx's *Communist Manifesto* as well as some writings of Lenin, Karl Kautsky, and other Marxists of the time. However, in Mao's surviving writings of this year, there is no indication that Marxism made a particularly huge impact on him, even though many later Chinese scholars have compared Mao's encounter with Marxism at Beida to a lightning bolt awakening him from his alleged slumber.

More consequentially at the time, Mao received notice in early 1919 that his mother was gravely ill. He left Beijing without regret to travel back to Hunan. He took a job teaching in Changsha and began writing for and editing his own journal, the *Xiang River Review*, modeled after *New Youth*.

May Fourth 1919

Shortly after Mao's departure from Beijing, Beida became the site of the unfolding of one of the major formative incidents of modern Chinese history:

the May Fourth Movement. The movement began as a protest against provisions in the Versailles Treaty that concluded the Great War. The Chinese had joined the side of the allies and provided some one hundred thousand laborers to dig trenches in France. In return for their contributions to the allied cause, the Chinese expected to recover German-owned territories in China. In addition, the American president, Woodrow Wilson, had promised self-determination to colonized peoples, thus helping fuel Chinese expectations. They were disappointed at Versailles: German territories were handed over to Japan, not to China.

Japan had been eying its enormous resource-rich neighbor to the north since 1895. The failure of the Republican Revolution to solve its political problems had left China even weaker and more fragmented than it had been under the dying Qing dynasty. Once Britain, France, and Germany had turned their backs on Asia to fight the Great War in Europe, Japan had moved in. The Versailles Treaty thus merely confirmed the facts on the ground: Japan was now China's biggest threat, and the world powers would have to take Japan seriously.

Chinese students at Beida were already politically engaged by the domestic problem of poor governance, militaristic warlordism, and inadequate financing of education. Their concern for world affairs was greatly facilitated by the telegraph lines recently laid under the Pacific that brought news quickly to China from abroad. Reports of the Versailles Treaty provisions galvanized students to action. Beida became the organizational site of an angry nationalist and anti-imperialist uprising that quickly spread beyond the bounds of the university, soon reaching Shanghai and other major urban areas. This was a political cause—a humiliation—that unified workers and industrialists, as well as petty merchants and shopkeepers. Demanding a boycott of Japanese products and demonstrating in the streets behind banners festooned with angry, pithy slogans calling for an end to imperialism and the strengthening of the Chinese nation through democracy and science, this coalition of urban classes became a new force in Chinese society and politics. It was to form and re-form, with shifting constituencies, from this time forward.

Mao, in Changsha, wrote from afar about these events for his *Xiang River Review*. In his essays and editorials, he was ambivalent about the idea of violent revolution, even though he was all for the boisterous demonstrations of students and urbanites in the name of "democracy." He condemned Japan's oppression of China, and encouraged the boycott of Japanese products as well as the activities of the "popular masses" against imperialist aggression and the betrayal of China by her leaders and the Western powers. The *Xiang River Review* was soon suppressed by the Hunan militarist then in power because of its critique of the Chinese leaders' lack of backbone in failing both to stand up to Japan and to protest the international betrayal of China at Versailles.

Miss Zhao's Suicide

In November 1919, a local Changsha event grabbed Mao's attention and galvanized his pen anew. This was the suicide of one Miss Zhao. The precipitating incident involved a woman of no fame or social standing, who was betrothed by her family to a man whom she detested. In the covered bridal sedan chair transporting her to her future husband's home, Miss Zhao killed herself by slitting her throat. The role of modern women in social and political life was a prominent issue in the new culture discussions of the day. Indeed, almost all male (and female) participants in new culture debates were, to one degree or the other, feminists. As such, the formerly routine matter of a common woman's suicide in the face of an arranged marriage became, for social critics such as Mao, an occasion for impassioned commentary.

Mao begins the first of his nine commentaries on Miss Zhao—all published in the Hunan newspapers—with a seemingly prosaic statement: "When something happens in society, we should not underrate its importance."[2] Signaling with this comment that common daily events were as worthy of social discussion as huge national or international ones, Mao went on to pose the question of whether Miss Zhao's suicide was evidence of her free will or of her subjection to an evil social norm. That is, was she an active agent in her own death or a passive victim of life? Did Miss Zhao have a personality that she was able to express through suicide? Or was suicide the ultimate expression of a powerless woman faced with a society that conspired against her individuality?

Construing the everyday relationship of women to society as an inherently violent one—Mao characterizes it as a relationship of daily rape— Mao concluded that women such as Miss Zhao (thus, most women in China) could not develop individuality in life, but could only assert free will in death by suicide. As such, Miss Zhao's predicament was symbolic, Mao wrote, of the socially charged marriage question in general: should women (and men) submit to marriages arranged by parents, or should they be allowed to choose their partners freely? If the latter, society would need to accommodate women in public places, where they still did not appear in great numbers. In this sense, for Mao, any solution to the problem of marriage and of female free will would require a complete overhaul of social norms, from those regulating the family to those regulating citizenship and the state.

By coincidence, at approximately the same time that Mao was discussing Miss Zhao, Henrik Ibsen's *A Doll's House*—newly translated and in performance on the Shanghai stage—provoked a huge debate within new culture intellectual circles. Inspired by the angry departure of the protagonist, Nora, from her stifling home and oppressive husband, many urban Chinese feminists—male and female—promoted Nora as a role model for all women trapped in bad marriages. All women should be Nora, and abandon stifling homes if they so chose. However, Lu Xun, China's most famous and accomplished modern writer, posed the startling question: what happens to a Chinese Nora when she leaves home? That is, if society is not prepared for independent women, such women have no choice other than to become whores or die. What, then, he asked, would a host of Chinese Noras do when they left home? This sobering question and all it implied was to shape, for Mao and his generation of male and female radical activists and thinkers, a determination to liberate women from the strictures of traditional family constraint by making society receptive to independent women.

Toward the Communist Party

The intellectual scene in China in the early 1920s had begun to fragment. For, even while the new culture and May Fourth movements had identified a large number of problems that all progressives could agree upon— including opposition to imperialism, support for nationalism and democracy, rejection of traditional values and ideas, and promotion of feminism —there was no agreement about their solutions. The problem with anarchists, believers in the most radical and widespread philosophy of social transformation then available, was their intentional lack of organization. Liberals, meanwhile, were split on how to achieve the social transformations for which they called. And among the political leaders of China— where no central government existed and where the forces of the erstwhile

Republican Revolution were attempting to regroup in the South—there were few who could articulate any solution either to the dire political or the long-term cultural issues that China faced. In this fragmented situation, more and more intellectuals came to view the Russian Bolshevik solution —which called for a centralized party of committed activists who could lead society toward a common goal—as an attractive one.

At this point, even as Mao was in Changsha writing on Miss Zhao and other matters of everyday and social concern, the Soviet-sponsored Communist International (the Comintern) decided to foment interest in the establishment of a Communist Party in China. Surveying the scene from Moscow, Comintern agents determined that Li Dazhao, Chen Duxiu, and their followers at Beida were likely candidates for such interest. They also identified a group of intellectuals in Shanghai who could possibly form the nucleus of a Communist Party. The Comintern search fortuitously converged with a social-intellectual context also urgently in search of a solution.

Mao, for his part, had also been moving towards Bolshevism, as he came to understand the Russian Revolution more thoroughly and as he became disillusioned with both anarchism and liberalism. By mid-1920, aided by his friend Cai Hesen's letters from France analyzing communism's virtues and explaining the basics of Marxism, Mao declared his support for the "total solution" and common ideology embodied in Bolshevist Communism.

Under the influence of all this internal and external activity, small communist groups began to form around the country. Mao headed the one in Hunan, and Yang Kaihui, not yet married to Mao but the beloved daughter of his favorite teacher, also participated. Finally, in July 1921, these groups began to merge into a national organization, when twelve delegates from the various small cells met secretly in Shanghai to establish the Chinese Communist Party (CCP) under the direction of the Dutch Comintern agent known as Maring (Hans Sneevliet). Mao attended the Shanghai meeting. The two ostensible founders of the CCP, Li Dazhao and Chen Duxiu, did not attend. The twelve delegates, it turned out, represented a total of fifty-seven self-identified communists.

The formal founding of the CCP was a totally unremarkable event in a country rife with political and social chaos, fragmented under the leadership of innumerable militarist warlords, and with urban areas controlled by foreigners. Yet, with the founding of the CCP, Mao returned to Hunan, and the other delegates returned to their home provinces, where, in their respective locations, everyone was to start to learn systematically the very Marxism that was presumably the ideological basis for the Communist Party. At the same time, the delegates were charged with recruiting new members, expanding into the working classes, and putting the CCP on a firm ideological and social foundation.

3 Toward the Peasant Revolution, 1921–1927

A theoretical and practical paradox immediately emerged with the founding of the CCP. Marxist revolutionary theory calls for the working class—the proletariat—to lead a social revolutionary movement to overthrow capitalism and seize state power. Yet, China in the 1920s was an overwhelmingly agrarian society, with only small pockets of industrial manufacturing dominated by Western and Japanese capitalists located in the coastal treaty port cities. The question immediately presented itself: How were Chinese Communists to reconcile a revolutionary ideology that presumed an industrial social structure with the reality of Chinese society, which was composed of primarily impoverished peasants? Who was to lead this revolution? And against whom was the revolution to be targeted?

Communist Revolution and China—A Mismatch?

China in the 1920s was divided amongst rapacious militarist warlords who ruled over disparate territorial satrapies in the inland areas. The coastal cities were under the rule of the Western and Japanese powers. There simply was no centralized or unified Chinese state. Against which social forces—domestic and imperialist—was a Communist Revolution to be launched? The question at its most abstract as well as its most practical became: How could a national Marxist revolution be mobilized in a country that lacked the social elements of a Marxist revolution and a central state apparatus, and where foreign imperialism played such enormous but uneven socioeconomic and political roles? This was the theoretical, political, social, and cultural dilemma that any Chinese Marxist and Communist revolutionary faced. These issues were not taken up in systematic theoretical fashion by Chinese Communists until after 1927, and yet they lurked behind the practice of all revolutionary mobilizers through the 1920s.

Directly confronting the issues in practice, Mao began to organize labor in Hunan. He discovered that the tin and coal miners in Anyuan (north of Changsha) and the workers on the Hankou-Canton Railway, whose route was through Hunan, comprised the largest concentrations of proletarian labor in the province. Thus, in late 1921, he went to Anyuan to unionize miners, working out of a cousin's house located at the foot of the mines. Much later, in the 1960s, a heroic painting, *Chairman Mao goes to Anyuan*, was produced and circulated nationwide as poster art to commemorate this earlier organizing effort of Mao's. The poster shows a young and slim Mao in a plain blue scholar's gown, with windswept hair and a fierce gaze directed into the distant future; he is framed by the mountains and mines as the backdrop to his coming greatness. This portrayal, of course, is entirely retrospective, since in the early 1920s, the going was extremely tough, and Mao's future as leader of China was not even a glimmer on the horizon.

Yet, Mao proved to be an impressive and effective organizer. By May 1922, as secretary of the Hunan branch of the CCP and now joined by his classmates, who had returned to Hunan from their work-study program in France, Mao had helped organize more than twenty trade unions among such groups as miners, railway workers, municipal employees, and printing press workers. In early 1923, Mao estimated that there were twenty-three major unions in Hunan, with over thirty thousand workers participating. In only a couple of years, there had been at least ten strikes, which had extracted some key gains in wages and ameliorated work conditions for over twenty-two thousand workers.

In the midst of this very busy period, Mao married Yang Kaihui in a low-key ceremony in Changsha. By late-1921, pregnant with their first child, Yang also became very active in the unionization movement, focusing on the peasant communities near the Anyuan mines, where she worked for women's rights, female literacy, and general educational improvements. Mao's brothers, Zemin and Zetan, also joined the struggle in the mines, establishing consumer cooperatives and workers' clubs with educational and recreational facilities.

This combination of activities was to become a common model for the Communist labor movement, and later the peasant movement: organization of male workers and a focus on women's issues in the communities, underpinned by a commitment to literacy and education for all. Mao and his Hunanese comrades were not the only ones to engage this model, nor were they its creators; but Mao was certainly one of the more successful in implementing it. His success drew the attention of Chen Duxiu, the Beida professor and *New Youth* editor Mao had met during his library stint in Beijing, who was now chairman of the CCP. Chen was so impressed with Mao's achievements that, in January 1923, he invited him to become a member of the Party's ruling Central Committee in Shanghai.

Right before Mao's departure for Shanghai to take up his new Party post, the February Seventh Massacre took place. Ordered by Wu Peifu, a hugely powerful warlord in the north, the action was targeted against restive railway workers who were building a north–south rail line in central China that Wu considered essential for the consolidation of his own power. The violent action was intended to crush all worker solidarity; it resulted in the deaths of dozens of workers, the arrest of countless labor organizers (mostly Communists) along with the summary execution of many of those, and the brutal suppression of the most powerful and militant workers' organization in all of China. Wu Peifu's move emboldened other holders of local power, who, in collaboration with their local business leaders, began to move against the burgeoning labor movements in their areas. The Hunan labor organization that had been built over several years by Mao, his wife, his brothers, and his comrades, was destroyed overnight.

The United Front—Nationalists and Communists in Alliance

Disheartened, Mao arrived in Shanghai shortly after this incident, at a moment of a great rethinking of Communist strategy. The February Seventh Massacre had revealed the fragility of the very labor movement the Communists had determined would be their main social support. It had also revealed the urgency of stopping warlords from their destructive amassing of personal power, and thus the necessity of establishing a strong political and military alliance for the unification of state power and the strengthening of society.

The Communist Party's formal membership still numbered below two hundred at this time. Only one large-scale organized modern political party existed in China: the Nationalist Party, known as the Guomindang (GMD). With roots in Sun Yatsen's Republican Revolutionary movement that had overthrown the Qing dynasty in 1911, the GMD by 1923 had transformed itself from a small band of conspirators into a party with a mass social base. It was organized along Bolshevist lines—that is, as a centralized Party—and had a large contingent of advisors from the Comintern. Indeed, Soviet Comintern advisors were also assisting the GMD build a modern and strong army at the newly founded military institute in the south, the Whampoa Academy.

The GMD's political-social base was in Canton in southern China, where it vied for power with several local warlords while also entering into fierce competition with the British colonial government farther south, in Hong Kong. In May 1922, the GMD co-sponsored one of the most spectacular strikes in modern Chinese history, the Hong Kong seamen's strike. This action shut down the British colony as well as immobilized Canton and its environs. The longevity of the strike and GMD solidarity with the workers, along with successful wage and employment settlements for the seamen, garnered great prestige for the GMD among workers and radical organizers.

In this domestic context, the Communists and the Nationalists—despite their vast differences—were induced to form a United Front by the Comintern agents stationed in both camps. These agents had been charged by Stalin in Moscow with welding together a unified political movement in China that could contest the chaos of warlord power. The form of the United Front the Comintern advocated was called a "bloc within." It was designed to have Communists join the Nationalist Party, even while they retained their CCP membership. This required the much smaller CCP essentially to fold itself into the much larger GMD, with the Nationalists providing the organizational, administrative, and ideological umbrella and infrastructure. The Communists would retain a subordinated organizational identity, but no independent overarching structure. Many Communists, including the CCP chairman Chen Duxiu, were quite skeptical about dissolving their Party organization into the Nationalist Party. Many Nationalists were also very hostile to the idea of allowing Communists in their midst. For, the basic differences between the Nationalists and the Communists were huge and primarily revolved around the parties' respective analyses of China's present and the desired shape of its future.

The Nationalists were convinced that China's major problem was its poverty and inability to compete on the global capitalist stage. For them, establishing a strong sovereign state was absolutely essential, and encouraging capitalism was the only viable method to quickly enhance China's wealth and power. Their goals, therefore, were the unification of the country under a strong state and the establishment of a state-capitalist-landlord partnership for the accumulation of national wealth based upon the protection of individual property rights. This type of socioeconomic analysis led to a strategy that called for the development of urban-led industrialization funded by private capital with state guarantees. Rural areas were to play a supporting economic role at best. The GMD thus aimed to avoid any revolutionizing of social class relationships that might prove destabilizing to smooth economic growth. It also called for cooperation with global capitalism, albeit from a position of strength and equality rather than weakness and subordination. For the GMD, the overriding priority and concern were a strong unified state able to direct the economy and contain social strife.

Communists, by contrast, defined the issue in almost polar opposite terms. For them, capitalism was the *problem* not the *solution*. As far as they were concerned, capitalism in its imperialist form in China had combined with the existing pre-modern landlord economy to produce a rapacious monstrosity. They called this monstrous social form "semi-feudalism and semi-colonialism," or "the two semis." According to the Communists, this social form produced two problems for China. First, as an imperialized country, the nation was subordinated and subjected to the domination of predatory global capitalism that would never be a partner in developing China. As a consequence, capitalism had to be resisted not only in China but globally. Second, China was a partially colonized country. Its social structure was unable to transform itself from its pre-modern agrarianism because of the collusion of native landlords and dependent industrialists (named "compradores") with foreign capitalist forces. This collusion in turn allowed foreign capitalists to prey upon China's socioeconomic weaknesses without developing China's overall economy. Thus, domestically, landlords and compradores had to be overthrown, and their properties redistributed. While unification of the country was deemed absolutely necessary, for Communists the real transformative target was national and global capitalism as well as domestic landlordism and compradore capitalism. This type of analysis led to a social revolutionary strategy calling for the complete transformation of property relations—encapsulated in the concept of class struggle—that would overthrow domestic landlordism at the same time as national and international capitalism. In this sense, for Communists, the social struggle had at least as high a priority as the struggle for the unified state.

These irreconcilable analytical differences between the GMD and the CCP at first yielded to a shared hatred of the militarist warlords, a hatred producing a shared conviction that social and economic progress could only be achieved through strong and unified state power. By 1923, opposition to the United Front in both parties was transformed into grudging and wary acceptance. Mao was instructed to join the Nationalist Party in the summer of 1923, even while he was elected to the CCP's ruling Central Executive Committee.

Mao's Wife and Other Women in the Early CCP

In late 1923, Mao briefly returned to Changsha from his Party work in Shanghai. He and Yang Kaihui had already had their first son, Anying, in early 1922. Their second boy, Anqing, was born in December 1923. Meanwhile, the situation in Hunan was becoming dire, with a daily escalation in warlord-inspired violence against any and all perceived political rivals. Peasant organizations that had sprouted up to oppose the rapacious taxation policies of self-aggrandizing holders of local power, were being crushed; Changsha's factories were being closed due to the incessant warfare; and workers' organizations—even innocuous clubs—were being suppressed. Faced with these tough circumstances, Yang Kaihui, a CCP member herself and thus potentially a target of political suppression, but also the mother of a fourteen-month-old baby and a one-month-old infant, begged Mao to stay by her side and not return to Party work immediately.

In a pattern that was to repeat itself often enough for female Party members, Yang's own political work clashed with her husband's work and her family obligations. Yang's decision was to stay with her children, sacrificing her own Party career for her boys and her husband. Other women who became involved in the CCP faced similar problems. Yet unlike Yang, who remained close to her natal family, most women had to sever their family relationships in order to liberate themselves from traditional norms and marriage expectations. Many, in fact, were formally disinherited by their families. The CCP became the equivalent of a family for them, and they formed complex liaisons with male comrades in the exciting, dangerous, and often intimate context of Party work. The children that were born from the sexual relationships that often resulted became a hindrance to their mothers' further advancement in the Party. Thus, while the essential openness of the CCP to women and their declared policy of support for women's liberation attracted large numbers of women to the Party, the Party's rhetoric often was mitigated in practice by the relegation of women to menial and maternal roles. The great internal Party debate about the relationship of women to political work and family life of these years was not resolved before other urgent events overtook it.

Mostly immune to Yang's pleas to stay with her in Changsha, Mao left for Canton in late January 1924 to take up his duties in the Nationalist Party. Already an accomplished poet, Mao wrote a despairing verse for Yang upon his departure:

"Waving farewell, I set off on my journey.
The desolate glances we give each other make things worse . . .
From this time on I'll be everywhere alone.
I'm begging you to sever these tangled ties of emotion.
I myself would like to be a rootless wanderer.
And have nothing more to do with lovers' whispers."

In Canton, Mao plunged into the fraught and contentious environment of political cooperation within the framework of the United Front. Demonstrating a singular ability to synthesize a debate and focus a discussion, Mao's organizational and political analytical skills were honed. Nevertheless, his initial support for the Front soon turned to discouragement, despair, and then depression. Realizing that the goals of the two parties were too different to meld into one program, Mao's faith in Sun Yatsen, the titular head of the United Front and the revered leader of the 1911 Revolution, was severely shaken when Sun proved more willing to cut deals with power-hungry warlords than to confront them directly. And by the end of 1924, Sun Yatsen was dead of illness. The Nationalist leadership was taken over by military men. Mao went back to Shanghai, now joined by Yang Kaihui and their two sons. He was exhausted, dispirited, and ready to take a break.

Return to Hunan and Discovery of the Peasants

Pleading illness, Mao returned to Changsha and thence to Shaoshan. He missed meeting after meeting of the CCP, and his formerly prolific pen fell silent. In the quiet of Shaoshan, surrounded by his wife, sons, childhood friends, and others, Mao had plenty of time to indulge his favorite pastime: reading. He had restocked his library in Shanghai in anticipation of his retirement from politics and he contentedly embarked on a life of calm and contemplation.

Yet, through 1925, spontaneous peasant unions started to spring up all around Hunan and adjacent provinces in reaction to worsening economic, social, and political conditions. These soon drew Mao out of his self-imposed seclusion. While some scholars have suggested from retrospect that Mao must have returned to Shaoshan with the explicit intent to build an autonomous power base amongst the peasants, there appears no evidence for this. By the same token, because of Mao's silence through this period, there is no way actually to trace the evolution of his social commitments or his thought, or to find any definitive explanation for why peasant organizing so grabbed his attention at this time. Mao had never previously expressed much interest in the peasantry as a potentially revolutionary force but had instead adhered to the more orthodox Marxist view of the urban proletariat as the leading revolutionary role. But we do know that after the spring of 1925, Mao became more and more enthusiastic about the revolutionary potential of the peasantry, an attachment that marked an enormous departure from the urban-based political and social emphases of both the Communists and the Nationalists.

As peasants organized, radical political attention remained riveted on the cities. On May 28, 1925, a Chinese factory worker in Shanghai was murdered by a Japanese foreman in a Japanese-owned cotton mill. This provoked an enormous demonstration on May 30. Winding their way through the streets of Shanghai behind streaming banners, thousands of Chinese demonstrators—students, teachers, workers, and regular city folk—arrived at the International Settlement, where most foreigners lived and which was heavily guarded by foreign troops and police. The protestors were fired upon by British-commanded police. Dozens of workers and students were killed—including for the first time in such urban political violence, a female student. This event was immediately labeled the May 30th Incident.

A year later, after another episode of political violence, in Beijing, China's most famous writer, Lu Xun, wrote despairingly in memory of a female student killed by Japanese troops: "Miss Liu Hezhen, one of the more than forty young people killed [on March 18, 1926], was my pupil . . . She is no pupil now of one dragging on an ignoble existence like myself. She is a Chinese girl who has died for China."[1] Signaling an end of the era of timid teachers such as himself and the beginning of an era of youth movements and politics (along with the horrible sacrifices those were to entail), Lu Xun articulated a widespread shift just then gathering momentum.

The deaths on May 30 and the circumstances leading up to them—including Japanese high-handedness, British-commanded troops (who were actually Sikhs from British colonial India and Chinese police), and the shock of a student death—crystallized a huge amount of building anger and frustration. This sparked an outpouring of strikes, anti-foreign boycotts, demonstrations, and militant anti-imperialist activity that engulfed China, from north to south and east to west. Most urban social classes—students, merchants, petty shopkeepers, workers, and even vagrants and rickshaw pullers—participated in this loose movement of protest in a renewal of the "May 4th spirit," by occupying the streets, closing down business as usual, pressuring political leaders, and fashioning elaborate banners, songs, and protest slogans. The May 30th Incident and its aftermath helped usher in a new hope for social mobilization and revolutionary upsurge.

The essentially urban movement was joined—in a historical first—by burgeoning rural peasant movements, such as the one Mao was becoming excited about near Shaoshan. By mid-1925, over two million peasants had mobilized against the intolerable conditions they were forced to endure under the twin oppressions of landlords and warlords. The peasant movements were spreading quickly, and while the urban and rural movements had different catalysts and did not explicitly link up, anyone who wished to notice could see that the whole country finally was ready for action. This energy injected a sense of hope into dispirited revolutionary-minded activists. It also suggested the future social coalition—petty urbanites and peasants—that was to become so essential to a distinctive Maoist Marxism.

In the summer of 1925, invigorated by the various social movements, Mao threw himself into the peasant world with a new sense of purpose. His activity, however, soon attracted the attention of the Hunan warlord then in power, and he was forced to flee for his life to Canton. There, Mao again took up his abandoned Party activities.

The Northern Expedition and the "Report on an Investigation of the Hunan Peasant Movement"

In the wake of the May 30th Incident and its aftermath, the GMD and their CCP allies finally found themselves in a position to launch the long-awaited Northern Expedition from Canton. The intentions were to wipe out the warlords and reunify the country under one central government, and its initial destination was Nanjing, the capital of the early Ming Dynasty. With his Soviet-trained army, Chiang Kaishek, a GMD militarist soon to become paramount leader of the GMD-controlled Chinese state, began the march north. In a winning strategy, CCP agents were sent out to the peasant organizations in advance of the army, to assist them in opposing landlords, who were the financial props of the warlords. After the peasants and their CCP allies had weakened the social foundations of the combined power of warlords and landlords, the Northern Expeditionary troops led by the GMD would sweep away military resistance. This process of simultaneous peasant organization and military action represented the highpoint of cooperation between the GMD and the CCP.

Through this period, Mao worked feverishly in Canton in the United Front headquarters. He advocated the further radicalization and mobilization of peasants, as well as the adoption of peasant-friendly land reform policies that called for the confiscation of landlord property. Mao soon became a severe critic of the CCP chairman Chen Duxiu and others, who insisted that the CCP's most important social base remained in the cities and that peasants were merely functional to an urban revolutionary strategy. This urban-centeredness was, of course, the orthodox Marxist position, as well as the viewpoint of the Moscow-directed Comintern agents in China. Paradoxically, in this period, the more left-leaning of the GMD members, with whom Mao closely worked at Canton, were far more sympathetic to Mao's peasant advocacy and to the peasant movements than were Mao's CCP comrades. As a consequence of his pro-peasant views, Mao was appointed by the GMD to be the principal of the Peasant Movement Training Institute near Canton, where, from May to October 1926, he was able to act directly on his convictions by instructing many leaders who soon became peasant organizers.

As the Northern Expeditionary troops got farther from Canton, and thus as the pace of work in the United Front headquarters slowed, Mao returned to Hunan to engage in a study of agrarian conditions and peasant organization. His February 1927 "Report on an Investigation of the Hunan Peasant Movement," written for CCP leaders, resulted from this study. It is one of the most passionate of all his surviving early writings. In the brilliant rhetoric of the Report, Mao called into being the very revolution he was to lead; he produced the revolutionary unity that a new politics of mass mobilization demanded; and he established a poetics and a politics that constituted and reflected the revolutionary situation.

The point of the Report was to convince urban-based CCP leaders that peasants were the key to China's revolutionary movement. It demonstrated that peasant organizing was already so far advanced that those who wished to count themselves as revolutionaries had only three choices: "To march at their head and lead them? To stand behind them, gesticulating and criticizing them? Or to stand opposite them and oppose them? Every Chinese is free to choose among the three, but by the force of circumstances, you are fated to make the choice quickly."[2] The "choices" Mao offered left no doubt that any true revolutionary had no real choice at all.

In Mao's view, the significance of the peasant organizations was that they had been spontaneously organized by peasants themselves. That is, in the face of centuries of oppression, during which peasants had been systematically convinced that their difficult lot in life was *fated* by the heavens, they had finally decided to take their lives into their own hands so as to transform them. This, for Mao, was a revolutionary turn in consciousness. This, for Mao, was what all genuine revolutionaries needed to learn how to do. As far as Mao was concerned, the *historic mission* of China's revolution now rested not in the urban areas alone, not among CCP or GMD leaders alone, but rather upon the shoulders of the peasants. As Mao articulated it, the peasants' mission was to overthrow landlordism, to help the proletariat oppose capitalism and imperialism, and to unite with the other revolutionary social classes in a joint urban-rural coalition to rid the country of its oppressors. In this view, peasants, formerly understood as the most backward of China's population, now vaulted into the forefront of progressive history: they were the true bearers of revolution; they were the ones on whom China's Marxist revolution was to rest.

To those who sat in the urban areas and lamented from afar the violence of the peasants' organizations, Mao responded: "It is fine. It is not 'terrible' at all. It is anything but 'terrible.' . . . 'It's terrible!' is obviously a theory for combating the rise of the peasants in the interests of the landlords; it is obviously a theory of the landlord class for preserving the old feudal order and obstructing the establishment of the new democratic order; it is obviously a counterrevolutionary theory." To those who objected to the peasants' lack of respect for the landlords and the violence of the movement, Mao responded: "a revolution is not like inviting people to dinner, or writing an essay, or painting a picture, or doing embroidery; it cannot be so refined, so leisurely and gentle, so 'benign, upright, courteous, temperate and complaisant.' A revolution is an uprising, an act of violence whereby one class overthrows the power of another." And to those who were appalled at the thoroughgoing nature of the peasants' revolutionary fervor, Mao responded: "A man in China is usually subjected to the domination of three systems of authorities: (1) the state system (political authority) . . . (2) the clan system (clan authority) . . . (3) the supernatural system (religious authority). . . . As for women, in addition to being dominated by these three, they are also dominated by men (the authority of the husband). These four authorities—political, clan, religious, and masculine—are the embodiment of the whole feudal-patriarchal ideological system, and are the four thick ropes binding the Chinese people, particularly the peasants." In view of these "four thick ropes," according to Mao, all aspects of society needed to be violently ripped apart.[3]

Mao ended his Report with a description of the constructive changes Hunan's peasants had wrought in their own villages through their organizations. Starting with bans and prohibitions on gambling and opium, the improvements included such matters as bandit suppression, the abolishment of exorbitant levies, the establishment of schools and consumer cooperatives, and the building of roads and irrigation embankments to enhance commercial and agricultural productivity. From the larger level of village association to the smallest level of everyday life, peasants had taken their lives into their own hands.

The Report marks a complete shift in Mao's revolutionary commitments. He called upon no political party to discipline or lead the peasant movement. The CCP was merely exhorted to join the peasants or be left behind. Indeed, as far as Mao was concerned, and no matter what orthodox Marxist theory might say, from this time forward, the Chinese revolution would stand or fall with the peasantry.

Nationalist Betrayal

The Northern Expedition was for the most part successful in destroying the warlord strongholds in southern China (even while the re-conquest of the north was postponed indefinitely). And yet, the mass movements of 1925–27 that had been crucial to this success increasingly came to be seen by the right-wing members of the GMD, including Chiang Kaishek, as a threat to their political, military, and social control. For, once peasants and workers had been mobilized to prepare the grounds for the Northern Expeditionary troop advancements, their demands for land, wages, and social transformations became more radical. As the peasants were radicalized, they threatened landlords' property rights, capitalist industrialization, and the centuries-long cultural legacy of entitlement assumed by the landed and wealthy elites. The Hunan peasant movement about which Mao was writing with such enthusiasm was a prime example of such radicalization. Standing on the side of landlords, urban capitalism, and social stability, Chiang and his GMD comrades found it more and more expedient and increasingly urgent to suppress these radical demands. Over the course of late 1926 and into early 1927, the alliance between the CCP and the GMD frayed badly over these and many other issues.

By April 1927, Chiang's forces had reached Shanghai. He finally was able to turn the fury of his counter-revolutionary convictions against the very revolutionary forces that had sustained him and his army. Beginning with a brutal assault on Communists and workers in Shanghai that eviscerated the CCP and their urban-based labor unions, the attack soon spread to the rural areas, where peasant leaders, organizers, and everyone close to them were summarily killed. The ensuing "White Terror" proceeded over several years. It took the lives of more than one million people, most of them the very peasants of whom Mao had written so glowingly. The White Terror led to the near extinction of CCP membership. And, in a strangely grisly outcome of anti-revolutionary fury, short-haired women with natural-sized feet, presumed to be radicals because of their untraditional hairstyles and unbound feet, became specific targets of the terror. Their shorn heads and mutilated bodies—with breasts cut off—became favored public displays amongst those local GMD officials who now wished to warn a cowed populace against further mobilization or opposition.

The rout of CCP social and organizational forces was complete. Of 60,000 Communist Party members, only 10,000 survived the end of 1927. Those not killed or imprisoned fled from urban areas, some to their familial homes in villages in the countryside despite the risk of endangering their extended families. Others went deep underground in large cities. And yet others fled to remote rural areas. Mao chose the last course.

The possession of an army turned out to be one key to political power. This lesson was not lost on Mao or on others. In addition, the seeds of extreme distrust in Moscow's directives were also sown, for, throughout the beginning of the terror, the Stalin-directed Comintern remained wedded to the United Front, advising the CCP to continue to work for national unity. By the time the Comintern and Stalin in Moscow realized the scale of disaster and betrayal befalling the CCP, it was much too late to save anything but their own skins. Comintern agents fled China forthwith.

The painful task of regrouping, rethinking, and revitalizing got under way among the remaining Chinese Communist Party members. Henceforth, this process was to take place primarily amongst the poorest and remotest of the peasants, amongst whom the remnants of the CCP were encouraged to gather. Communists in urban areas were hunted down like wild animals. Li Dazhao, erstwhile Beida professor and one of the cofounders of the CCP, attempted to take refuge with Soviet embassy officials in Beijing. They handed him over to GMD soldiers, who executed him. Made scapegoat for the disasters, Chen Duxiu was ousted as the Party Chairman. While Party Central continued to operate clandestinely out of Shanghai's French Concession area—for the moment, out of the reach of Chinese law enforcement—most surviving Communists dispersed to the countryside and went underground.

From the very bleak view of 1927, all seemed lost.

4 Establishing Revolutionary Bases

FROM JINGGANGSHAN TO YAN'AN, 1928–1935

On the northwest side of the Jinggangshan Mountains in Jiangxi Province, just east of the provincial border with Hunan, stands a remote and forbidding promontory known as Huangyangjie. Overlooking the site is a monument, a poem of Mao's engraved on it. The poem—which every Chinese schoolchild used to be able to recite—commemorates an important victory won in August 1928 by Mao and the embryonic Red Army. This ragtag bunch of Communists was in the process of establishing a revolutionary base in the area amidst the ongoing disaster of Chiang Kaishek's White Terror. Pushed farther and farther from urban centers by pursuing militias, the Red Army—trained as a mobile guerilla force— was compelled to stand and fight in the summer of 1928 against a superior enemy. Mao's verse describes the heroic encounter:

> At the foot of the mountain, our flags and banners can be seen,
> At its peak our drums and bugles are heard to respond.
> The enemy troops besiege us thousands strong,
> We stand alone and will not be moved.
> Already our defense was like a stern fortress,
> Now do our united wills form yet a stronger wall.
> The roar of gunfire rises from Huangyangjie,
> Announcing the enemy has fled in the night.[1]

The Jinggangshan Base

Jinggangshan was at best an accidental site for a revolutionary base. It was a remote bandit hideout known for its undisciplined lawlessness, not for its potential to harbor a disciplined revolutionary organization such as the CCP. Yet, in this territory and society, Mao, and a little later, Zhu De, the brilliant military general who became one of Mao's closest associates, decided to settle and regroup. There they began to experiment with those social, cultural, military, and economic practices that later became the hallmarks of "Maoism." For about one and a half years, under the protection of the Red Army—popularly known as the Zhu-Mao army—Jinggangshan's social, cultural, and economic life was transformed: land was redistributed (a task in which Mao's brother Zetan was engaged), basic literacy was promoted, and non-hierarchical organizational relationships were encouraged. These practices attracted many local admirers, including educated youths and ordinary peasants as well as lower-level elites from surrounding areas. The practices also attracted the anxious notice and virulent opposition of the big landlords, provincial-level elites, and government entities. After the Red Army's arrival, Jinggangshan, never an entirely peaceful area, soon became the target of concerted suppression campaigns by militias and armies.

Jinggangshan was not the only rural site where Communists settled in the post-1927 flight from the cities. Yet, in later Party histories it became iconic because Mao's subsequent rise to power endowed it with retrospective significance. At the time, Jinggangshan was important because Mao's faction of the CCP there began to overcome its dependence on the Stalin-dominated Comintern, setting up a showdown with Moscow-trained CCP members who continued to espouse an urban-centered revolutionary movement. Through the Jinggangshan experience Mao became convinced that, rather than pursue futile and costly attempts to regain the lost urban areas, the CCP should harness itself to the peasantry by rooting in rural base areas. Out of this conviction arose the Maoist strategy to mobilize the countryside in order to "surround the cities." At Jinggangshan were sown the seeds of this specifically Chinese path toward Marxist revolution, a path that would see its unlikely fruition two decades later.

In light of subsequent events, Mao's commemorative poem takes on greater significance. For, aside from celebrating an unlikely (and temporary) victory, the poem proclaims a theme that was to become Mao's unwavering refrain from this time forward. Not only would the CCP need to strengthen its own military capacity to fight against a well-armed and well-funded foe, but, even more important, it would need to define and forge a united revolutionary will that would weld its military capacity to the Communist Party and to the mobilized peasant masses. It was toward the development of this unified revolutionary will that Mao worked tirelessly for the rest of his life. In tying his personal fate directly to the fate of the Chinese revolution, Mao became inseparably identified with the revolution, even if the Communist Party often did not follow Mao's will.

Settling in and Settling down

Mao was frantically busy in 1927–28 establishing Jinggangshan as a base area, fending off militias, establishing the ideological building blocks of his revolutionary philosophy, waging intra-Party struggle with opponents, and experimenting with socially transformative practices among the peasant communities in which he was operating. With his family far away and inaccessible, he was not too busy to engage in romance. The woman on whom his amorous attention was soon fixed was a young revolutionary named He Zizhen.

From a local elite family, He Zizhen at age fifteen attended a school run by Finnish missionaries. There, she became politicized through reading radical journals and experiencing personal outrage over the May 30th Incident in Shanghai that had brought Mao out of semi-reclusiveness in Hunan in 1925. One year later, having been expelled from school allegedly for her politics, He Zizhen returned home to set up revolutionary organizations aimed at raising women's consciousness and establishing peasant associations. Until the spring of 1927, she mostly worked in small urban areas in and around the Jinggangshan region. Once the White Terror set in through the end of 1927, however, she was forced to flee into ever more remote regions to escape capture. Showing great bravery and capacity for military tactics, He Zizhen had much opportunity to demonstrate her ability to shoot both left- and right-handed from horseback. She soon became central to the Jinggangshan revolutionary cause and came to be known as "the Two-Gunned Girl General."

Shortly after her flight into the mountains, in October 1927, He Zizhen was introduced to Mao. There was evidently an immediate mutual attraction. By May 1928, they were married in a small ceremony, attended by several sympathetic bandit leaders from the area, some local Communist cadres, and a few of He's family members. Mao and He apparently spent the weeks after their marriage working together redistributing land among the peasants.

He Zizhen was Mao's constant companion from 1928 to 1937. Yet, Mao's first wife, Yang Kaihui, was still alive in Changsha and still married to Mao, until her execution by the Nationalists in 1930. There was simply no way for her to reach Mao in his mountain fortress, however, or for Mao to reach her in Changsha. The enforced separation took its toll, and in the loose social arrangements indulged by many Chinese men (no matter how revolutionary their politics), Mao simply married He Zizhen without formally divorcing Yang Kaihui.

Through their sojourn in Jinggangshan, He Zizhen continued her own revolutionary activities, with and without Mao. At the same time, she also struggled to keep Mao supplied with the one thing he could not get in the mountains, but without which he could not live: current newspapers. The newspaper-reading habit formed twenty years previously as a student in Changsha had now become an addiction and even a political necessity for Mao, as National papers gave hints of government policies and strategies that could have a big impact on Mao's own plans. He Zizhen devised an ingenious method to circumvent the embargo placed around Jinggangshan by the GMD military. She instructed the smugglers of salt and the small-scale peddlers of other blockaded goods to use newspapers as wrappers for the items they brought to the region. She then unwrapped the items and smoothed the papers for Mao's perusal. In this manner, Mao maintained access to the latest news, even if it came in scattered and wrinkled sheets.[2]

Mao and He Zizhen had six children together: three boys and three girls. Some died in infancy, and others were left in peasant households and subsequently lost to their parents during the many and various CCP escapes from disaster, leaving only their daughter, Li Min.

The Red Army, Guerilla War, and Political Relations

Although the Red Army beat back the GMD offensive commemorated in Mao's poem in August 1928, by early January 1929, with provisions dwindling, salt blockaded, and winter storms threatening to close all routes off the mountain, the Jinggangshan base ceased to be viable. The Zhu-Mao army and 3,500 followers decided to abandon it. Thrown back into a wandering mode in their escape, they were burdened by many noncombatants and pursued at all times by hostile troops. They had no definite notion of where they were headed; they just needed to flee from immediate peril to find a more hospitable sanctuary elsewhere.

Two keys explain the survival of the Zhu-Mao army through these lean times in the remote mountain regions: its prowess at a specific form of guerilla warfare—known as protracted war—and its adherence to strict rules of discipline. Unlike the predatory armies of the warlords or the Nationalist government troops, who were usually not paid or fed and who often pillaged their way through villages in their path, the soldiers of the Zhu-Mao army had ideological coherence and a reason to fight. The Red Army soldiers neither were mere mercenaries nor had they been press-ganged into warlord armies. Their participation in the Red Army was voluntary, and beyond its military significance, it was also a social endeavor. As such, they were respectful and considerate of the villagers, on whose good will they relied for provisioning and quartering.

Mao helped Zhu De write the code of the Red Army soldier, which included the following eight precepts:

1. Replace all doors [used under mats for a bed] when you leave a house; 2. Return and roll up the straw matting on which you sleep; 3. Be courteous and polite to the people and help them when you can; 4. Return all borrowed articles; 5. Replace all damaged articles; 6. Be honest in all transactions with the peasants; 7. Pay for all articles purchased; 8. Be sanitary, and especially establish latrines a safe distance from people's houses.[3]

As fame for their unusually polite behavior spread, the Zhu-Mao troops were able to recruit freely from peasant families, whose sons—and sometimes daughters—were enthusiastic about serving with such principled comrades.

In addition to forging and maintaining good relations with local villagers, the army was able to survive because of their adoption of guerilla tactics. Mao's version of guerilla warfare contrasted sharply with the instructions he had received from the Central Committee of the Communist Party, situated in Shanghai. In fact, Party Central's doctrinaire policies had little to do with the realities faced by Mao and his followers on the ground. The Central Committee—under the direction of Moscow-educated, urban- focused Li Lisan—instructed Mao to break up his large force into small bands and to disperse them throughout the immediate area. Mao refused, believing that was a recipe for the annihilation of his troops.

Keeping his men together, Mao articulated a strategy of "luring the enemy deep" into hostile territories, where *they* would disperse and thus become sitting ducks for the concentrated forces of the Red Army. Combining these tactics of concentration and luring with the classic hallmarks of guerilla warfare—mobility and flexibility—Mao and Zhu were able to keep the bulk of the army intact. At the same time, they inflicted defeat after defeat on the numerically and technologically superior forces of the government troops.

During the long months of retreat from Jinggangshan and the circuitous search for another sanctuary, one of the major ideological issues that emerged was the optimal relationship between the political and the military in the fashioning of strategy and tactics. Mao was acknowledged as the political leader: he set the ideological tone and provided the political rationales. While Mao was also involved in military matters, day-to-day command of the army was firmly in the hands of Zhu De. In this manner, civilian Party control over the army became a core principle of Maoism. This principle of civilian command over the armed forces is elaborated in the well-known, but oft-misunderstood, Maoist slogan: "The Party commands the gun; the gun shall never be allowed to command the Party."

In early 1930, after many months of wandering, battle-hardened and now thoroughly exhausted, Mao and his followers settled on the southern plains of Jiangxi Province. Their headquarters was in a small city named Ruijin. Here, the Zhu-Mao army was joined by the army of Peng Dehuai. Peng had been left to retreat more slowly from Jinggangshan so as to draw some enemy troops off the pursuit of Mao and Zhu. Peng's army, initially smaller than the Zhu-Mao army, but now swollen by new recruits, miraculously escaped annihilation. Through a similar circuitous route, they arrived in Ruijin in April 1930. The armies were integrated through reorganization, thence reapportioned between Zhu and Peng.

At this point, Li Lisan, still in Shanghai and still focused on an urban-centered revolutionary movement, re-established contact with Mao. Li ordered the Red Army to attack and attempt to take Changsha, the capital of Hunan Province. This order derived from Li's belief that the Red Army's only utility was to launch assaults on cities, rather than to build a revolutionary movement slowly in rural base areas. Reluctantly, Mao instructed Zhu and Peng to commit some of their forces to this Changsha endeavor. The Red Army troops were destroyed in the doomed effort to take what was now a heavily garrisoned and defended city.

Trapped in Changsha were Mao's first wife, Yang Kaihui, and his sons by her; his sister, Mao Zehong; and the wives of his two brothers. Yang Kaihui was arrested and given the chance to save her life by repudiating Mao and the Party. She refused to recant and was shot. His sister was executed for no other reason than her kin relationship to Mao Zedong. Mao's two surviving sons—Anying and Anqing—ended up in Shanghai, living hand-to-mouth. They were reunited with their father only in 1936 after concerted CCP efforts to locate them.

The sole long-term silver lining to emerge from this military and personal debacle was the rethinking soon thereafter of what came to be known as Lilisan'ism or the "Li Lisan line." This refers to the strategy that called for Red Army attacks on cities in the hope of stirring proletarian uprisings. This urban-based strategy merely led to the sacrifice of Red Army soldiers, as demonstrated in the Changsha disaster. For, in face of the ongoing White Terror perpetrated by Chiang Kaishek's GMD, the proletariat was now not likely to risk themselves in revolutionary adventures. It was totally quiescent.

In the immediate term, however, the attack on Changsha had catastrophic consequences for the Jiangxi base and Mao's leadership.

The Bloody Origins of the Jiangxi Soviet Base Area

Settling in and around Ruijin and combining a number of smaller CCP base areas, Mao proclaimed a soviet-style government in southern Jiangxi by mid-1930. This new amalgam was both a much larger and much more viable socio-political and economic entity than anything Mao had presided over in Jinggangshan. The Jiangxi base presented an opportunity to further hone revolutionary practices and to build a Communist administration.

Mao's arrival in Jiangxi, however, was superimposed on an indigenous Communist movement not particularly eager to be incorporated into his expanding military-political complex. In addition, Mao's evolving ideology of peasant-centered revolution presented the Central Committee in Shanghai with an explicit challenge to its urban-based ideology. The tensions between Mao and the Central Committee—particularly after the Changsha debacle—as well as those between Mao's followers and the indigenous Jiangxi Communists, broke out in December 1930 in a bloody orgy of internal conflict that almost paralyzed the Communist movement.

Known as the "Futian Incident," the internal conflict had multiple sources, including calls by Mao and his followers for radical land redistribution—a policy opposed by local Jiangxi Communists in part because of their personal ties to local society—and the military tactics for defending the Jiangxi base against Chiang Kaishek's Nationalist troops. In this regard, Mao continued to insist on his tactic of "luring the enemy deep." Yet, local Communists worried the immediate impact of such deep luring was the inevitable destruction of local property and loss of life, including their own friends and families. Infusing all of this was the loyalty of the Jiangxi Communists to Li Lisan, counterposed against Mao's clashes with Li and Party Central. Distrust was rampant.

In late 1930, a rumor about a hostile infiltration by Nationalists into the Jiangxi Communist base areas began to circulate. Panic ensued. Initially, Mao and Zhu were engaged in their doomed efforts at Changsha and were not involved in the onset of events. Upon his return to Jiangxi, Mao ordered over four thousand officers and soldiers of the Red Army arrested on suspicion of betrayal. The vast majority of these were local Jiangxi Communists. Over half of those arrested were induced to "confess" their guilt and were summarily executed. The purge sparked the mutiny of a division of Jiangxi soldiers, who suspected they would be the next targets. After a good deal of fighting back and forth, the mutineers were suppressed by troops loyal to Zhu and Peng (and thus to Mao). Order was restored, at a great cost in lives and to unity.

Concurrent with this internally divisive and bloody set of events, Chiang Kaishek launched the first and second of his self-proclaimed "extermination campaigns" against the "Communist bandits." The CCP attacks on Changsha, and even earlier on Nanchang, the capital of Jiangxi, had raised alarms about the growing Communist menace. The Communists now no longer seemed contained in remote regions but apparently were contending for power in the urban areas. This struck fear into Chiang's heart. In early 1931, in the first "extermination campaign," Chiang sent a hundred thousand Nationalist troops to take care of the "bandit problem." He was confident his overwhelming force would easily emerge victorious. Lured deep into Communist strongholds, the Nationalists were all but wiped out by Mao's forces. In his second effort several months later, Chiang sent over two hundred thousand troops to encircle and exterminate the Communists. This force also failed.

Coinciding with the second extermination campaign was another round of purges loosely related to the original Futian Incident. This round was immediately tied to the ousting of Li Lisan in Shanghai as Chairman of the

Party. In a tortured pseudo-political logic, suspected Nationalist infiltrators, who had been the targets of the first round of purges, came to be labeled Li Lisan loyalists. Through extension, all forms of behavior and attitude suspected to be insufficiently loyal to Mao—including supposed Nationalist spying, alleged fealty to Li Lisan, opposition to Mao's land reform policies—were lumped together and labeled "counter-revolutionary." In such a context, the purges took on a surreal dimension. Having labeled many loyal Communists—Jiangxi natives and others—as traitors, Mao loyalists took the lives of thousands. Mao vigorously participated in and expanded this stage of the purge in order to suppress any possible loyalty to Li Lisan, his internal foe.

The internal purges had taken their bloody course and had mostly abated when the third extermination campaign was launched by Chiang Kaishek, in late 1931. The three hundred thousand Nationalist troops thrown at Jiangxi were also defeated by the Red Army with the now unassailable "luring the enemy deep" strategy.

This third Nationalist defeat coincided with the Japanese invasion of Manchuria in September 1931, which led to the establishment of the puppet state, Manchukuo, under the rule of the last Qing emperor, Pu Yi, who had been deposed. In early 1932, the Japanese bombed Shanghai in an attempt to force Chiang formally to cede Manchuria; these attacks temporarily drew the attention of Chiang's forces away from Jiangxi and gave Mao's base a respite from Nationalist assault.

The Xunwu Report

In the midst of fending off Chiang's extermination campaigns, and despite the internal purges, the revolutionary transformation of local society remained a top priority of the CCP during the Jiangxi base period. The Jiangxi policy on land distribution and the transformation of peasant society was conceptualized and organized on the basis of Mao's acknowledged expertise in rural affairs. Mao's "Xunwu Report" of 1930—named after the administrative center of the area—provided the local specifics on which the plans were implemented.

At the beginning of the Jiangxi base period, in May 1930, Mao had taken the opportunity to investigate the area as he had the Hunan area for his report of 1927. Based on a ten-day examination of the region, Mao's meticulous analysis of the rhythms and structures of everyday peasant life—the barbers, the prostitutes, the usurers, the telegraph and postal services, the medicine shops, etc.—once again proclaimed his faith in the capacities of peasants to transform their own lives, if only they had the socio-political conditions for so doing.

Equally important at the time to this proclamation of faith, were the specific details recorded of how peasants lived their lives. These details provided guides as to how peasant society could be more equitably structured through revolutionary activism and transformation. In other words, the revolution was not something that was to happen above and elsewhere; rather, the revolution was brought into the everyday lives of local people. It was to become a *lived* experience of everyday life, not merely a rumor of other people's activities.

An outgrowth of this Report was the appearance of yet another of Mao's maxims: "Without investigation there is no right to speak." Criticizing his fellow Communists who "keep their eyes shut all day long and go around talking nonsense,"[4] Mao insisted book learning—or, abstract theory—needed to be subordinated to reality and practice. In the immediate sense, this was clearly an attack on the detached ideologues and dogmatists of Party Central. In a longer-term sense, the unambiguous announcement here of an inextricable relationship between theory and practice became another hallmark of Maoism. Mao was to return repeatedly to this issue in the fuller articulation of his revolutionary philosophy in the late 1930s and beyond.

For the moment, the Xunwu Report informed the organization of Mao's new base area. The core of the Jiangxi Soviet covered a territory of close to fifteen thousand square miles incorporating around three million people; its extended zone could count more than six million under its administrative sway. The establishment of a short-lived but stable polity there gave those who later survived the fall of the base valuable experience as political administrators; it also gave those, whose lives were transformed, a taste of revolutionary practice.

The central aspect of the Jiangxi polity revolved around the transformation of social relations in the rural areas. This included the redistribution of land and the rearticulation of the cultural bases of rural society. Having learned from Jinggangshan that too radical a redistribution policy would alienate would-be supporters, the policy in Jiangxi was relatively more moderate. Not only were the poorest of peasants invited to participate in the land redistribution, but those categorized as "middle peasants" were also induced to participate. Only "rich peasants" and "landlords" were dispossessed of their excess land—defined as any land they could not till themselves but for which they needed to hire labor. On this standard, families were allowed to retain as much land as family labor could till, and all excess was thrown into a common pool for redistribution to the land-poor. The Jiangxi Soviet also minted its own currency, usable only in the Jiangxi base area itself. Nevertheless, the symbolism of this currency was enormous, particularly insofar as its exchange value remained stable, while Nationalist currency exchange rates fluctuated wildly.

The CCP took many initiatives on the social and cultural front. Recognizing top-down approaches did not teach peasants to be active in the transformation of their lives, Party workers urged peasants to take land redistribution into their own hands and to reorganize their villages. Meanwhile, the CCP took aim at arranged marriages and anti-female family practices by elaborating the most progressive marriage laws in China or anywhere else. These provided the conditions for local women to divorce husbands they had been forced to marry; to detach themselves from marital families who were mistreating them; and to own and till their own land. The Party also took literacy campaigns seriously. They opened schools for children and adults (male and female) using locally produced textbooks filled with CCP-friendly learning devices. For the first time, peasants had the opportunity to learn, contesting centuries of elite control over "culture." At the same time, the Party launched public hygiene campaigns and dispersed rudimentary clinics and hospitals throughout the area, giving peasants access to basic medical care in an attempt to wipe out common, but easily vanquished, health problems.

The combination of internal purges and serial assaults by the Nationalists had created extremely difficult conditions for building trust and unity within the Party, and between the Party and the society within which it was embedded. Mao had retained the personal loyalty of the vast majority of the Red Army because of the success of his strategy to thwart Chiang's forces. However, he had lost the support of Party Central, which was staffed almost entirely by Moscow-trained ideologues and dogmatists who were suspicious of Mao's commitment to rural revolution. From 1932 on, although Mao remained Chairman of the Jiangxi Soviet in name, real power was transferred by Party Central to others. Zhou Enlai, a returned student from France who had joined the Communist Party with Mao's old friend from Changsha, Cai Hesen, took over the reins of political power. The Red Army remained in the hands of Zhu De and Peng Dehuai.

The year 1932 was relatively quiet at the Jiangxi base. Land redistribution and cultural transformation took on their own momentum; Chiang Kai-shek was busy fending off the Japanese in Shanghai. Mao was ill for much of the year with the return of malarial attacks and then was diagnosed with tuberculosis. He took the opportunity of his effective fall from power to accompany He Zizhen to neighboring Fujian Province for the birth of their second child, a son, Anhong. Mao stayed in a Communist-friendly sanatorium there until his tuberculosis abated. In early 1933, He Zizhen gave birth to their third child, a daughter who died in infancy. Anhong lived with his parents until he was two years old. In 1934, with the retreat of the CCP from Jiangxi, he was left with Mao's brother, Zetan. After Zetan died in combat, Anhong was cared for by Mao's former bodyguards. After Jiangxi was overrun by the Nationalists in 1935, Anhong was never heard of again.

The Fall of the Jiangxi Soviet and the Long March

At the end of 1932, leaving the Japanese to their Manchurian conquest, Chiang Kaishek again decided the greater menace to China and his rule was not the Japanese but the Communists. He launched a fourth extermination campaign against the Jiangxi Soviet. Again, this one was decisively defeated, albeit at much greater cost to the Red Army than the previous three. By October 1933, Chiang finally hit upon a winning formula to dislodge the Communists from Jiangxi. Called the blockhouse strategy, it was in part designed and implemented by newly hired Nazi German advisers. Mobilizing over a million troops and outnumbering the Red Army ten to one, Chiang's forces refused to be lured deep without adequate preparation. They meanwhile deployed their mechanized artillery and air force to great advantage. By careful advancement through fourteen thousand newly constructed concrete blockhouses, Chiang's troops tightened the noose around the now-shrinking Jiangxi Soviet. Faced with this strategy and now advised by the dogmatic Comintern agent, Otto Braun, the Red Army abandoned its mobile warfare in favor of a conventional positional battle. This was a disaster for the Red Army, which could not hold out in face of vastly superior numbers and technology possessed by the Nationalists.

By the summer of 1934, Braun and Zhou Enlai decided the Jiangxi base had to be abandoned. This meant leaving their erstwhile peasant collaborators as well as their wounded comrades to what turned out to be a hideous fate at the hands of the GMD. In July, approximately ninety thousand people—among whom were a pregnant He Zizhen and nineteen other women—broke through a weak point in the Nationalist encirclement. This main force of the Red Army, along with civilian administrators and bearers, was able to elude Nationalist detection long enough to escape the immediate area.

What came to be known as the Long March began. Born of the terrible political and military defeat symbolized by the fall of the Jiangxi base, the Long March retrospectively took on an aura of heroism and triumph. However, few of the original escapees from Jiangxi survived the rigors of what turned out to be a yearlong "odyssey" across China. As with the escape from Jinggangshan five years earlier, the destination this time was also unknown. Mao's forces recognized, in order to survive, they needed to settle in a much more remote region than had hitherto been considered possible or desirable. Relentlessly pursued by Nationalist ground troops and air force, the cumbersome CCP columns were vulnerable to attack. Unable to maneuver with sufficient flexibility and mobility, the slow-moving mass could not be defended. Within several months, at least half of the original columns had succumbed. Many of Mao's closest friends and comrades fell along the way. In the breach, it was decided, on arriving in Zunyi, a city in Guizhou Province, the columns would stop and evaluate their present and future directions.

At the Zunyi Conference in early 1935, the forty-one-year-old Mao emerged as first among the leaders of the CCP. Almost completely deposing the Moscow-clique, Mao declared his and the CCP's independence from the Comintern, Stalinism, and Moscow dogma. Instead, Mao advocated, should the Red Army and the CCP survive the current crisis, the main purpose of CCP policy would be to oppose the Japanese, struggle against the Nationalists, and transform peasant society. All of this would have the final long-term goal of taking state power and unifying the country under CCP (and Mao's) rule.

While Mao gained a limited internal political victory, his and his followers' very survival was still in the balance. The Red Army had already been reduced to thirty thousand exhausted and demoralized troops who wanted to know where they were headed. Mao decided to aim for the last known surviving Communist base area, in far-away Shaanxi Province. Separated from Zunyi by huge rivers, snow-capped mountains, deep ravines, rough terrain, and potentially hostile local populations as well as absolutely hostile warlords, the attainment of Shaanxi seemed impossible. Pressed at all times by Nationalist and now also warlord troops, it took another nine months of extreme hardship and loss to reach the destination.

Mao's and He Zizhen's fourth child was born along the way. A daughter, she was left in a sympathetic peasant household and never heard of again.

The Long March Ends

On February 28, 1935, Mao and the Red Army were mired in the mountains of Sichuan Province, in the far west of China, where the climb toward the Tibetan plateau begins. Commemorating in verse a major military victory as well as the spectacular vista of Loushan Pass, Mao seemed upbeat, despite the difficulties he and his troops were facing. He wrote:

> Do not say that the strong pass is hard as iron,
> For this very day we'll stride across its summit.
> Across its summit,
> Where blue-green hills are like the seas,
> And the setting sun like blood.[5]

As was often the case with Mao's poetry, the classical spatial imagery—hills as seas—combined with the reality of a supercharged moment in time—the bloody setting sun—to produce a curious but effective emotional state of both elation and despair.

It was October 1935 before Mao entered northern Shaanxi province with the scarcely eight thousand half-starved troops who remained from the initial ninety thousand escapees from Jiangxi. There, in the shadow of the Great Wall, they finally found sanctuary among a small band of Communists who had an operational base and had heard rumors of the Red Army's plight and made preparations for its arrival.

Although in subsequent Party histories, the Long March was hailed as a major triumph, Mao clearly recognized it as a huge defeat for the Communist movement in China. Most of the Red Army had perished; the bases in the interior of China had been destroyed, and most of the Communist presence there had evaporated. Ideological struggles had taken a toll on the unity of the Party. The economic, political, and social foundations of Communism in China would need to be rebuilt from the ground up. The psychological toll on the survivors was heavy. In an ominous turn, their Communist mission now took on the quality of a sacred quest to avenge their fallen comrades. The revolutionary loyalty and sheer will to survive of veterans of the Long March became the standard to which all revolution-aries were held. In subsequent years, few measured up. In this context of exhaustion, defeat, psychological depression, and depletion, however, there were flickering renewals of hope. With such flickers did the Yan'an period begin.

5   Yan'an, the War of Resistance against Japan, and Civil War, 1935–1949

Upon arrival in Yan'an, Mao and the CCP were faced with rebuilding the Communist movement while administering a sprawling territory sparsely inhabited by a mostly subsistence-level peasant population. The conditions of life were characterized by a semi-desert environment with poor natural resources and little surplus agricultural production. There were no access to capital for investment, few urban centers, and little industrial capacity. To this unpromising region, the CCP brought its army, battle hardened but exhausted after a year of fighting its way across China, as well as a tiny number of educated people with medical, scientific, and cultural expertise. On this material and social basis, Mao and the CCP set about constructing a viable socialist-inspired polity, economy, and culture.

Yan'an became the unlikely location where the socially transformative practices of and ideological rationale for Marxist revolution in China were articulated, implemented, and honed. In part for this reason, the Yan'an period holds a hallowed place in Chinese Communist Party history. Policies implemented here developed into the real-life crucible of Chinese revolutionary practice. Yet, Yan'an also became a mythologized time and place recalled for its spirit of plain-living camaraderie and its relatively nonhierarchical communal ethos of sharing. Forged out of the morale and sensibilities of Long March veterans, Yan'an was supposedly uncorrupted by considerations of individual wealth or aggrandizement. In CCP lore, "Yan'an" represents an extended moment of creative cooperation in the overcoming of hardship and impossibility.

Mao's Yan'an Life and the Elaboration of "Mao Zedong Thought"

Settling into the type of cave residence peasants had long been carving into the loess hillsides near Yan'an, Mao recovered from the Long March if not in luxury at least in some peace. He was able to enjoy the company of his newest daughter, Li Min, born in the summer of 1936, the only one of Mao's and He Zizhen's children raised to maturity. Yet, the relationship between Mao and He became increasingly tense. In 1937, pregnant again, He Zizhen requested to be sent to the Soviet Union for medical treatment. Shrapnel fragments acquired during the Long March were causing her pain, and she was considering having an abortion. She remained in Moscow, where, upon reflection, she decided to have the baby. The child soon died of pneumonia. When she was two years old, Li Min was sent to Moscow to be with her mother; Mao's two sons by Yang Kaihui, who had been found and retrieved, went to Moscow to join them. He Zizhen was divorced from Mao in 1939.

In Yan'an, Mao set up a new household with a beautiful film actress, Jiang Qing, who had arrived in the revolutionary base area along with a huge influx of left-leaning artists and intellectuals after fleeing Shanghai in the wake of the Japanese occupation in 1937. With few revolutionary credentials, although having several leftwing film credits to her name, Jiang was much resented by most inner Party members, who admired He Zizhen and were annoyed at Mao's faithlessness. Jiang Qing was to become and remain Mao's wife until his death in 1976. Their only daughter, Li Na, lived to adulthood.

Despite these personal upheavals and the rigors of establishing the Communists in a new location, Mao took the opportunity of being settled in one place to read systematically through some Marx and Soviet economic and philosophical texts, as well as some Lenin. He was aided by his secretary, Chen Boda, a Soviet-trained Marxist philosopher critical of Stalinism, who had arrived in Yan'an with the exodus of leftist intellectuals from Beijing in 1937. During this period of study, Mao became familiar with the historical materialist method, Marxist dialectics and categories of analysis, and other theoretical components of a revolutionary historical philosophy. His commentaries and annotations on some of the works he read at the time provide insight into his thought process, and what clearly emerges is Mao's visceral objection to Stalin's mechanical interpretation of the relationship between history and ideology. It was in this context that Mao established his own theory of politics, a radical reinterpretation of the tenets of Marxism, Leninism, and Stalinism. This theory, known as "Mao Zedong Thought," is the product of these years.

While Mao Zedong Thought is usually said to be the result of the collaborative thinking of Party leaders, it is clearly based on Mao's idiosyncratic explorations into Marxism and Chinese history. Mao Zedong Thought is also usually said to be a "sinification" of Marxism, or the making of Marxism Chinese. This formulation is inadequate, however, as it takes Marxism as a unified dogma and considers Chinese as a settled cultural predisposition. Marxism was (and continues to be) a much-contested matter, and, in the 1930s, "Chinese" was the subject of intense struggle. It is more appropriate to see Mao Zedong Thought as the product of Mao's simultaneous interpretation of Chinese history and China's present through Marxist categories and the interpretation of Marxist categories through the specific historical situation of China. This mutual interpretation is the motivating dialectic of Mao's theory and revolutionary practice.

Mao's self-education at this time assisted him in his ongoing ideological and power struggles with Moscow-educated Party members, who again were sharply criticizing his rural revolutionary approach. It also allowed Mao to argue with theoretical precision for the historical and contemporary bases for a Marxist revolution in China, for building socialism in such impoverished circumstances and, most immediately, for resistance against Japan. In addition, from the Yan'an period onward, Mao Zedong Thought became the standard for disciplining the Communist Party and for waging guerilla warfare. Perhaps most important, Mao Zedong Thought became the guide for the creation of a culture of revolution and of a revolutionary culture capable of sustaining a long-term social movement that could capture and harness the imaginations and productive potentials of a broad cross-section of the Chinese people facing insuperable odds against a powerful enemy: the Japanese.

The Japanese and the Second United Front

At the same time that the Red Army was fighting its way across China during the Long March, with the GMD dogging its every step, the Japanese had consolidated their grip on Manchuria. By 1935, they started moving into North China. As attacks on China by Japan increased, several generals within the GMD tried to convince Chiang Kaishek he needed to dedicate troops to fighting the Japanese. However, Chiang stubbornly insisted that wiping out the Communists was more important to the nation's security than confronting Japan. The disagreement came to a head in what is known as the Xi'an Incident of December 1936, when General Zhang Xueliang moved against Chiang. Zhang was originally a warlord in Manchuria, who had been displaced by the Japanese and put in charge of the GMD attacks on the CCP from his new base in Xi'an. Unhappy with his new assignment and convinced that Japan was the more immediate threat to China, Zhang organized the kidnapping of Chiang Kaishek, whom he held hostage for two weeks until Chiang agreed to begin negotiations with the CCP for unified military action against the Japanese.

Meanwhile, in addition to his preoccupation with Party and personal survival on the Long March and with establishing the CCP in Yan'an, Mao had kept a close eye on Japanese advances. He had lost no opportunity to write and distribute analyses of what he called the traitorous behavior of Chiang Kaishek. Throughout 1935 and 1936, Mao's writing and speeches consistently connected "Japanese imperialism" to "Chiang Kaishek's sellout." According to Mao, Chiang was "the most diligent trailblazer for Japan in swallowing up China."[1] In laying the responsibility for the ease of the Japanese occupation of China on Chiang's doorstep, Mao was able to position himself and the CCP at the forefront of anti-Japanese resistance. In a telegram written to General Zhang on his kidnapping of Chiang, Mao declared the arrest of Chiang an opportunity not only to exhort the GMD to resist Japan, but also to "drive out the fascist elements within the armed forces, and . . . proclaim to all officers and soldiers Mr. Chiang's crimes in selling out the country and harming the people."[2]

Mao clearly wished for Chiang to be permanently sidelined. This was not to be. Rather, the CCP was forced to negotiate with Chiang for renewed cooperation between the two parties. These negotiations took eight months before resulting in the second United Front. Unlike the first United Front, this second effort at unity ensured the independence of both the GMD and the CCP. As Mao wrote to Zhou Enlai, the leader of the CCP negotiating team in the GMD capital, Nanjing, "the principle is to ensure our absolute leadership" over the Red Army; "the principle is to ensure our Party's independence. Concerning these aspects, we absolutely cannot compromise."[3]

The full-scale Japanese attack on China commenced in July 1937 with the Marco Polo Bridge Incident, a manufactured excuse to invade and to occupy Beijing. Given the disarray of the GMD military, the Japanese pushed south from Beijing with lightening speed. By December 1937, they had reached Shanghai, which was valiantly, albeit futilely, defended by GMD troops. The Japanese proceeded to the GMD capital, where they perpetrated one of the most notorious episodes of the war, the "Nanjing massacre." As GMD troops evacuated the city under orders from Chiang to retreat inland, Japanese forces moved into the undefended capital. They slaughtered, raped, maimed, and enslaved hundreds of thousands of defenseless Chinese civilians in an orgy of violence tracked in the Japanese press for entertainment value at home. This set a pattern of cruelty toward the Chinese that was to characterize the next eight long years of occupation. Indeed, this was to be simplified by the late-1930s into the official doctrine of the Japanese military known as the "three-all" policy: burn all, loot all, kill all.

In light of these developments, arrangements for the second United Front took on great urgency. Mao ceased his verbal attacks on Chiang, and Chiang lifted the GMD blockade on Yan'an. The United Front was finalized in the autumn of 1937; it held for several years, always frayed and fraught. Mao remained rhetorically committed to the United Front, even as the unity broke down in the early 1940s.

On Protracted War

Faced with the Japanese, a vastly superior foe, whose technological and military capacities rested upon a vigorous military-industrial foundation geared towards total war, Mao was required to update and elaborate his theory of protracted war. As had its earliest versions during the Jiangxi Soviet, the theory still emphasized the necessity for "luring the enemy deep." But now it had to account for the potentially national scope of operations, the endless local variations of the opposition, and the impossibility of central coordination.

When Mao delivered his famous set of lectures, "On Protracted War," to Party cadres in Yan'an in May 1938, Chinese forces had suffered numerous defeats. The GMD had continued its retreat inland under its policy of "trading land for time," and was busy setting up its wartime capital, Chongqing (Chungking), deep in the mountains of Sichuan Province. The CCP guerilla capacity was not yet mobilized. Meanwhile, the Japanese had pushed far into China's most productive agricultural regions, occupying urban centers, seizing internal market routes, requisitioning supplies, and terrorizing the population. Added to this bleak internal situation, no country had come to the aid of China in fending off the Japanese. According to Europeans and Americans, the Japanese attack on China was a regional problem requiring a local solution. As long as the Japanese neither occupied nor touched European and American territories or assets in China, they were not considered a threat. While the Soviets were concerned to have Japan stopped at the China-Soviet border, neither they nor others saw this conflict as part of a global struggle against fascism or as a harbinger of a second world war.

Mao saw the issue otherwise. In his lectures of May 1938, he worked hard to convince his audience that China could survive the current moment, could fight a war against Japan, and could win the war, if only the Chinese unified and found the correct path. The lectures opened with a description of two major immediate dangers. First, Mao warned, a growing sense of defeatism in parts of the country could lead to capitulation to or compromise with the Japanese. This danger in fact was realized in 1939–40 when Wang Jingwei led a breakaway faction from the GMD and set up a collaborationist government in Japanese-occupied Nanjing. Second, Mao warned against an unrealistic hope in quick victory, encouraged by the idea an outside power—usually assumed to be Britain or the United States—would come to save China. Mao argued that, on the contrary, only the Chinese could save China, and they could do so only in a protracted war.

For Mao, protracted war is defined in three ways simultaneously: 1) an objective necessity, indicated by a dispassionate evaluation of the current situation; 2) a strategy for pursuing the war by actively protracting it; and 3) a method of analysis elaborating the historical relationship between global and local situations and deriving contemporary conclusions therefrom. Mao notes: "The war between China and Japan is not just any war; it is specifically a war of life and death between a semi-colonial and semi-feudal China and imperialist Japan, fought in the Nineteen Thirties." He further specifies: "The present war was launched on the eve of the general collapse of world imperialism and, above all, of the fascist countries; that is the very reason the enemy has launched this adventurous war, which is in the nature of a last desperate struggle."[4]

In other words, according to Mao's historical analysis, imperialism and fascism are part of the dying world order of the global 1930s. The war launched by the fascist-imperialist Japanese is a sign not of the growing strength but rather of the death throes of that world. In this way, Mao directly links Japan to a global situation—fascism and imperialism—and rejects the idea that the events in China are merely a regional or local problem. Furthermore, the "semi-colonial and semi-feudal" designation indicates China's current backwardness in relation to Japan: neither fully capitalist nor fully sovereign. Yet, Mao asserts, through "life and death" struggle this backwardness will lead beyond fascism and capitalist-imperialism, beyond Japan and the dying world it represents, toward national sovereignty and a new world. The nonfascist world, Mao felt sure, would eventually wake up to the fascist threat in its midst, and, if China could hold on until then, the nonfascists would come to the assistance of China, even if only to save themselves.

Mao's conclusion to the historical portion is: "Taking an objective and all-sided view, we recognize the two possibilities of national subjugation and liberation, stress that liberation is the dominant possibility, point out the conditions for its achievement, and strive to secure them."[5] A successful historical outcome, Mao notes, could only be secured through the creative and revolutionary activity of the unified Chinese masses. This is the contemporary burden of the Chinese, and it is the historical task of the Communist Party to protract the war while leading the Chinese in this direction.

In the ensuing detailed analysis, Mao argues the key to securing the conditions for success is correctly recognizing the local situations, in all their interconnected complexity at each moment of the struggle. In rapidly changing circumstances and different terrains, guerilla commanders needed to understand what would be best for their locale at any given time: whether to go on the offensive, to retreat, to engage in mobile warfare, or to melt into the populace and become invisible. Protracted war therefore is not a centrally designed blueprint. Rather, it is an overall strategy or approach requiring what Mao calls "jigsaw" tactics. It is a puzzle—or, in Mao's terms, a game of *go* (or *weiqi*, Chinese chess)—with an overall pattern that can only be discerned in its particulars. Correct recognition of what is required at any given moment rests upon good military knowledge and judgment.

Even more important, correct recognition rests upon what Mao calls "politics." Mao's distinctive concept of politics is intimately related to his idea of creating a culture of revolution and a revolutionary culture. It is also central to the method of protracting the war. Practicing politics, in

Mao's terms, is part of everyday life. Politics entails the self-mobilization of the masses through the activation of a consciousness and determination to transform the quotidian conditions of their lives. Different types of conditions, however, take priority over others at different times, depending on the situation of the particular moment. For example, in the context of the war of resistance against Japan—in which a backward China confronts an advanced enemy and opposing Japan takes priority over all other matters—mobilizing the masses means activating a broad sense of patriotism and the desire of the masses to live as a sovereign people. Such mobilization allows not only the guerilla armies to embed themselves amidst the masses, but also each and every person to become a combatant when needed. Simultaneously, in the context of the revolutionary struggle, politics means helping create the socioeconomic circumstances in which the masses can become conscious of, and thence overturn the conditions of life keeping them oppressed. Politics in this sense is class struggle, or the struggle to overthrow oppressive social relations.

Central to the Maoist theory of politics is a theory of the historical role of mass revolutionary consciousness and mass activity in transforming the structures of social life. In Maoism—particularly as compared to orthodox Marxism or even Leninism—consciousness and politics take priority over the givenness of social structure. That is, the structure of social relations may constrain the pace and degree of certain transformative activities—how power and wealth are redistributed; how the rural and urban relations of production are recalibrated; how the cultural level of the populace is raised; and so on. Nevertheless, according to Mao, the conscious activity of the masses can alter these given historical conditions of constraint. While many scholars have called this emphasis "voluntarism," it is more appropriate simply to recognize there is no concept of politics in Maoism divorced from mass politics. For this reason, politics in Maoist theory and practice cannot be abstracted from everyday life, engaged in only by distant elites. It is, rather, part of quotidian existence itself, and most important, it is part of the struggle to transform social existence.

A necessary element of politics in Maoism is the integration of theoretical precepts—based upon education and wider knowledge—with the everyday experiences and existence of the masses, generally confined to local concerns. This is where the Maoist method, the "mass line," comes in. The mass line is a method through which theory is refined in practice. Specifically, theory and historical analysis must inform the formulation of an initial policy; yet, in the encounter with the real world, the policy and theory must be revised to suit the conditions of implementation. Finally, the revised theory becomes the guide to "correct" practice and policy. In Maoist language, this is made into the slogan: "to the masses-from the masses-to the masses," a process requiring CCP cadres—who are charged with formulating and implementing policy—to be endlessly flexible and constantly analytical. They cannot be bookish or reliant on abstract theory, for in Mao's terms, the only correct theory and practice are theory and practice that interact constantly in the concrete here and now of specific conditions.

During the Yan'an period, political practice centered on activating a double movement of mass consciousness: resistance (against Japan) and social transformation (of the conditions of life). Through this practice, a culture of revolution and a revolutionary culture would be simultaneously created and embedded in the lives of the masses. And the proof of the correctness of theory and practice of politics in Yan'an would be the survival of the CCP and the progress made in the war against Japan. Mao's "On Protracted War" articulated this politics precisely.

Practicing Politics in Yan'an and New Democracy

Even as the war absorbed Mao's energies from mid-1937 on, building and consolidating the base area in Yan'an was also urgent. The urgency was in part dictated by the necessity to provision the CCP central administration and its supporters, along with creating the educational and medical facilities the CCP had pledged to bring to the peasants. It was also dictated by the necessity to build an industrial capacity that could produce the military equipment needed by the CCP armies for their fight against the Japanese. Finally, the urgency was dictated by the desire to put into practice the revolutionary theories of social transformation and political consciousness Mao called "new democracy." The achievement of all these goals would make Yan'an a model of a new socialist society and a magnet for Chinese and foreign sympathizers.

With the slogan "everything subordinate to the war,"[6] the first goal of the CCP in Yan'an was stabilization of local society and of its rule in it. An election system was established to absorb the energies and utilize the capacities of the local elite. Meanwhile, large-scale programs were launched to educate peasants in electoral methods, since they would be involved in their own self-government. Land was redistributed, albeit in moderate fashion, and youths mobilized for war through a system of incentives including family tax relief and free schooling for their family members. The CCP also passed and promoted woman-friendly marriage laws. Most important, peasants formed mass organizations from the grassroots up to put into practice the "mass line" cornerstone of Maoist politics. Even though the Party remained the ultimate arbiter of correct practice and the formulator of all basic policy, nevertheless, mass organizations gave the hitherto disempowered peasant populace a greater sense of their own stake in the transformations of their lives. Party membership grew by leaps and bounds.

Problems that were to plague the post-1949 Chinese state emerged at this point. One was the inherent contradiction between bureaucracy and mass politics: Bureaucracy emanates from on high and aims at predictability; mass politics, which requires mobilizing people, entails a certain amount of instability. Another problem surfaced between male peasants and their newly empowered wives and daughters: men came to resent their loss of mastery over women. By the same token, the needs of the army often clashed with basic civilian provisioning. The freedom of the organs of propaganda and communication—journals and newspapers—came into conflict with ideological and policy standards crafted and enforced by the Party. And, finally, the dispersed private nature of most industry—encouraged as a mode of maintaining and enhancing productivity, and of corralling local elites into the CCP fold—faced pressure from centralized planning.

Despite these problems, economic development was quickly fostered. Cooperatives were formed to maximize labor power and productivity; individual household industries, such as textiles, were turned into small-scale cottage industries; and for the first time a way was discovered to smelt crude pig iron in the region.[7] Several badly needed arsenals were established. These and many other achievements made it clear that what had seemed impossible not only *was* possible but even likely, given appropriate priorities, good leadership, and a unity of social forces.

The theory guiding this social unity was called "new democracy." It was articulated by Mao in an essay of early 1940, just as the Yan'an region's territory was being expanded and development was proceeding. New democracy calls for a gradual transition to socialism under a coalition of classes led by the CCP. Thus, rather than mobilize sharp class struggle—through the dispossession of capitalists, landlords, and other elites in favor of the proletariat and peasantry—new democracy aims for the nationalist unity of all "patriotic classes" who help resist Japan and can assist in developing the productive forces needed for the war and beyond. In Maoist terms, new democracy is the politics and socioeconomic arrangements commensurate to the historical era and needs of the United Front in the context of the global antifascist War of Resistance against Japan.

In Mao's theory, new democracy contains three intertwined analytical components: 1) the Chinese revolution is part of a global revolution against imperialism and fascist-capitalism; 2) it is, however, a revolution launched in a semi-colonized country, where national liberation is the primary task; and 3) thus, the Chinese revolution is also a national revolution to create a sovereign nation and a new culture. In the course of liberating China, a new culture would be elaborated; this new culture would be guided by a new type of Marxism, which drew simultaneously from general Marxist theory and also from the particularly Chinese historical conditions of its creation. This new culture would produce a new China.

Mao's concern in his elaboration of new democracy was to give a historically and theoretically precise account of China's current and future transition to socialism. Arguing against Soviet dogmatists (who called for collectivism as the only correct socialist path) and ultra-radicals (who called for the confiscation of all private property), Mao urged restraint. Indeed, Mao's theory of new democracy specified the relatively enduring place that a mixed economy comprised of small-scale capitalism coexisting with state-ownership of banks and core industries had in China's present and future. Moreover, Mao cautioned land reform and redistribution would need to exhibit a certain inequality to ensure productivity.

And yet, realizing that none of this was going to occur without problems, another pressing issue Mao addressed in his new democracy essay is the increasingly bureaucratic nature of Party work in Yan'an. For already in this period—and for the remainder of his life—Mao saw bureaucratization as the enemy of revolution, the enemy of mass politics, and the potential death of the CCP. By 1940, Mao was concerned with setting out the broad parameters of a culture of political and Party work that would be the antithesis of bureaucracy and theoretical rigidity, a culture of political work that would exemplify his method of mass politics. In this culture, the role of mass democracy is enshrined. Yet, the right to mass democracy was to be guaranteed only to the "revolutionary masses" and not to counter-revolutionaries, a distinction that set up a potential problem of definitions. Who is included in which category? For the moment, in the context of the War of Resistance against Japan, the revolutionary category was quite capacious: all anti-Japanese people in China, regardless of class, could qualify. In subsequent years, the inclusionary breadth of the definition frequently changed.

Mao's Talks on Literature and Art—Redefining Culture

Along with the formation of a mass guerilla army and the development of mass politics under the banner of new democracy, another key component to the establishment of a culture of revolution and revolutionary culture was the redefinition of what constituted "culture." For Mao, the goal of mass mobilization for war was not only to beat back the Japanese but also to achieve socialist national liberation. According to him, in order to attain both goals simultaneously, a cultural army had to work side by side with and be embedded in the army. In his famous "Talks at the Yan'an Forum on Art and Literature" in 1942, Mao established the parameters of this revolutionary culture and its "army."

Of first importance to the formation of a revolutionary culture and a culture of revolution is what Mao calls "class stand." No artistic work is innocent of class, according to Mao. A classical European still life, for example, reflects a bourgeois lifestyle, while a classical Chinese landscape painting expresses the detachment of artists from everyday life and the subordination of human beings to nature. In Mao's view, it is important for an artist—renamed a "culture worker"—to ask and answer the question: What constitutes the consciousness of the work of art or literature? For art or literature to be "revolutionary," in Mao's terms, it must express the consciousness of the "proletariat." Since the largest revolutionary constituency of the CCP was the peasantry, not industrial workers, the "proletariat" is a loose definition of the revolutionary masses. Or, more clearly still, it is what the Communist Party represents.

Of second importance for a culture worker in pursuit of revolutionary culture is what Mao calls "attitude." Revolutionary culture must expose the duplicity of enemies; it must praise and criticize allies (such as the GMD); and it must praise the masses, while helping to unite, encourage, and promote their revolutionary progress. In this sense, revolutionary culture can be ambiguous, but not with regard to the masses, who must be depicted in a positive light. Third is the problem of "audience." Acknowledging that art and literature are generally made for and appreciated by elites, Mao insists revolutionary art and literature must expand its audience to workers, peasants, soldiers, and revolutionary cadres, who are not necessarily as educated as traditional art consumers. Revolutionary art and literature thus must address and reflect problems faced by these new constituencies, rather than only the romantic or material aspirations of an urbanized elite intellectual and bourgeois class.

Next in importance is work style. How are intellectuals, unfamiliar with their intended mass audiences, to write on themes that appeal to this audience? In what kinds of language are intellectuals to write, if they are to be understood by this audience? How are they to learn the language of the people and to turn it into a literary language? To address these problems, Mao calls for the invention of a new type of literature and art using revolutionary mass vernaculars. This would be a new literature and art not only in formal terms, but also in terms of content. This is what Mao calls the "mass style." Cultural workers were not merely to represent the masses in their art, they were to give the lives of the masses literary expression. In order to learn and perfect this mass style, intellectuals—or, those now relabeled cultural workers—would have to live with the masses, experience their lives in all of its dirt and lack of refinement, and trade in their intellectual pretensions for the simplicity and earthiness of the masses.

Finally, the problem of "popularization" also needed to be handled properly. Mao did not recommend the dumbing down of culture, but rather its reorientation toward a different audience and purpose. Popular art and literature were to be measured, therefore, not in terms of market viability or eliteness, but rather in terms of its acceptance by the masses. To fulfill all these criteria, one must ask and correctly answer: For whom is literature or art produced? And yet, at the same time, revolutionary literature and art cannot be anti-foreign, nor can it repudiate the native past. Rather, it must combine the best of foreign things and the best of the native past to become truly progressive, not only in national but in global terms as well.

As Mao notes in general terms, literature and art are subordinate to politics, but in their turn exert a great influence on politics. That is, art cannot be purely for the sake of art, but rather is always an ideological project serving a particular class. Thus, if, in capitalist society, art serves the bourgeoisie and is beholden to the market, in socialist society, art must serve the proletariat, or the revolutionary masses, and must be beholden to them. In this sense, art must be subordinate to politics. This formulation, as many at the time cautioned and foresaw, soon lent itself to great interpretive abuse. Indeed, art and literature's subordination to politics came to mean subordination to the Party: To the extent that the Party came to control and enforce what was defined as revolutionary, it was also the Party that came to define and enforce what was the culture appropriate to the moment.

INTERLUDE—THE COMMUNIST UNDERGROUND IN SHANGHAI

Even as the center of Communist activity remained in Yan'an, the Party persisted in its efforts to rebuild a presence in Japanese-occupied Shanghai. These efforts were connected to the broad United Front policies of the CCP and were aimed at uniting all patriotic classes under the banner of anti-Japanese resistance. At the same time, they were to weld the CCP's concern with mass organization to the broad urban elite.

In May 2007, I interviewed one of the last living members of the Shanghai underground Communist Party from the 1940s, Mr. Wang Yuanhua. From the 1940s on, Mr. Wang made a reputation as a literary scholar and critic, a college professor, and political activist; by the time of his death from brain cancer in March 2008, his huge corpus of work on classical and modern Chinese literature and history, as well as on Western literature was being systematically reprinted in China. No less important to his current reputation are various anthologies of his memoirs, occasional essays, and opinion pieces that have appeared over the past decade or more. Best known as a man of integrity and honesty, Mr. Wang had an inner circle composed of those who could keep pace with his lively mind and critical attitude, with whom he enjoyed the give and take of intellectual tussle. I was lucky to be counted among them. I asked him to comment—for this book—on his earliest memories of how he, as an underground Communist cultural activist in Japanese-occupied Shanghai in the 1940s, remembered the promotion of Mao's "Yan'an Talks on Art and Literature" among his Communist comrades. The interview he granted me was the last of his life. I excerpt part of it below.[8]

> **Q:** Your activities in the Shanghai underground party in the 1930s and 1940s were mostly concerned with cultural issues?
>
> **A:** Yes. Culture is connected to the future of the whole country and the nation.
>
> **Q:** Culture is a big field; in what activities did you engage?
>
> **A:** Mainly we organized art festivals . . . activities in literature, opera, and the

social sciences. We also held discussions at night schools. . . . We just wanted to do something useful for society; we had no targeted plan . . .

Q: Did you write for newspapers? What were the topics?

A: . . . . We launched art and literature organizations which intended to organize youths from every walk of life. We taught them how to write essays and reportage literature about reality. I was appointed [by the Communist Party] to do the organizing. Over two hundred people participated, and we published their essays in Shanghai's newspapers.

Q: How did the refugees [in the Shanghai camps] respond to the plays your group performed for them?

A: I remember, we sang a song called "Long Long Ago" [in English]. The refugees had no idea what we were singing and kept wondering aloud: "What kind of 'go' [dog] are they speaking of?" We had a lot of laughs then. We were all educated university students . . . they were all peasants . . . We often talked to the refugees and assisted them in their lives.

Q: When you joined the revolution in the 1930s, why did you choose the Chinese Communist Party?

A: I resented the GMD's "nonresistance" policy toward the Japanese . . .

Q: So, it wasn't Communism or Marxism?

A: No. I knew nothing of Communism or Marxism. I joined the [only] Party that fought against the Japanese. I had no knowledge of Communism.

Q: Did your anti-imperialist activities in the 1930s only mean fighting against Japan? Or, did you have a broader aim?

A: I opposed all invasions and occupations of China by outside powers. Of course, my activities at the time were mainly targeted against Japan because Japan was attacking China then.

Q: In the 1930s, what did it mean to you to have an anti-feudal consciousness?

A: My anti-feudal consciousness was very vague. . . . I was deeply influenced by [the writer] Lu Xun and thought Chinese medicine was bad and Confucius was evil. But, because I was born into a Christian family, I did not grow up with feudal elements. We had no feudal rituals: We believed rituals for ancestors were bad, as were those for the emperors. My consciousness [about these things] was quite simple, very vague.

Q: When did you get to know something of Maoism?

A: I became a propaganda committee member at the end of 1942. The committee was comprised of three persons. . . . We belonged to the Changjiang Bureau, led by Zhou Enlai. Shanghai's situation was quite different from the Great Rear [the occupied areas] and even more different from Yan'an. We did not follow Mao's standard of "transforming" ourselves so strictly. The 1942 "Talks at the Yan'an Forum on Art and Literature" were the starting point of Mao's thought re-education movement [aimed at intellectuals].

Q: What did you think when you first read that lecture?

A: I couldn't accept it. This was an important Party document and we began to read and discuss it [among underground Party members].

Q: What did you think of Mao's "art and literature for the masses" articulated in his "Yan'an Talks"?

A: I also suspected it. I thought: how could it be possible that your thought will progress once you step in a pile of cow dung? The massification of art and literature was not originally proposed by Mao; leftwing literary associations had already proposed the question of massification. I was deeply influenced by the nineteenth-century version of massification in Russian literature, French and German literature, as well as in American literature by those such as Mark Twain. I could hardly accept Mao's crude massification proposal when I was so obsessed with nineteenth-century literature.

Critique of the Party at Yan'an

As the CCP established itself deeply in Yan'an, and as Mao's theories of mass politics, mass culture, and mass mobilization became clearer, a multisided critique developed of certain practices from within the Party itself. One of the most famous of these critiques was launched by the feminist literary figure, Ding Ling.

Ding Ling had come to literary prominence in the 1920s as part of the May Fourth generation of writers. Her literary practice had evolved from an advocacy for cultural reformism into a profound belief in the need for revolutionary culture and a cultural revolution. As a target of GMD attack for many years—her husband, Hu Yepin, was executed in 1930 by the GMD—Ding Ling arrived in Yan'an in the late-1930s. Her work there centered on cultural matters and on pushing the CCP to make good on its longstanding commitments to gender equality.

In 1942, to commemorate International Women's Day (March 8), Ding Ling wrote an essay critiquing the gender politics of the CCP. She begins bluntly: "When will it no longer be necessary to attach special weight to the word 'woman' and raise it specially?"[9] She acknowledges women are better off in the CCP areas but points to the double standards with which "women comrades" are treated. Specifically, they are subjected to incessant gossip, and even censure, based on whether and whom they do or do not marry, whether or not they have children, how they conduct their personal lives, and how their personal lives allegedly influence their professional lives. Ding Ling charges that women are expected to "transcend the age they live in"; they are supposed to be perfect and "hard as steel." However, she notes, most "woman comrades" had to fight through many social obstacles to become communists and revolutionaries. As such, "the mistakes women commit" should be considered "in their social context." Despite rhetorical support for women and feminism among male and female Party members, Ding Ling urges it would be "better if there were less empty theorizing and more talk about real problems, so that theory and practice would not be divorced."[10] Thus using Maoist revolutionary language to argue her point, Ding Ling was also arguing the politics of individualism over the politics of collectivism. Rather than subordinate and sacrifice the individual (woman) to revolutionary necessity or Party needs, Ding Ling insisted on the autonomous meaning of "woman" and on a recognition of the distinctiveness of woman's personal and daily life.

For a brief few weeks after the publication of Ding Ling's essay in March 1942, many other Party members took the perceived opportunity to critique the Party on other grounds as well. Ding Ling was quickly accused of harboring a "narrow feminist" and "subjectivist" sentiment—a nonrevolutionary view of the relationship between women's liberation and class struggle. She was fired from her literary journal editorship and ordered to "reeducate" herself among the masses. Her strong revolutionary credentials and populist belief in the necessary relationship between literature, language, and the masses allowed Ding Ling to politically survive her temporary fall from favor, and she returned to the center of cultural affairs some time later. Others were not as lucky as she in escaping severe punishment, however.

Rectifying the Party and the Mao Cult

Party membership and the Red Army expanded rapidly after the CCP's arrival in Yan'an. Certain problems in the quality of new recruits had surfaced. A Party Rectification campaign was launched in 1941, originally intended to weed out the weakest new recruits and train the stronger ones in correct practice and theory. However, in the wake of Ding Ling's and others' critiques in 1942 and after Mao's "Talks" on art and literature, the Rectification soon became a campaign to impose an ideological litmus test on new and old members of the Party and Army alike. Mao's texts on the interpretation of Marxism and Chinese history and on the relationship between culture and revolution became required reading and study matter for all. A uniform ideology was molded. Passages from Mao's texts were now often cited in Yan'an publications, almost as incantations. Deviators— real or imagined—from accepted interpretations were punished. Some were sent to "learn from the masses," to reeducate themselves (such as Ding Ling); others were jailed for long or short terms; some were executed.

The emphasis on ideological purity had a traumatic dampening effect on the vibrant intellectual society characterizing Yan'an until this time. It was certainly recognized by most that Mao's military theories and strategies, as well as his methods for mobilizing mass enthusiasms and productivity, had already been quite successful. Mao's dominance within the collective leadership group was assured. Yet now "truth" became whatever Mao said it was. Contravening his own philosophical and interpretive method, Mao's texts were canonized in precisely the dogmatic fashion Mao had warned against. From this grew the beginnings of the Mao cult.

Mao's close associate, Zhou Enlai, who eventually became Premier, wrote in 1943 an assessment of Mao: "Comrade Mao Zedong's style of work incorporates the modesty and pragmatism of the Chinese people; the simplicity and diligence of the Chinese peasants; the love of study and profound thinking of an intellectual; the efficiency and steadiness of a revolutionary soldier; and the persistence and indomnitability of a Bolshevik."[11] Yet, Mao's personal dictatorial style came to have more and more destructive effects. The extent of these effects did not become clear until later, but the Rectification gave many leftist intellectuals and many Party members pause.

For the moment, the exigencies of the wartime situation seemed to explain the ferocity of attacks on so-called internal enemies. And, for as long as Mao's protracted war theories staved off and helped roll back Japanese advances, Mao's personal practices could be forgiven.

United Front Strains

Public unity between the GMD and the CCP was maintained until January 1941, even though a number of incidents had led to severe strains. At the national level, the establishment of a puppet government in Nanjing by one of Chiang Kaishek's associates (albeit a rival for power), Wang Jingwei, led to increasing CCP suspicions that the GMD itself was preparing to succumb to Japanese pressures to join an anti-Communist front. Closer to home, constant disputes over territory in the northwest had led to some bloody clashes between the ostensibly allied armies. Most egregiously, in late-1939, the GMD had resumed its blockade of the CCP base area centered on Yan'an. However, only with the "New Fourth Army Incident" in January 1941 did the increasingly fictive unity become defunct.

The New Fourth Army was, along with the Eighth Route Army, the strongest CCP military force. Operating behind the lines in the north, by 1939 the New Fourth Army had pushed its way south of the Yangzi River, the heart of Japanese occupation and of GMD opposition. As with all guerilla operations, the New Fourth Army organized peasants for resistance and revolution simultaneously; they also recruited heavily in the very villages from which the GMD tried to find troops to fill their depleted ranks. The GMD became increasingly suspicious of the CCP Army's intent and ordered it to retreat from its new southern positions. Meanwhile, the Eighth Route Army had successfully infiltrated and organized much of North China behind Japanese lines.

In 1940, the Parties convened in the GMD wartime capital, Chongqing, to negotiate the borders of operation for the CCP armies. Deadlines were set in late 1940 for the New Fourth Army to move north of the Yangzi, and for the Eighth Route Army to move north of the Yellow River. Who did what to whom has never been agreed; each side has its version. What is clear is that in January 1941, the New Fourth Army headquarters was still south of the Yangzi. This force of around nine thousand men was surrounded by GMD troops on January 4. A vicious battle lasting over ten days ensued. Top commanders of the New Fourth Army were killed, along with seven thousand of their troops.[12]

The Incident was clearly a military disaster for the CCP, and the CCP immediately blamed the GMD for traitorous behavior. It also led to the tightening of the GMD blockade around the CCP base areas. As Mao wrote in a telegram to his associates, "All of Chiang Kaishek's talk about virtue and morality is a pack of lies and should under no circumstances be trusted."[13] Chiang's declaration of January 17 that the New Fourth Army was mutinous, provoked Mao to write this "marks the beginning of a sudden emergency on a national scale . . . and the breakup of the whole country."[14] And yet Mao was concerned to keep a public facade of cooperation and warned his commanders that "until Chiang announces a complete break . . . , we shall not raise anti-Chiang slogans. . . ."[15]

The New Fourth Army Incident provoked a realignment of forces within the CCP armies. It marked the rise of Liu Shaoqi, who was to become one of Mao's closest associates in the post-1949 period. It also marked the freeing from United Front constraints of CCP organizing and guerilla warfare. It was a public relations coup and became a call to arms to all patriots, regardless of political affiliation, who now could believe the CCP was all that stood between them and the Japanese. The Japanese noted the split in Chinese forces and began a ferocious anti-insurgency campaign continuing through the rest of the war.

After his month of frantic telegram exchanges sorting out the Incident, Mao took the time on January 31 to write to his sons in Moscow. His letter praises Anying and Anqing for their diligence and their correspondence, while also cautioning them to concern themselves "less with politics" and more with studying natural sciences. He warns them not to listen too much to praise, as it may make them "conceited, dizzy with success, and complacent." He also advises them to "plant your feet on the ground and be realistic."[16]

War Triumph

When the United States joined the war against Japan in the wake of Pearl Harbor in December 1941, the tide of war in China began to change. In order to gain time to rebuild the Pacific fleet and to put the country on a wartime footing, the United States needed China to tie down the huge number of Japanese troops now mired there. Soon, weapons and financing began to flow to the GMD, along with American advisors. While the CCP was still stranded—the Soviet Union, after all, was pressed to the limit by the Nazi German assault after June 1941—nevertheless, the strain on the Japanese army began to take its toll.

In the course of the eight long years of war in China, the Red Army expanded to over one million ideologically committed and battle-hardened soldiers. The CCP's unwavering policies to confront the Japanese, as well as its organizational prowess on the ground, had won it the strong sympathies and support of the north Chinese peasantry and of many city dwellers, who had labored under Japanese occupation and GMD waffling. Local peasant militias had been formed throughout the country as bulwarks against the Japanese, and for the first time in Chinese history, many rural areas were thoroughly organized.

Nevertheless, at the Japanese surrender in August 1945, the GMD army numbered over four million. Chiang Kaishek also possessed an air force and advanced weaponry—tanks and artillery—supplied by the United States through the wartime lend-lease program. Moreover, the GMD was backed by the only wartime power—the United States—not to have suffered devastating territorial and financial destruction during the war. Finally, Stalin had secretly signed a treaty of alliance with Chiang Kaishek, forcing Mao into an attempt at a coalition government with his archenemies. If Mao's distrust for Stalin had been sown in 1927 with the debacle of the first United Front, and then nurtured over the years through his clashes with the Moscow-clique in his midst, this 1945 betrayal of the CCP by Stalin was even harder to swallow. For the moment, Mao did not publicly renounce the global "communist fraternity" of which Stalin was the acknowledged head.

As the U.S. Army Air Corps and U.S. Navy ferried GMD commanders around the country to accept Japanese surrender, and as the United States sent fifty thousand troops to occupy North China until the GMD could arrive in sufficient strength to secure the region, Mao went to the GMD wartime capital, Chongqing, to negotiate a coalition government with Chiang.

Coalition Negotiations and Civil War

The initial six weeks of negotiations from August to October 1945 were probably doomed from the start. Mao and Chiang hated one another, and no trust existed between themselves personally or between their parties. Although a surface atmosphere of seriousness was maintained, both were merely trying to appease their big-power supporters: Chiang was being encouraged by the United States not to resume the civil war; and Mao's hand was forced by Stalin. When this first round of talks broke down, fighting between the CCP and the GMD commenced in Manchuria, a territorial prize desired by both parties. With an infrastructure left behind by the surrendering Japanese, it had the most developed industrial capacity of any place in China.

In December 1945, U.S. President Harry Truman dispatched General George C. Marshall to China to help mediate a settlement. Zhou Enlai and a team of CCP negotiators stayed in the newly relocated GMD capital, Nanjing, to hammer out an agreement under the guidance of Marshall's group. A nominal truce between the CCP and GMD held through the spring of 1946. At this point, Marshall departed, the United States declared it was washing its hands of the China problem, and the CCP and GMD were set loose against one another again.

The final civil war was quite bloody, albeit relatively quickly resolved. Even though the GMD possessed far superior arms and a numerically stronger army—GMD generals boasted of a ten to one advantage over the CCP—they had little support on the ground. In addition, corruption and demoralization within the GMD army made it much weaker in reality than it appeared on paper. Finally, Mao's faith in the human will—in mass politics now directed toward a civil war rather than toward a war of resistance against Japan—led him to depend greatly on the ability and desire of the Chinese people to complete the CCP-led Chinese revolution. Mao's faith was not ill-founded.

Fierce fighting ensued in Manchuria, where Mao and Chiang took personal control of their respective armies. The Manchurian campaign significantly weakened Chiang's military through huge casualties and large numbers of desertions among the best troops, who joined the Communists. The CCP Fourth Field Army—commanded by Lin Biao—gained a large influx of men along with the huge cache of American-made weaponry they carried with them. In addition to tried and true military tactics—"luring the enemy deep" and mobile warfare—the peasantry's support became key to CCP victory. Providing bodies, intelligence, safe havens, and economic support, the peasants of north China rallied to their wartime saviors to help defeat the GMD. This is what Mao called a "people's war."

Fighting continued for another year, but in unexpectedly quick fashion, the GMD military caved in and retreated south. Along with them went the Nanjing-based administration, whose last toehold on the mainland was Guangzhou. With the final collapse of GMD resistance, Chiang Kaishek and his followers packed whatever they could on boats and planes supplied by the United States and precipitously fled the Chinese mainland to the island of Taiwan. The dispute between the GMD and the CCP remains today a vestigial territorial problem of the Chinese nation.

Meanwhile, in Beijing, Mao proclaimed the dawning of a new era for China.

6 Stabilizing Society and the Transition to Socialism, 1949–1957

In September 1949, as final victory against the GMD was at hand, Mao opened a session of the Chinese Political Consultative Congress in Beijing. The Congress gathered together independent parties committed to working under the CCP's leadership. Facing the assembled representatives, Mao announced, "Chinese people have begun to stand up." He continued: "We have united ourselves and defeated both our foreign and domestic oppressors by means of the people's liberation war and the people's great revolution, and we proclaim the establishment of the People's Republic of China [PRC]."[1]

Having survived more than twenty years of remote exile, brutal war, civil strife, power struggles, decimation and growth, Mao and the Communist Party he now led had, against all odds, reached the pinnacle of Chinese power. For the first time in over a century, China was a unified state and also a sovereign nation. This was a monumental achievement the CCP could claim as its own. As a consequence, the year 1949 marked an absolute divide: the demarcation between "pre-liberation" and "liberation." In historical accounts, political statements, movies, dramas, and everyday speech, everything now would be identified by this chronology, with darkness and gloom characterizing the before-time, light and hope characterizing the after-time.

As Mao prophesied during his speech at the Congress, "An upsurge in cultural construction will inevitably follow in the wake of the upsurge of economic construction. The era in which the Chinese were regarded as uncivilized is now over . . . Let the domestic and foreign reactionaries tremble before us. Let them say that we are no good at this and no good at that. Through the Chinese people's indomitable endeavors, we will steadily reach our goal."[2] Pledging to quickly overcome the remnants of Chiang's GMD and to move rapidly into the task of development, Mao declared even though the civil war had been won, the revolution was far from complete.

At ten o'clock in the morning on October 1, 1949, Mao stood atop Beijing's Gate of Heavenly Peace, the traditional center of the Chinese state, crowds massed before him. One participant described the scene: "Above the sea of people thousands of banners were unfurled, waving in the autumn breeze, their colors transforming the shabby city. The crowd was shouting slogans . . . and singing revolutionary songs. The enthusiasm was contagious . . ."[3] No longer in his ubiquitous army fatigues but now sporting a brown Chinese-style suit and a worker's cap, Mao was flanked by a number of non-Communist personalities, Sun Yatsen's widow, Song Qingling, among them. Speaking a version of Mandarin heavily accented by his native Hunanese dialect, whose lilting rhythms and unaccustomed emphases soon became familiar to all Chinese, Mao formally proclaimed the founding of the People's Republic of China.

People's Democratic Dictatorship

At its founding, the PRC took the form of a "people's democratic dictatorship." This apparently contradictory form had a theoretical logic in Maoism. In Maoist politics, revolutionary consciousness and activity were crucial elements distinguishing "the people" from counter-revolutionaries. Enshrining this distinction as a principle and right of citizenship, "the people" were defined in the PRC as those who supported—through word and deed—the revolution and, by conflation, the CCP. For these, "democracy" would be guaranteed. This democracy was not of the bourgeois or "old" type (as practiced in capitalist countries); it did not rely on elections or parliamentary procedures. Rather, this was to be the "new" type of democracy, as promoted by Mao in Yan'an. It was a democracy comprised of the united revolutionary classes and supportive political parties under the leadership of the CCP. It depended on the "mass line" and called for centralized rule. It was democratic centralism. All those designated "the people"—the vast majority—could and in fact were expected to participate and contribute to the flourishing of this type of democracy. For all others—

counter-revolutionaries, or the "non-people"—dictatorship would be the form of government imposed upon them. They could re-educate and reform themselves to become "people," but, those classes and individuals designated the "non-people" would be dealt with harshly, through dictatorial and coercive methods. The "non-people" were not permitted to participate in the life of the socialist nation, until their re-education by "the people" was completed (as decided by the Party).

With this theoretical justification, a dual state form was promoted: a democratic one for "the people" and a dictatorship for all others. There was no pretense to non-partiality. The PRC state was a state for the revolutionary peoples—the coalition of peasant and proletariat as well as all those who could claim to have the correct revolutionary consciousness. Others could either join by developing the correct revolutionary consciousness, or leave, or suffer their fates. Very quickly, of course, the problem of who qualified as "people" emerged. As Mao Zedong Thought became more dogmatically construed, and as the CCP using Mao Zedong Thought came to be the exclusive arbiter of "revolutionary truth," the boundaries of the "people" became more fluid and arbitrary. These issues plagued Chinese political society from this time forward.

An Economy in Ruins

As the People's Liberation Army (renamed as such in 1937) took control of the country region by region from the fleeing GMD military, the extent of China's disrepair became apparent. In their hasty flight from the mainland, the GMD had stripped the country of all liquid assets such as gold, silver, and dollar reserves; they had also packed up and moved—on boats and planes supplied by the United States—the "cultural patrimony" of China, including the treasures of Beijing's Forbidden City and other moveable artistic and archival items of value. They had attempted to firebomb industrial sites to prevent them from falling into CCP hands. However, many workers acted to protect their factories from destruction.

Adding to the problems, bandits roamed the scorched countryside, preying upon a weakened people; displaced refugees from the Japanese occupation and from the ravages of the civil war wandered the nation and clogged the cities. Commerce had been destroyed, first by the wars and then by rampant inflation; the national currency was worthless, and a barter economy had emerged. Portions of the urban intelligentsia and technologically proficient elites had fled with the GMD, leaving cities without administration and institutions without management. Daily necessities were scarce and prohibitively expensive. Urban unemployment was rife; rural productivity was at an all-time low. With the often enthusiastic, although sometimes only tepid, support of the majority of China's war-weary people, Mao's and the CCP's duties were daunting.

One of their first tasks was to have the CCP armies, upon entry into the cities, stabilize the social and financial situations. For many of the peasant troops, this was their first taste of modern life. As destroyed as the cities were, remaining urban amenities were still more advanced than those of the Yan'an caves or of the wartime front. Realizing the danger of temptation in leading troops astray, Mao felt compelled to issue a directive in late October 1949 to his armies to "always keep to the style of plain living and hard struggle" characterizing the Yan'an spirit.[4]

As a top concern, the CCP was committed to cleaning up the socially destructive habit and century-long symbol of Chinese colonial subjugation: opium smoking. Under the GMD, particularly in the civil war years of hyper-inflation, opium had become a widespread item of barter as the opium gangs had increased their stranglehold on GMD finances. Drug usage had skyrocketed. Under CCP rule, big opium dealers were summarily executed. By contrast, common opium users as well as prostitutes were targeted as the two socially parasitical populations who should be saved through re-education. The CCP enforced draconian drug rehabilitation measures requiring cold-turkey withdrawal. Meanwhile, they dragooned prostitutes into centers, to treat them for their medical problems and re-educate them to be productive members of a new society. Within two years, opium had been stamped out, and prostitution had been drastically curbed.

The state-sponsored Women's Federation assisted in these tasks, as prostitution in particular was understood to be a part of the "woman problem." In order to boost economic productivity and reduce social chaos —whether because of refugees, war-torn families, or child-selling due to poverty, prostitution, or drug use—women and families became important subjects of policy. Indeed, a cornerstone of the Maoist notion of a strong family was women, who were happy and secure enough in their marriages to be productive members of society and strong bulwarks for family unity. As such, in early 1950, one of the first laws passed by the CCP state was the new marriage law, guaranteeing freedom of choice in marriage, as well as divorce on demand and property rights to women. Thus addressing a concern formed at least since the time of Miss Zhao's suicide in 1919, Mao delivered part of the legal conditions for women's equality, even though these conditions were to tie women more firmly than ever to the family structure. With Mao's proclamation "women hold up half the sky," the Women's Federation became a symbol of the PRC's commitment to a particular form of feminism sponsored and guaranteed by the state.

Aside from urban work, the other major tasks to stabilize society were to get agricultural production going and to resume trade and commercial ties between the rural and urban areas. An initial requirement was to get rural refugees clogging the cities to return to the land. In the longer term, however, raising agricultural production had to go hand in hand with land reform and redistribution, which was going to prove disruptive before its potential of enhanced productivity could be realized.

Despite their best efforts, the CCP's administrative and financial capacities were soon stretched beyond the limit. To stave off complete crisis, Mao was forced to go hat in hand to Stalin.

"Lean to One Side"—Mao Goes to Moscow

Immediately upon the CCP victory, the United States slapped an embargo on the PRC, cutting off any and all trade with or aid to the mainland. America's global allies followed suit. Mao, who had had illusions about good relations with the United States and western Europe following CCP victory in the civil war, was left with no choice. He had to "lean to one side"—the Soviet side.

Until April 1949, Stalin had remained an ally of Chiang Kaishek's. When the CCP's imminent victory in the civil war could no longer be ignored, Stalin was forced to acknowledge Mao, even though an independent Communist movement to his south was hardly to his liking. After the formal founding of the PRC in October 1949, Stalin invited Mao to Moscow for talks. In December 1949, Mao boarded a special train in Beijing for the ten-day journey north. Mao's Moscow visit seemed to confirm to cold warriors in the United States there was one monolithic Communist bloc directed from Moscow's Red Square; the McCarthy witch hunts got under way in large part based upon this assumption. Yet Mao had no intention of delivering China to Stalin's control. In fact, Mao's struggles with Soviet-trained ideologues in China as well as Stalin's frequent betrayals of the CCP since the 1920s had conditioned Mao to be very wary of Stalin. Yet, Mao's position was not strong, given the international isolation of China and the disintegration of the economy.

On his arrival in Moscow, Mao stated in his formal address to the welcome committee: "For me to have the opportunity at this time to visit the capital of the Soviet Union, the first great socialist country in the world, is a very happy event in my life."[5] However, Mao's nine-week stay in the Soviet Union—one of only two sojourns abroad in his life—was by all accounts a very unhappy time. With hard negotiating, he managed to extract from Stalin a pledge of the Soviet Union's assistance if China were attacked by the United States or Japan, but he also had to allow the Soviets continued occupation of ports in Manchuria. Stalin refused to assist the CCP in planning a conquest of the GMD on Taiwan, even though he enthusiastically supported a show of Chinese force in Tibet. Most important, the economic aid Stalin offered was, in absolute terms, tiny. Yet, for China's industrialization efforts, it became a crucial contribution, coupled as it was with the number of Soviet scientific and technological advisors who were sent to China in the 1950s.

Aside from negotiations, while in the Soviet Union, Mao sat for an official portrait, met cultural figures, and toured many factories and farms. He also visited Leningrad. Speaking at the Moscow train station upon departure, Mao noted in the course of his visits and talks that he had "seen the great achievements of the workers, peasants, and intellectuals of the Soviet Union . . . [and] observed the work-style of combining a spirit of revolution with a spirit of realism and practicality." On February 17, 1950, Mao thanked the people of the USSR, in particular Generalissimo Stalin, and boarded his train home.[6]

Through the 1950s, Mao continued his verbal fealty to Stalin even though his ideological differences from the Soviets were huge. These were differences that, by 1960, erupted in an all-out divide between the two Communist giants. For the moment, Mao returned to Beijing carrying the Sino-Soviet Friendship Treaty, with the bare minimum of what he'd gone to Moscow to seek.

Mao Settles into Life in Beijing

Upon resettlement from Yan'an to Beijing, Mao and the top leadership of the CCP had moved into a portion of the former imperial palace grounds called Zhongnanhai, behind the Gate of Heavenly Peace and next to the Forbidden City. Each leader—Mao, Liu Shaoqi, Lin Biao, Zhou Enlai, Peng Dehuai, and others—had as a place of work and residence a one-story courtyard house comprised of several wings connected together by corridors and hallways. Each compound was separated from the others by walls, fences, and armed guards. Those leaders, such as Mao, who had families, settled into routine family life; others, getting a later start, married and began having children, resulting in a minor baby boom in Zhongnanhai.

Mao's compound housed himself and his enormous study, lined with the thousands of books he had been collecting since his Changsha student days. In addition, there was Jiang Qing, his third wife, who occupied one wing of the house with his daughter by He Zizhen, Li Min, who had returned earlier from Moscow; and Li Na, his daughter by Jiang. The two girls were enrolled in a nearby school in Beijing. Joining them in the compound was Mao Yuanxin, the seven-year-old son of Mao's brother Zemin, who had been killed in 1943 in the far northwest.

Mao's eldest son by Yang Kaihui, Anying, who had fought with the Soviet army on the Eastern European front, had recently married. He had his own residence and worked in a machinery plant in Beijing. Anqing, Mao's younger son by Yang, was at first stationed in Manchuria engaged in land reform. On his return to Beijing, he was diagnosed as schizophrenic; he kept a low-profile job as a Russian translator.[7] Anqing mostly lived in the Zhongnanhai compound prior to his 1962 marriage to Shao Hua, the sister of Anying's wife.

Jiang Qing and Mao led mostly separate lives. Rumors of Mao's active extramarital sex life immediately began to circulate. Many retrospective exposés of Mao—most sensationally, by his private doctor, Li Zhishui—concentrate on the supposed relationship between his sexual appetites and his dictatorial style. These prurient accounts are used to dismiss Mao as a lecherous tyrant. Whatever the alleged sex-tyrant linkage, it is true that Mao's sexual liaisons with a number of women did create great difficulties between himself and Jiang Qing.

Mao remained in vigorous physical condition until close to his death. His five-foot ten-inch frame was amply filled out, as he gained a good deal of weight after moving to Beijing from Yan'an. Mao swam daily in an indoor pool set aside for his use in Zhongnanhai; when he left Beijing to tour the country—as he did for many months each year—he walked for long distances. He continued, against his doctor's advice, to eat the greasy, chili-laden foods of his Hunanese childhood, often challenging guests to eat with him, exclaiming "if it is not spicy, it is not revolutionary." Mao also was a heavy smoker: in the early 1950s, his favorite brand was British "555" cigarettes; thereafter, it was China's "Panda" brand, which became famous (and unobtainable) because of his habit. He preferred to work at night and sleep through the morning, continuing a schedule he'd maintained as a guerilla warrior, when night maneuvers were the only ones possible. Most affairs of state had to wait until late afternoon or early evening to be handled.

Mao eschewed proper clothing. Upon his death, his closet reputedly contained mostly old and patched outfits. He hated suits and leather shoes, and only agreed to put these on when receiving guests of state or presiding over formal meetings. His bodyguards broke in new shoes on his behalf, when required. He usually wore flexible cloth shoes and mostly preferred to be naked, other than a draped robe around his shoulders and a towel loosely thrown around his middle. In this fashion he received friends and colleagues. He disliked sit-down toilets, preferring the squat variety, and continued his lifelong habit of cleaning his mouth with tea leaves rather than a toothbrush.

Land Reform

After his return from Moscow and before the rice planting season in June 1950, Mao decided to launch the long-promised land reform. In consultation with the Communist Party leadership group—who continued as a strong unified presence at this early stage of CCP rule—the decision was taken to destroy once and for all the gentry-landlord class, which had been China's elites for millennia. Most landlords had stayed in China rather than follow the GMD to Taiwan. Their assets, after all, were not exportable. While many landlords confidently looked forward to the return of the GMD, others hoped for leniency. All were disappointed.

Land reform was a political and an economic commitment made by the CCP to the peasantry. And yet it held different meanings for the different parties involved. To the peasantry, the CCP victory promised the fulfillment of desires to own land, free of landlord control and perennial indebtedness to predatory rural usurers (such as Mao's father had been). For the CCP, land distribution to the peasants was to be the first step in a protracted process. The initial step was intended to break the back of the landlord class by expropriating the material conditions of their economic and cultural power: their land. The next steps were, necessarily, to lead to collectivization.

Communist economics is not predicated upon private landholding; it is not intended to shore up what Marxists call the "petty bourgeois" economy of small cultivators. Its goal is to achieve agricultural economies of scale without the waged-labor and private-ownership structure of capitalist agribusiness or the immiseration of tenants in feudal land relations. In theory, collectivized agriculture would not only enhance productivity; it would facilitate state accumulation of surplus for urban industrialization and national social programs. It would also provide a more stable basis for peasant livelihood than the precarious ones generally marking the rural areas from time immemorial.

Land reform proceeded unevenly. In keeping with the tenets of Maoism —revolutionary politics needed to be practiced as part of everyday life—it was the peasants themselves who undertook the land redistribution, with the guidance of the CCP. In the old northern base areas, where the CCP had been in power since 1935, land redistribution had already begun long before. During the civil war, these bastions of CCP support had been further radicalized. In 1950, land reform quickly turned even more violent in these areas. Landlords—big and small—were rounded up by local peasants with scores to settle. They were subjected to brutal people's tribunal sessions, where their and their family's crimes against the poor—current and historical—were enumerated in public "struggle sessions," after which they were sentenced to death and killed. In these areas, in fact, local CCP cadres tried to rein in the excesses. Mao weighed in on this matter, albeit ambiguously. He urged caution against what he called "ultra-Left deviations" and encouraged adherence to the new democratic social unity appropriate for this transitional period.[8] And yet Mao also repeated his phrase from the Hunan Peasant Report of 1927—"a revolution is not a dinner party"—thus seeming to sanction the violence.

In the south, where land reform had not before been attempted because of GMD control, and where land was owned by large, sprawling clans rather than single landlords, peasants were unfamiliar with the processes. The redistribution went more slowly and less antagonistically. In fact, unlike in the north, one problem the CCP had in the south was convincing poorer peasants that the land of their richer neighbors—often kin from the extended clan—should be expropriated at all.

With ebbs and flows in the process and much regional variation, by 1952 the momentous social revolution of land redistribution was completed. The landlord-gentry was destroyed as a class. Many individuals had been executed, although most landlords, after admitting their historical crimes, were permitted to have their own plots of land. In the course of the movement, cultivated acreage had been expanded, anti-pest campaigns undertaken, irrigation canals re-dug or strengthened, and insecticides and fertilizers made more widely available. By 1952, rural productivity increased hugely, and agriculture was on a firm footing.[9]

All this proceeded just as China was forced back into war.

"Resist America, Aid Korea"

In the months of consolidation of CCP rule in the mainland, there were numerous fears among leaders about the fragility of their victory. Nobody expected Chiang Kaishek to take defeat lightly. Paramilitary groups of the GMD funded by the CIA operated out of Tibet and on China's borders, hoping to foment rebellion or chaos. Paranoia about internal spies and enemies was rife. In the midst of this uncertain situation, the Korean War broke out in mid-1950. This was a civil war fought as a product of the incomplete independence of Korea from the Japanese after the Second World War. In the context of the military protectorate the United States threw around the GMD on Taiwan and of CCP fears of counter-revolutionary activity, the U.S. entry into the war appeared as a direct threat to China. In mainland opinion, and in many public statements from the United States, the American involvement was immediately construed as an action preparatory to a potential invasion of China. The GMD-aligned "China Lobby" in Washington did all it could to encourage U.S. policy in this direction.

By October 1950, U.S. troops had almost reached the Yalu River, the border between Manchuria and Korea. A faction of U.S. senators loudly supported the "nuking" of China, or at least, an invasion to overthrow Communism. Anxiously noting the developments, Mao issued an order on October 8 for "the Chinese People's Volunteers . . . to move immediately into the territory of Korea, to join our Korean comrades in their fight against the invaders, and to strive for a glorious victory." Enjoining Chinese troops to "repel the attacks of the American imperialists and their running dogs,"[10] Chinese participation in the Korean War began.

Commanded by the veteran guerilla general, Peng Dehuai, the Chinese lured the enemy deep, onward toward the Yalu. When General MacArthur took the bait, Peng sent wave upon wave of troops to attack, inflicting upon the American army its greatest defeat. American forces were pushed back down the Korean peninsula. By mid-1951, fighting stabilized at the Thirty-eighth parallel, where the war had first begun. For two and a half years thereafter, a war of attrition was fought before the truce could be arranged that is still operative today.

Popularly known in China as the "Resist America, Aid Korea" period, the war placed huge strains on an already fragile economy and society. With Soviet military aid in shorter supply than originally expected, the Chinese were forced to produce, substantially on their own, the clothing, food, and equipment needed by their troops fighting in the frozen northern climes of Korea. This they had to do in addition to providing for civilians, who might chafe against further privations so soon after the completion of the civil war. Exhortations to production were the order of the day, even as a measure of political terror descended upon suspect populations out of fears about internal subversion.

At the beginning of the war, Mao's eldest son, Anying, requested to join the effort. Mao agreed. Though Anying wanted to be in the infantry, Peng Dehuai decided it was too risky. Now twenty-eight years old, Anying was assigned to be a Russian translator at Peng's headquarters. In late November 1950, Anying's position was hit by a U.S. incendiary bomb; he was killed and immediately buried in Korea. Peng told Mao in person of his loss. In his public pronouncement, Mao was brief: "In war there must be sacrifice. . . . To sacrifice my son or other people's sons is just the same. There are no parents in the world who do not treasure their children. . . . There are so many common folk whose children have shed their blood and were sacrificed for the sake of the revolution. They are in need of consolation, and we ought to pay more attention to showing them greater concern."[11]

Despite Mao's public stoicism, Anying's death took a huge personal toll on him. Due to historical circumstances, Mao had never spent much time with his sons by Yang Kaihui. Now settled in Beijing, Mao had looked forward to the routines allowing him to enjoy his grown and smaller children, and later, hopefully, some grandchildren. While Jiang Qing was never close to Mao's children by his previous wives—nor, reputedly, to her own daughter, Li Na—Mao was a loving father. Anying's childless widow, Liu Songlin, remained close to her father-in-law long after her husband's death; in her memoirs, she writes of the concern he showed her and the long hours she spent with Mao reminiscing about Anying.

Development vs. Revolution

Once stabilization had been achieved and the Korean War fought to a stalemate, it was time to turn to longer-term plans. The dilemma now facing the CCP was a practical problem of culturally and politically transforming a society that rested upon a very weak economic foundation. In dealing with this, Mao tirelessly attempted to impress upon his fellow CCP leaders that there is a vast difference between advocating development for its own sake and advocating development in the pursuit of revolutionary transformation.

In the quest for high growth rates, capitalism had already shown its historical superiority in comparison to any other system. Yet, capitalist growth comes at the expense of huge inequalities within nations and between them. Mao had long since rejected capitalism and embraced revolutionizing social relations. He was intent on developing China, not as an end in itself, but as part of deepening the transformation of and creating the conditions for equality in society. Others disagreed. As early as 1953, ideological divisions began to emerge within the Party over the relative importance of development and revolution, and the methods by which each would be achieved. These differences were not empty power struggles, as some scholars have claimed. Rather, the power struggles reflected real ideological disagreements over the course and direction of the Chinese nation.

The disputes in the Party leadership introduced an issue, already foreshadowed in Yan'an, that characterized the Maoist period: the contradiction between bureaucracy and revolution. As the Party in power, the CCP was *both* the bearer of revolution *as well as* the bureaucracy in charge of economic policy and social transformation. These were inherently contradictory roles. From 1953 on, during times of emphasis on economic development at all costs, the CCP's bureaucratic role grew, social hierarchies proliferated, and the revolutionizing of society slowed in pursuit of growth and economic efficiency. Conversely, at times of emphasis on social revolution, the CCP, as a bureaucracy, became an object of revolutionary attack, mass politics came to the fore, and social hierarchies were mitigated, while economic efficiency took a backseat to radical politics. These oscillations largely shaped the Maoist era.

Industrial Policy and Self-Sufficiency

In 1953, the CCP opted to follow the Soviet path of development. This called for modernization based on the maximum extraction of surplus from the rural areas to fund heavy industrialization located in the cities. It was a plan subordinating the rural to the urban and calling for a centralized state to allocate and distribute resources according to economic not social dictates. The decision to follow this path was made in part because the

Soviet model was the only existing socialist one; because Soviet advisors counseled their Chinese counterparts to do so; and because Chinese economic weaknesses were so thoroughgoing and the Euro-American-Japanese embargo so crippling, that the Chinese had to produce almost everything they needed on their own. Finally, the decision was made because the economic developmentalist faction within the leadership temporarily won the ideological debate over the Maoist faction.

Mao made a virtue of necessity. Designating China's vast population its most precious resource—in the absence of technology and capital investment, what China had in abundance was human labor power—Mao promoted the idea of labor-intensive self-sufficiency, or autarky. Self-sufficiency in grain and other foodstuffs, in cloth, fuel, and all basic necessities, became the hallmark of Maoist-era economic policy and practice.

With land reform providing stable conditions for a steady source of agricultural surplus, the first five-year plan, lasting from 1953–57, saw the annual rate of industrial growth average 16 percent. Total industrial output more than doubled over the course of the five years. The industrial working class grew from six to ten million, and urban population rose. Large industrial workplaces were organized on socialist principles. They provided subsidized housing, cradle to grave medical care, permanent jobs, educational facilities from pre-school through high school for workers and their families, vegetable markets and butchers, barbers, entertainment, and so on. As the basic structure of labor and everyday life, the "work unit" (*danwei*) came to define and police the political and economic parameters of the everyday lives of the majority of urban residents.

Centralization and Decentralization

Organizing the national economy required a delicate balance between centralized decision making and local-level activity and needs. As Mao noted in a speech made in August 1953, "Centralization and decentralization are constantly in contradiction with each other." According to his method, then, one needed to analyze each moment to find whether the one or the other was more appropriate to the situation. In raising this issue, Mao was issuing a veiled critique of Party ideologues, whose insistence on centralization was often out of step with local conditions. As he recounted in the same speech, "Recently I made a trip to Wuhan and Nanjing and learned a lot about conditions. . . . When I stay in Beijing I hear almost nothing; from now on I will go out and take trips."[12] Mao went further. He called the urban focus of the Party a "sugarcoated bullet of the bourgeoisie." Indeed, he accused the Party of establishing a "gentleman's agreement" with urban capitalists and of betraying revolutionary principles. This so-called capitulation to the urban bourgeoisie was an ominous indicator of potential counter-revolution within the Party for Mao.

Nevertheless, at this point, Mao grudgingly recognized that the nationwide scarcity of resources required central distributive controls and the new democratic transition to socialism required firm Party leadership. Soon enough, Mao became thoroughly disenchanted with the ways in which plodding bureaucratic routines squashed mass initiative; in which urban and rural inequalities were proliferating; in which the continued existence of private industry and private property in the mixed economy was hindering the fulfillment of socialist principles in the cities; and, finally, the ways in which Party cadres quickly became a privileged social sector, taking urban comforts and perks of power as entitlements. By the late 1950s, Mao was to attack all of this by whipping up a mass movement.

For the time being, in keeping with its broad cultural concerns, the CCP immediately embarked on literacy campaigns, educational programs, and wide-ranging plans to deepen the reach and content of revolutionary culture around the country. For these initiatives, the Party needed to tap the expertise, participation, and enthusiasms of intellectuals and educated people. Yet, Mao had always had a conflicted relationship to intellectuals, and his ambivalence was to erupt frequently through the years, as it already had in Yan'an during the Rectification. As independent thinkers, intellectuals were not to be wholly trusted. They were elitist, bookish, and urban based. Even if nominally Marxist, their commitments to the revolution were not in tune with Mao's cultural revolutionary policies of massification. Nevertheless, intellectuals possessed the expertise and specialized knowledge required of a functioning modern society. Thus, almost from the very first days of the PRC in October 1949, Mao wrote letters and telegrams to major literary and cultural figures, urging them to remain on the mainland to help reconstruct the Chinese nation. Many of these figures—including many non-Communists deeply disillusioned by Chiang Kaishek's and GMD corruption—decided to stay in the PRC to contribute their skills and knowledge to the revolutionary transformation of China.

State-sponsored cultural organizations were established shortly after the PRC's founding, often led by non-Communists. These organizations provided an umbrella for cultural activities, which now no longer relied on marketability for survival, but rather needed to conform to political criteria. In the initial years, these criteria were rather capacious. Not long after, ideological control over cultural production began to narrow dramatically the parameters of the possible. At the same time, elementary, secondary, and tertiary educational facilities were set up or revived after the wartime destructions and displacements. Mandarin was proclaimed the national (spoken) language to unify a country of mutually incomprehensible dialect speakers. Linguists embarked on what was to become the simplification of the written language aimed at boosting literacy. Physical education was widely promoted, to strengthen the bodies of the new socialist people; in these campaigns, Mao's lifelong devotion to swimming was cited and promoted.

The CCP provided basic medicine to the remotest of communities, intending to wipe out the diseases that had often been fatal only because untreated. After quickly training teams of what came to be known as "barefoot doctors" in rudimentary aspects of diagnosis and care, public hygiene campaigns were launched at the same time as common ailments were brought under control. As a consequence, fertility rose, infant mortality declined, life expectancy began to climb, and the population stabilized and then grew for the first time since the Japanese invasion of 1937.

Mobile drama troupes were sent on nationwide tours to bring culture and propaganda to the farthest corners of the country. Mobile film groups transported projectors and screens on oxcarts and shoulder-carrying poles to the remotest of villages, to teach peasants how to watch moving pictures and how to understand the narrative forms of new media. Most of the emphasis was on the grassroots spread of medicine, education, and culture rather than on urban-based specialized institutes and knowledge accessible only by the few for the few. This bias toward massification of culture, begun during the Yan'an years, consistently was promoted by Mao from 1949 on.

Hu Feng and the Counter-Revolutionary Clique

At the beginning of the 1950s, relations between the Party and intellectuals were tentatively cooperative. With Mao's public attack on the prominent Confucian philosopher Liang Shuming in 1953, the atmosphere started to change. In 1955, the "Hu Feng affair" put intellectuals on permanent guard about Mao's control over "revolutionary truth." Hu Feng was a literary critic with a huge reputation and a distinctive style. Loosely a Marxist, Hu was no admirer of Party strictures, and he refused to submit to Party discipline. He had been in debating dialogue with Communist literary figures since the 1930s, particularly with Zhou Yang, now in charge of cultural policy. Hu Feng had consistently warned against the creation of a "cultural desert," should Party-dictated conformism be enforced or followed. Nevertheless, he had elected to stay in CCP-controlled China to assist in the rebuilding of the nation. In early 1955, he was accused of exhibiting "bourgeois" tendencies and "subjectivist" deviations. By mid-1955 and much more seriously, Hu Feng was accused of being the leader of a subversive counter-revolutionary clique allegedly intent on preparing the way for the restoration of GMD rule. In July 1955, Hu was arrested. Only in 1980, after decades of incarceration, was Hu released. He died in 1985.

Mao was personally involved in this affair. He wrote a preface to the published anti–Hu Feng materials, in which he hurled one politically loaded accusation after another. Most ominously, he wrote: "The Hu Feng elements were counter-revolutionary elements who appeared in disguise; they gave people a false image and hid their true face. . . ." In explaining how such elements could have hidden in plain sight, Mao notes: " . . . the task of distinguishing and purging bad persons can be done only by relying on the integration of correct leadership on the part of the leading organs and a high degree of consciousness among the broad masses. . . . All these things are lessons for us." He concludes, "We are taking the Hu Feng affair seriously, because we want to use it to educate the broad masses of the people, first of all those literate working cadres and the intellectuals."[13]

INTERLUDE: WANG YUANHUA ON HU FENG

Q: When did you start to have doubts about the Chinese revolution?
A: It started from the anti–Hu Feng campaign. At that time, Hu was regarded as a counter-revolutionary. The chief of police [of Shanghai] came to speak to me. He said, in essence: "If you admit that Hu Feng is a counter-revolutionary, I will let you continue to work; if, however, you do not, the consequences will be severe." He asked me to think about my answer carefully. I was detained. I spent a very sleepless night. The next day, he came back and I replied to him: "I think Hu Feng certainly maintains an anti-Marxist line, but he is not a counter-revolutionary."

Q: So you became suspicious at that time?

A: Correct. I think so. They did not allow people to speak honestly. Once, I went to have a cup of tea with Hu Feng at a teahouse in a park. They accused me of being part of Hu's counter-revolutionary clique. This was ridiculous. Later, I realized that in a political campaign [such as the anti–Hu Feng one], there is no truth; there is only meeting the needs of the movement defined by the leaders. One could be framed at will. I could not understand this principle at that time—thankfully!—so I was dismissed from the Party.

Q: So the whole direction of the Chinese revolution was in doubt for you after that?

A: . . . Hu Feng turned out to be only the beginning. Those in the Party who disagreed with Mao came to be detained. This was to completely distort truth!

As Wang attests, the Hu Feng affair turned out to be only a mild harbinger of what was to come next for intellectuals.

Bandung and Third Worldism

By the mid-1950s, the global Cold War was subjecting all nations and peoples to its divisive logic. The Indian leader, Jawaharlal Nehru, and President Sukarno of Indonesia, among others, insisted there was a different way through the global political minefields. They called for a conference of the unaligned Asian and African nations and peoples to be held in Bandung, Indonesia, in April 1955. The PRC was among the twenty-nine participating nations. Its delegation was headed by Premier Zhou Enlai. Zhou had just attended the Geneva talks in 1954, during which the de facto division of Vietnam after the defeat of French colonialism had been a major point of contention. An urbane, multilingual, sophisticated man, Zhou had spent time in France in the 1920s. He was a CCP insider, Long March veteran, and Yan'an survivor. The international spokesperson for Maoist-style communism and the PRC, Zhou was much respected inside and outside of China. Mao kept him close for the entirety of his rule.

Zhou went to Bandung to represent the PRC not as a Communist nation but as a third world country, whose historical legacy of colonialism and of imperialist-induced developmental distortion had much in common with other African and Asian countries. At Bandung, Zhou promoted the "new democratic" developmental plan theorized by Mao in 1940. He also promoted what he and Mao called the "five principles for peaceful co-existence." These were intended to create the global conditions for peace, beyond the tensions of the Cold War. Indeed, China's participation in Bandung was a firm sign not only of Mao's growing attachment to third world identifications but also of his increasing estrangement from the Soviet Union.

With the high point of the PRC's normally isolated international presence achieved at Bandung, two events in 1956 presented Mao with an explicit ideological challenge: the Hungarian uprising and Krushchev's denunciation of Stalin. Combined with new developments on the domestic front, these created a particularly tense situation in China by the late 1950s.

Dealing with Stalin's Ghost

Dead in 1953, Stalin was idolized in official Chinese propaganda as a great socialist leader. However, nothing in Nikita Krushchev's secret speech to the Soviet Politburo in 1956 detailing Stalin's terrible crimes and brutality was news to the Chinese. What needed to be explained publicly was how the most advanced socialist country in the world could have permitted such crimes to proliferate, and, moreover, what the relationship of those individual crimes was to the socialist endeavor in general. This ramified into the larger question of what was the proper relationship between leader (the "cult of the individual") and the Party (the collective), and between Party and society? In turn, this question was directly related to the increasingly fraught relationship between Mao and the CCP, and between the CCP and Chinese society.

In 1956, Mao echoed, while mitigating, Krushchev's condemnation of Stalin. Acknowledging Stalin was responsible for crimes, Mao also credited him with building Soviet socialism. In a balance sheet approach to become a familiar form of evaluation, Mao proclaimed Stalin mostly correct and partially wrong. This allowed Mao to continue to promote Stalin as a major socialist leader, even while he launched critiques of the Stalinist method and of Stalin's cult of personality.

Of even more momentous concern was the outbreak in Hungary in November 1956 of a direct challenge to communist rule and the dispatch of Soviet troops to quell the challenge. For Mao, this presented a real conundrum. Mao recognized how the hyper-bureaucratization of the Soviet system—in Eastern Europe as in the Soviet Union—and the mechanistic nature of its implementation had produced social alienation. The Party, rather than grow organically from society, was imposing itself upon society as an alien force. Always suspicious of the Soviet Union's bureaucratic tendencies and consistently critical of analogous CCP tendencies, Mao could understand the impetus behind the Hungarian uprising. Of equal concern was Mao's lifelong devotion as a Communist and a Chinese to keeping China independent from Soviet control. The reality of the Soviet army marching into Hungary was not a comforting one in this regard. It raised the specter of a similar action against China.

Nevertheless, an uprising weakening Communism by challenging the socialist system could not be countenanced by Mao. In his condemnation, Mao particularly focused on the supposed betrayal of socialism by Hungarian intellectuals and technocrats, who were, according to him, advocating the restoration of bourgeois rule. Conflating Hungarian desires to be free of the dead hand of Soviet-style bureaucracy with suspicions about the loyalty of intellectuals to socialism, Mao gave clear indications of where his domestic wrath would next fall.

On Rural Collectivization

By the mid-1950s, the Chinese economy was growing at a good pace, although agricultural production had slowed after the post-reform spurt. The second five-year plan was under discussion. At the same time, the problem of Party bureaucracy and privilege was becoming worse, as was the relative disadvantage of the rural areas in relation to the urban. Mao was galvanized to push forward on the next steps in China's transition to socialism. He decided it was time to abandon the new democratic mixed-economy approach by expropriating all remaining urban private property and industry and moving toward rural collectivization. These decisions were much contested within the Party. They not only represented inroads on the Party bureaucracy's vested interests but also an ideological shift in economic strategy.

The first problem to tackle was the rural areas. In 1953, peasants were given the option to join low-level agricultural cooperatives. These were not producers' collectives, but rather loosely configured mutual-help organizations. By the end of 1955, cooperativization had reached the majority of poor and middle peasants, who enthusiastically participated. With an initial impetus from above, this movement mostly was carried out at the grassroots level. Mao interpreted the grassroots upsurge as a "socialist tidal wave" overtaking the countryside, and as a spontaneous clamor for a more decisive struggle between capitalism and socialism.[14] Seizing the moment, Mao immediately decided to deepen cooperativization into collectivization.

But this was in explicit opposition to two recent Central Party Committee (CPC) decisions. The CPC had opted to wait on collectivization until China had the capacity to mechanize agriculture. Mao argued mechanization was fine in theory, but in practice it put people out of work, and what China had in abundance was people. The CPC also argued the "rich peasant economy" was most productive, and this economic form should be consolidated. Mao disagreed. He believed middle and poor peasants should be given assistance in opposing rich peasants and ex-landlords, who were attempting to reestablish their dominance. In Mao's view, forestalling this restoration could only be achieved through collectivization.

In an end-run around the CPC, Mao made a speech to local Party cadres in July 1955 urging further cooperativization and collectivization. The response was overwhelmingly supportive. Mao proclaimed, "A high tide in the new socialist mass movement will soon sweep across the rural areas throughout the country. Some of our comrades, however, are tottering along like a woman with bound feet, complaining all the time about others, saying: [You're] going too fast, [you're] going too fast. [They are given to] excessive nitpicking, unwarranted complaints, endless worries, and countless taboos and take this to be the correct policy for guiding the socialist mass movement in the rural areas. No, this is not the correct policy; it is a wrong policy."[15]

Collectivization required the incorporation of all peasants, not just the willing ones. It required the end of most privately owned land, the end of family farming, and the pooling of resources. Richer peasants were not enthusiastic, and many were downright hostile. However, they were overrun by enthusiasms among poor and middle peasants, who had everything to gain by collectivizing resources. The rich-peasant land, livestock, and implements were summarily incorporated into producer collectives, and by 1956 over 90 percent of the rural population was incorporated into collectives. The astonishingly quick movement had been completed mostly without violence. This agricultural socialization process stood in great contrast to the 1930s Stalinist version, which had entailed intense state violence and coercion accompanied by waves of executions. Mao took many opportunities to point proudly to the differences.

Two major issues emerged from the collectivization movement. In terms of production, while the process of collectivizing had been smooth, the actual running of the collectives was far less successful. They were plagued by confusions, insufficiencies in accounting procedures, inefficiencies in work allocations, difficulties in planning the larger units, and inequities in the distribution of the fruits of labor. Peasant enthusiasm quickly waned. Increasing coercion was required to forestall the stampede to withdraw from the newly formed collectives.

In terms of politics, Mao's end-run maneuver in 1955 brought into clear relief the problem of the relationship between leader and Party. In appealing directly to local cadres and the peasantry's own spontaneous activity, Mao began to separate himself from the Party's foot-dragging bureaucracy and to attach himself directly to the revolutionary people. The Party seemed to figure in Mao's speeches as a nonrevolutionary entity squashing the revolutionary enthusiasms of the people. The Party was becoming an enemy of the people.

On the Ten Major Relationships

For the time being, peasants were organizing into collectives, and the next problem was solving the recalibration of the overall economic relationships in society. In 1956, Mao spoke to this issue in a series of essays, speeches, and reports. All of these increased tensions between himself and the Party. They also addressed Mao's differences from Stalin. In Mao's view, the Stalinist approach to development refused to acknowledge the complexity of the relationship between a planned economy and the bureaucratic state. This had been one of Mao's concerns in Yan'an. His essay of 1956 "On the Ten Major Relationships" and his slightly later "Notes on *A Critique of Soviet Economics*" present his attempt to rethink the state's relationship to production under socialism, as well as the proper role of technocrats and intellectuals in the economic and social life of a socialist nation.

With the second five-year plan under discussion, the concrete problem facing Mao was the method by which the state could accumulate investment capital in a situation of domestic scarcity, and where attracting foreign capital was not an option. What Mao found most unpalatable in the Soviet system was the focus on extraction from the peasantry, who were made to bear the brunt of industrialization's costs. This was precisely the system put in place in 1953 in China that developmentalists within the Party wanted to continue into the second five-year plan. Yet the peasantry was Mao's strongest constituency, and their standards of living and access to commodities were actually falling in relation to their urban compatriots. This was intolerable.

The essay on the ten major relationships is a dense consideration of socialist economic laws, the particulars of which are of interest only to the specialist. However, the astonishing upshot of the essay was Mao's re-articulation of one of the major Marxist precepts of economic development. In orthodox Marxism—Stalinism included—the most important economic and thus social relationship is between the forces of production (the capacity for machinery, factories, electrical supply, etc.) and the social relations of production (the mode of exploitation and organization, e.g., waged labor, slavery, etc.). Orthodox Marxists hold that the relations of production are wholly determined by the level of the forces of production. For example, classical capitalism demands industrial waged labor aimed at garnering maximum profits for the capitalist; feudalism demands agricultural tenancy presided over by landlords, whose extraction of surplus is economically unproductive but politically empowering. And so on. As a Marxist, Mao accepted these basic elements. Yet, what Mao did in his essay was to reverse the determinations. That is, rather than the forces determining the relations, according to Mao, in the historical situation of scarcity in which China found itself, it would have to be the social relations of production that would determine the level of the forces of production. As such, even though China's forces were quite backward, advanced collectivized social relations of production would be the way to enhance them.

Translated into a matter of policy, Mao advocated the radical alteration of the relations of production, rather than work exclusively for the growth in productive forces as more orthodox Party economists were advocating. In the rural areas, this meant collectivization as a *means* for enhancing productivity; in urban industry, it meant overhauling the organization of factory floors to enhance worker participation in management. Overall, it required a much tighter integration of rural and urban economies than the essentially extractive one currently being pursued. It called for the spatial reorganization of industrialization, so that it would no longer be located only in the cities, but rather dispersed through the countryside as well. This would bring the social relations of industrial production closer to the social relations of rural production. It would simultaneously fulfill Mao's desire to revolutionize society and to develop the Chinese economy.

All of this was monumentally contested. First, the reversal of deter-minations—relations leading production rather than production leading relations—meant the Party bureaucracy's role in directing the growth of the forces of production would be demoted. This was a direct attack on the Party. Moreover, the urban-located heavy industrial bias of all develop-ment policy was under assault. Second, Mao's theories seemed to be ques-tionable, relying as they did on faith in the revolutionary people's con-sciousness and activity in overcoming material limitations. Third, Mao was intervening in matters hitherto left to technocrats and specialists, whom he was critiquing for their urban, elitist ("bourgeois") biases. This set up the battle lines that were soon enough to be fought out at the mass and inner-Party levels.

On Contradictions among the People

In a third intervention into the problems of the late 1950s—following those on peasants and economic development—Mao reopened the ques-tion of "the people" and of politics under socialism. In his important "On the Correct Handling of Contradictions Among the People" of February 1957, Mao called for a people's movement to critique the Party and Party methods. Here, Mao specifically defined intellectuals as part of the revolu-tionary "people" and placed the burden of critique mostly on them. He noted that their critiques of the Party and of bureaucratic methods would have to be handled as friendly critiques, not as hostile ones. They should not be suppressed, as the critiques of enemies would be. Mao went further. He proclaimed in socialist society, where economic classes had basically been abolished, contradictions continued to exist. These contradictions were sometimes even of a fundamental, or antagonistic, variety. But, he specified, so long as these contradictions are "among the people," they are non-antagonistic. Only contradictions between "the people" and the "non-people" are antagonistic and must be dealt with dictatorially.

Much of this was familiar enough as Maoist analytical method or as settled ideology. What was extraordinary in the speech was Mao's pro-nouncement that in the China of 1950s, there was a contradiction "be-tween the leadership and the led" and it could be an antagonistic one. Clearly, for Mao, "the leadership" was not himself, but the Party. His insin-uation was that "the people" (and Mao as their spokesperson) were better arbiters of revolutionary truth than the Party. Intellectuals were invited to give voice to "the people."

The implications were staggering, and they were not lost on Party leaders. First, Mao implied, the Party was now, only seven years into socialism, thoroughly divorced from the society it ruled. It was a force above rather than a force of the people. It had lost its claims to revolutionariness. Second, Mao placed himself conspicuously outside the Party on the side of the people, from whence he and they could criticize the Party. This gave enormous impetus to the Mao cult. Third, and perhaps worst (from the Party's perspective), in proclaiming a contradiction between the leadership and the led, Mao seemed to be advocating popular struggle against the Party. He had transposed class struggle within society into struggle between the Party and society. The CCP was put on guard. Yet Party leaders remained silent.

Let One Hundred Flowers Bloom

One immediate consequence of Mao's invitation to the people to speak was the gradual opening of social spaces of critique. Newspapers published at first tentative and then increasingly vituperative criticisms of unjust Party methods, incredible inefficiency, poor planning, inadequate attention to everyday life and people's needs, and so on. Names were not often given in the articles, but they certainly were signed by their authors. Critiques appeared in wall posters, in pamphlets, and in any number of permanent and ephemeral written forms. The "blooming and contending" of the hundred flowers—diverse opinion—was astonishing in its range from May–June 1957. Equally astonishing was that most of the published or posted commentary was premised upon an absolute acceptance of the socialist system and the CCP as a ruling party. It was intended as honest suggestion to make the system work better not to overthrow it. The majority of the critique fell upon the Party's abandonment of its revolutionary principles, and the high-handed bureaucratic ways transforming Party cadres into a privileged social class.

Intellectuals, at first quite wary, soon found it safe enough to speak out. They did so in droves. And they came to regret it in droves.

Although much of the expressed critical sentiment paralleled Mao's own dissatisfactions with the Party, the flood of discontent was disturbing to Mao and, of course, to the rest of the Party leadership. On June 8, 1957, Mao endorsed an editorial in the Party mouthpiece, *The People's Daily*, declaring "poisonous weeds" had grown among the "fragrant flowers." This was a clear sign of a crackdown. Now joined by fellow CCP leaders, Mao accused right-wingers and counter-revolutionaries of abusing the invitation to "the people" to voice their opinions. Many observers thought, based on this indication, the crackdown would be limited in scope and token in nature. They were wrong.

Intellectuals were hounded and labeled as "rightists," or worse, counter-revolutionaries. They were summarily kicked out of the ranks of "the people." Purges ensued. Some intellectuals were subjected to house arrest and forced to write and rewrite self-criticisms confessing their thought crimes. Others were sent for re-education, their right to urban residencies revoked. A few were executed or harassed to death. Institutions where intellectuals were employed fell under a pall. Silence fell, except for the shrill denunciations proceeding in the newspapers and media. Intellectuals feared to speak out. Even worse, they feared to speak to one another, lest they be forced to report on colleagues or friends under suspicion. They hunkered down, waiting for their turn to come. Unlike the Stalinist purges, where a knock on the door after midnight heralded doom, in Maoist China, doom came through words, in newspapers and wall posters. It came in tortured interpretations of texts, that shortly before had appeared innocuous. It came in social shunning and rumors and insinuations. It came as social death.

With critics muzzled and the Party now back on his side, Mao went on to his next projects.

7 Great Leap and Restoration, 1958–1965

With the anti-rightist campaign in full swing, rural collectivization all but completed, and urban private property and industries now under state ownership, Mao was in a good mood in the summer of 1957. Even the Party leaders with whom he'd been at odds were back on his side. In a July article prepared for a meeting in Qingdao of provincial leaders, Mao noted that the difficulties China was facing were part of the struggle "between the two roads—socialism and capitalism." He added, "Complete victory in this struggle will take a very long time. It is a task for the entire transition period."[1] Clearly, capitalism as an economic system no longer existed in China. Here, "capitalism" meant "bourgeois thought" and "rightism," while "socialism" pointed to revolutionary consciousness, or, increasingly, loyalty to Mao himself.

Mao Goes to Moscow, Again

In 1957, Mao even had reason to feel more kindly toward the Soviet Union. His wife, Jiang Qing, had been diagnosed in late 1956 with Stage One cervical cancer. Her doctors advised her to go to Moscow for treatment, as Soviet cancer facilities were more advanced than China's. She had returned some months later by all medical standards cured, although, apparently convinced she was still ill. Her paranoia about her health only got worse.

When Mao was invited to attend Nikita Krushchev's celebration of the USSR's fortieth birthday in November 1957, he decided to accept. He was eager to go to Moscow, now not as the supplicant he had been in 1949, but as leader of the most populous Communist country in the world. He gathered a contingent of high-level Party insiders and staff to accompany him. The latter included, for example, his Chinese-style and Western-style doctors, his Hunanese chef and Western-style cook, a nurse, and others. The many Party leaders who went included Mao's secretary, Chen Boda, as well as Deng Xiaoping and Peng Dehuai. Song Qingling, Sun Yatsen's widow and the token non-Communist in state-level office, also attended.

Rather than take the train, Mao flew to Moscow on a Russian plane sent to pick him up, fully stocked with caviar and vodka. Krushchev ceremonially met him at the airport and took him directly to his living quarters, a former tsarina's palace. Mao refused to use the flush toilet adjoining his room, preferring to squat over the chamber pot he'd brought. He also refused to eat the food prepared by the Russian cooks, not for fear of poisoning, but because he detested it. His Hunanese chef cooked all his meals, which he ate in private. Otherwise, Mao seemed to enjoy the opulent setting, although only because it bespoke his high prestige in the Communist world.

On November 7, 1957, Mao stood with Krushchev on the leaders' reviewing stand. With St. Basil's cathedral and the crenellated walls of the Kremlin as backdrop, waves of impressive goose-stepping military contingents passed by on the cobblestone streets of Red Square. After issuing his Moscow Declaration, in which he lavishly lauded Soviet progress and international Communist unity, Mao returned to Beijing on November 20— also by Russian plane—elated with his international visibility and success.

"Go All Out, Aim High, and Build Socialism"

Mao turned immediately to domestic matters. At a meeting in Chengdu, Sichuan Province, in early 1958, the Maoist slogan that was to guide the next several years—disastrously, it turned out—started to make an appearance. It went (more succinctly in Chinese than is possible to render in English), "Go all-out, aim high, and build socialism with greater, faster, better, and more economical results." This was an opaque signal that economic planners and Party bureaucrats were going to take a backseat to a mass movement. The contours of the contemplated movement were not yet clear. What was clear was Mao's dissatisfaction with plodding progress and his wish to accelerate China's transition to socialism.

The relations of production had been at least partially transformed in rural and urban areas through rural collectivization and factory-floor reform. The next part of the transition was to rest on large labor-intensive infrastructural projects. Of priority among them was water conservancy, involving the building of reservoirs and dams for local irrigation and drinking. Other projects such as bridges and roads were also launched. The collectivization of agriculture and efficiencies of scale provided ample peasant labor to be siphoned off for this construction.

In order to signal the importance of these projects, in May 1958, Mao and other top leaders went to the outskirts of Beijing where a dam was being built. Mao worked there with a shovel for half an hour in the midday heat. A picture of him was snapped by an accompanying newspaper photographer. The next day, it was plastered across the front page of papers across the country. Provincial leaders immediately ordered dams and reservoirs to be built in their localities, and each went on a ritual shovel-wielding visit to demonstrate proximity to the laboring masses.

Yet, a rapid increase in modern infrastructure was only part of the "go all out, aim high" movement. More fundamentally and far more destructively, Mao announced China would surpass England in steel production within fifteen years and overtake America in grain and steel in thirty. A frenzy of activity set in to achieve these goals.

Great Leap Forward

From mid-1958 through mid-1959, China was gripped by this frenzy. For the two years after, the country was enveloped in lies and stalked by starvation and mass death. Maoism gone horridly awry was at the root of the problems; sycophantic and cowed advisors abetted them.

Mao believed in the capacity of revolutionary masses to overcome objective obstacles. This was as true of raising levels of production in grain or steel as it was of pursuing revolution or waging war against a superior foe. Mao had patience for neither plodding planners nor overly cautious bureaucrats. He had even less patience for leaders at any level who said higher production targets could not be achieved. Indeed, in Mao's view, one key to achieving higher production was "permanent revolution." This meant, for him, that revolution was not a one-time event, but a long-term, ever-deepening, neverending process. If revolution waned, bureaucracy took over. That spelled the death of historical progress. Mao's faith in the revolutionarily aroused people conditioned his rapidly evolving view of development. In 1956, he had already articulated the theoretical framework for the reversed relation between social and productive forces. Now he was going to test the theory in practice by mobilizing the people. This test was called the "great leap forward."

Mao offered the theory of a developmental "leap" in explicit opposition to the process of slow, steady development advocated by the Soviet economic crowd (and by economists of any persuasion). It postulated that if people worked with a high enough sense of purpose, all existing barriers to productivity could be shattered. A leap in social wealth and well-being could be achieved in very little time. This pursuit could be accomplished with activated masses. "Bourgeois" thinkers within the Party as well as go-slow bureaucrats in the localities were the main obstacles to this endeavor. Mao swept these obstacles aside with one sentence, uttered as he toured newly formed people's communes in the summer of 1958.

In Marxist theory, communes demonstrate a higher stage of the socialization of rural production than do collectives. In their formation in China, communes transferred economic decision making from central bodies to the local-level authorities working within the production units themselves. For full use of available labor power and local resources, it was people on the ground who knew best, not faraway bureaucrats. Most important, communes were a form of people's ownership, where private property was completely dissolved into the communal whole.

In China in the late 1950s, communes were created from the amalgamation of collectives. As larger units, they housed the production of crops and grain; but also as small- and medium-sized industries, they provided commodities for local use. Rural areas would no longer rely on urban industry for their consumer needs; everyday items chronically in short supply such as thermoses, toothbrushes, pails, and twine and rope would now be produced locally. This was the goal of self-sufficiency taken to a new level of self-reliance. It represented a true break from Soviet methods. It also held out the possibility for raising rural standards of living by employing seasonally underemployed rural labor in industry, without people migrating to the cities.

The size of the commune units also allowed for medical and educational facilities to be established at central locations within each; the surplus to fund these endeavors, rather than being sent to the central state, would remain local. In this way, communes were to replicate the combined productive and socio-cultural functions of the integrated urban work unit established earlier at the factories. This would produce in the countryside the ideal Chinese socialist citizen, both "red" (communist) and "expert" (educated).

As communization was getting under way, Mao and the Party leadership were in their summer retreat in Beidaihe, on the northeast coast. There, they combined meetings with family vacations and escape from the Beijing heat. Mao was increasingly stifled by a number of internal Party intrigues he had fomented himself. Jiang Qing's paranoia about her nurses' alleged intent to kill her was also a constant irritant. Mao took every opportunity to tour the country, to escape this stultifying atmosphere. Apprised of the commune initiative, he wanted to take a look. In August 1958, under a blazing summer sun, Mao was ushered to communes around the country by eager local cadres. Wearing a wide-brimmed straw hat, the sixty-four-year-old Mao outstripped all of them with his long strides and complete indifference to the heat. He and his flagging retinue were followed by reporters and photographers from the official New China News Agency. The crops were growing beautifully, the spring and summer weather had been perfect, the harvest promised to be abundant, and the mood was buoyant if a little torrid. At one spot, Mao proclaimed: "The people's commune is great."[2] The very next day, these words were banner headlines in newspapers across the country. In short order, communization drives were started or accelerated everywhere. The "spontaneous" movement took on a life of its own, and by the end of 1958, almost half a billion people were incorporated into these new structures. In a burst of exuberance, Mao hailed this movement as the transition from socialism into communism.

Meanwhile, Mao's rash promise that China's steel production would surpass England's within fifteen years and overtake America's in thirty had led to some strange developments. At a trivial level, many children born in 1958 and 1959 were named "Chaoying" ("Surpass England") or "Chaomei" ("Overtake America"). When the Great Leap was repudiated many years later, a number of this demographic cohort felt compelled to change their now embarrassing names. At a much more serious level, backyard furnaces were encouraged so that each family and locality could contribute to the overall targets in steel production. This was a waste of time, labor, and resources. Scarce fuel was burned to keep the furnaces going; household implements were melted down for their trivial amounts of iron ore; and labor better used for the harvest of bumper crops was eaten up by these schemes. And, the steel ingots produced in these furnaces were useless.

But for Mao, backyard furnaces showed mass enthusiasm, mass creativity, and mass participation in economic development. Rather than dampen this mass movement, Mao encouraged it.

The Great Leap Forward also called for the partial industrialization of the rural areas. Far from complete or adequate at the time, this early effort became one of the building blocks for the post-Maoist resurgence of the rural areas in the early 1980s (although most Chinese analysts and Western scholars do not acknowledge this history). The goal of self-reliance was never achieved, but small-scale commodity production was temporarily established in many localities. However, if China was to be a national market, as economic planners had striven to make it, the uncoordinated proliferation of local-level industrialization was redundant and wasteful. For, each locality now strove to produce everything it needed on its own, whether or not local production was efficient or sensible. Not only was the national-level economy sacrificed in the name of local self-reliance, but the same commodities were made (sometimes poorly) by each commune, thereby stunting regional exchange and markets. This soon led to the stockpiling of certain resources in certain areas and shortages in other areas; gluts of certain commodities in some places and scarcity of necessities in other places. With neither markets nor central planning, the economy ceased to function.

Iron Women

Another central aspect of the "Great Leap" was the total mobilization of all able-bodied people in agricultural and industrial production. This included women. While encouraging women to join production had been a fundamental policy from the beginning of the Maoist period, it was stressed even more in these years. There emerged at this time the phenomenon of the "iron woman."

Because of the lack of mechanization in China, all projects were labor intensive. Women's labor was particularly needed in the fields, as male labor was dedicated to the backyard furnaces and construction projects. "Iron women" were born, as it were, as more women began performing nontraditional tasks. In the fields, they drove water buffalo teams and tractors for plowing, traditionally a man's job. In the factories, women moved in droves into management, which combined administrative and labor roles. Women competed with one another and with men for high productivity. Those women who gained distinction in these competitions became nationally known as "iron women." This was the fulfillment of Mao's desire for and commitment to female "liberation through labor."

And yet, the problem to which the feminist literary figure, Ding Ling, had pointed in 1942 in Yan'an, and to which she had returned in 1957 during the "hundred flowers" movement, was exacerbated. Women's double burden became intolerably difficult to manage. With the invisibility of household reproductive labor in the productivity statistics, the fact that someone had to give birth to and take care of children, cook food, and clean the house, in addition to all the domestic maintenance women usually performed, disappeared from view. Women were celebrated in their public role as "iron women," for their heroic contributions to production. Meanwhile, they were forced to silently struggle with household chores. Ding Ling, who had courageously spoken out in 1942 and then again in 1957 on the issue, was sent for a second time for re-education among the masses during the anti-rightist campaign.

Focused as he was on productivity, Mao addressed the problem of household reproductive labor by encouraging the formation of communal canteens, where everyone would eat together. This was supposed to free women from family cooking chores. These were formed during the Great Leap period, but never became popular among the peasants. The quality of the food and the cooking was bad; the distances people needed to travel to get to the canteens were sometimes formidable; and rather than increase efficiency, the canteens proved to add to women's burdens.

Quemoy and Matsu, and Krushchev's Secret Visit to Beijing

In the midst of all these developments and after several routine provocations, in August 1958 the PRC took the unprecedented step of bombarding the islands of Quemoy and Matsu from the Fujian coast. These two islands in the Taiwan Straits were GMD-garrisoned buffer zones between Taiwan and the mainland located within shouting distance of China's Fujian Province. The Straits were patrolled by the United States Seventh Naval Fleet as part of the U.S. protectorate around Chiang Kaishek on Taiwan. With the bombings, everyone went on high alert, including Chiang's military and U.S. army troops and air force personnel based in Taiwan, Japan, Korea, and the Philippines. After an exchange of heated rhetoric, the Quemoy and Matsu crisis did not develop into a full-scale war. As Mao later said of the issue, "The United States wants to sign a declaration demanding Chiang Kai-shek not fight us and we not fight Chiang Kai-shek. We say no, because the question . . . is an internal matter and none of your business. The only question is that you move away."[3]

Even the Soviet leader, Krushchev, was nonplussed by Mao's brinksmanship. In the late summer of 1959, Krushchev sent an urgent message to Mao indicating he wished to visit Beijing in secret. Mao traveled in from Beidaihe to meet him. Krushchev was received poolside at Zhongnanhai, with Mao in swimming trunks and a robe draped around his shoulders. The Soviet leader had brought no swimming gear. He was lent a swimsuit. It turned out he did not know how to swim. Part of his talks with Mao took place as he bobbed in the pool enclosed in a life preserver, surrounded by bodyguards. The interpreters tried their best to translate from the pool's edges.[4]

Krushchev wanted to inform Mao personally of his change in policy toward the United States. At his meeting with President Eisenhower at Camp David in early 1959, Krushchev had pledged to engage with the Americans, rather than continue the purely confrontational path Stalin had trod. He wanted Mao to ratchet down tensions with the United States. After three days of inconclusive talks—and some uncomfortable swimming— Krushchev returned to Moscow in a towering rage.

Great Famine

The combination of enthusiasms and irrational initiatives, along with Mao's increasing dismissal of criticism of himself, his policies, and theories, produced a tragic situation in China by 1959. Provincial and local authorities, eager to be on the right side of history and of Mao, reported crazily inflated statistics intended to demonstrate the massive gains made in steel and grain production. Based upon these falsified numbers, it remained unclear for some time that crops were rotting in the field for lack of labor to harvest them. Women and children working sixteen-hour days were insufficient for what would have been the largest harvest in Chinese history. It was clear the steel produced in backyard furnaces was unusable in any form, and yet no one dared to call a halt to such projects.

Hunger began to stalk the land. Even in privileged locations, such as Zhongnanhai, scarcities of meat and vegetables began showing up. The military, usually the best fed of any group other than the Party leaders, tightened their belts and substituted coarse grains for rice. Urban dwellers found food more and more difficult to obtain, and rationing was established to ensure a certain minimum of necessities for each family. It often was not enough, and urban babies of this Great Leap generation were often physically stunted because of malnourishment. The worst hit, however, were in the countryside, where whatever grain there was had been requisitioned for urban use. This left peasants to fend for themselves. Soon they began to die of starvation. Local leaders were too afraid to inform central authorities of the extent of distress. After all, they had reported bumper crops and endless abundance. Those few who tried to make the problems known were accused of "bourgeois" thinking or "rightism." Most ducked their heads, hoping to survive physically and politically.

More people died.

The 1959–61 famine was enormous. In a contested retrospective numbers game, reliable statistics are impossible to find. Most responsible demographic estimates put the number of dead at some fifteen to twenty million. The vast majority of those were peasants, with the old, young, and female particularly vulnerable. City dwellers did not witness the pileups of corpses in rural areas. Rural refugees were barred from entering the cities. There was a total internal news blackout on the topic. Famine refugees who managed to escape to Hong Kong alerted Western China-watchers to the situation. Yet, they could only report about their own localities and had no sense of the scale of disaster. Only in the 1980s, after the official relaxation of some prohibitions on evaluating the Mao period, did the severity of the famine become known to the world and to the Chinese.

Shaoshan, the Lushan Conference, and the Fall of Peng Dehuai

Rumors of disaster began to reach Mao. Isolated from reality, he decided to travel to the one place he knew he could get a straight answer: his hometown, Shaoshan. In his first visit there since 1927, Mao re-encountered old friends, neighbors, and distant relations. He was apprised of some of the difficulties people were experiencing at the everyday level. And yet Shaoshan, Mao's birthplace, was accorded special administrative treatment by the Party; as such, conditions there were much better than in other places. The picture Mao got was not of absolute disaster but of certain difficulties. Mao stopped eating meat in solidarity with the people's troubles.

By the summer of 1959, the communes had more or less collapsed, and many of the Great Leap initiatives were faltering. Mao decided the coming Party Plenum would be devoted to discussion of developmental policy. Held in the mountain resort town, Lushan—where missionaries and foreign diplomats in the nineteenth century and early twentieth, and then Chiang Kaishek in the 1920s and 1930s had escaped the Nanjing and Shanghai summer heat—the Eighth Party Plenum turned out to be an extraordinary event. Party leaders were entirely aware of the human and economic disaster into which the country had been driven. Many had gone on tours of the country and discovered the enormity of the problems. They intended to use the Plenum to restore some measure of planning to the national economy. However, the meeting was soon overtaken by an irreparable conflict between the two old comrades in arms, Mao and Peng Dehuai.

Peng was now Minister of Defense. He was particularly unhappy about the Great Leap, believing it was weakening China just as the USSR was establishing a rapprochement with the United States. He also had witnessed the starvation in the country. Peng stood up to Mao at the Plenum, accusing him of "petty bourgeois fanaticism" and demanding an end to the policies. For two weeks, Mao patiently listened to one critique of himself after the next, led by Peng. Finally, he took the floor. In his speech of July 23, Mao affirmed the communes and the basic direction of the Great Leap, even while he called the backyard furnaces a "great catastrophe." He blamed falsified reporting and poor local implementation for the accumulation of problems, yet he acknowledged that he was ultimately responsible for the chaos in the country. Then he began to retreat: "Everybody has faults. Even Confucius made mistakes. I have also seen Lenin's handwritten manuscripts which had been altered so much that they looked a real mess. If he had not made mistakes, why did he have to correct them?"[5]

The Plenum wanted to reverse policy course. Mao called for the continued tapping of mass enthusiasm for communism. Most spectacularly, Mao warned, if the commune movement was suppressed, "I will go to the countryside to lead the peasants to overthrow the government. If those of you in the Liberation Army won't follow me, then I will go and find a Red Army, and organize another Liberation Army. But I think the Liberation Army would follow me."[6] Mao was threatening to go directly to the peasants to overthrow the CCP! The Plenum quickly fell into line, fearing a huge political and even larger social upheaval.

Mao's target was clear. Peng Dehuai, Minister of Defense and leader of the People's Liberation Army (PLA, renamed after 1949), was not following Mao. He would have to go. He was to be punished for standing up to Mao (and for the rankling phrase about petty bourgeois fanaticism). Peng had thought his longstanding personal loyalty to and comradeship with Mao would protect him; his extraordinary service in the Korean War; his brilliance as a general; his steadfastness as a Communist; his alliances in the Party. He was wrong on all counts. Peng was dismissed in disgrace. Mao's protégé, Lin Biao, took over as commander of the PLA. The country was stunned.

With famine and now bad weather gripping the land, Mao's victory at Lushan was fleeting. His exhortations to revive the commune movement found little resonance in rhetoric or practice. People were simply exhausted and famished; local officials were lying low. By the end of 1959, Mao recognized the magnitude of the economic disaster and resigned as Chairman of the PRC. Retaining his title as Chairman of the Communist Party, he gave up its daily management. Those tasks were transferred to Liu Shaoqi. By 1960, Mao had lost control of Party and state. Only the army, now under Lin Biao, was still in Mao's pocket.

From 1960 to 1965, Mao essentially withdrew from political center stage. Proclaiming, "Bourgeois elements have infiltrated our Communist Party,"[7] he operated from behind the scenes. He traveled in the country, avoided as much as possible Zhongnanhai, and remained aloof from what he saw as the bourgeois takeover of the Party.

Mao and His Wives

By 1960, Mao and Jiang Qing were living almost entirely apart. Jiang wintered in Guangzhou (Canton), where the weather was milder and less troublesome to her host of largely imaginary ailments than the cold of Beijing. She occasionally joined Mao on some of his trips, but mostly enjoyed watching movies (chiefly Western), dancing, engaging in photography (at which she was genuinely talented), and other leisure activities in specially built facilities for her exclusive use. On occasion, she invited others to join her. She was an intelligent, ambitious woman at loose ends.

In the summer of 1961, Mao was back at Lushan, nominally for a Party meeting. There, he had cause to send for He Zizhen, his second wife, now suffering from schizophrenia. She arrived at the mountain resort, and when they met, she apparently recognized Mao, but then went blank. Mao was immensely saddened by her aspect, mental state, and the signs of advanced old age. This was the last time he was ever to see He Zizhen; he gave her money and had her escorted away.

Revisionism and the Sino-Soviet Split

In 1960, China's self-induced economic crisis was exacerbated by Krushchev's recall of the 1,400 Soviet scientists and technology specialists and advisors working in China. Most of these were involved in urban-based industrial sites of major national importance. The blow was enormous. Many projects came to a screeching halt. Over time, much of China's machinery, imported from the Soviet Union, was impossible to fix, as spare parts became unavailable when relations between the countries deteriorated completely and trade relations broke down.

Problems between China and the Soviet Union had been brewing for some time. In addition to the ideological differences, there was no love lost between Krushchev and Mao personally. In September 1959, China and India fought a border war in a territorial dispute left over from the colonial period. The dispute had been reactivated due to the PLA invasion of Tibet. At the time, Chinese troops made a number of incursions into what Indians said was India but what the Chinese claimed as their own territory. The Indians counterattacked, and Krushchev upheld Nehru. In addition to Krushchev's disapproval of the Quemoy and Matsu events, his refusal to support China against India also infuriated Mao. Most recently, Krushchev had been critical of Mao's Great Leap, and had mocked Mao for claiming China was entering communism without having consolidated socialism. Then there was the matter of the visit to Beijing and the swimming pool.

In 1960, the Sino-Soviet split became official with the withdrawal of advisors. A round of mudslinging ensued, in the public space of a meeting of the Romanian Communist Party in Bucharest. Krushchev verbally attacked China; Peng Zhen, the Chinese delegate to the meeting, returned the attack in kind. It appeared to most observers that China and the USSR would come to open warfare. Yet, cold warriors in the United States refused to see the Sino-Soviet split, preferring to uphold the bogeyman of a monolithic Communist bloc for another decade.

Verbal vituperation against the Soviet Union followed in China. Political language became particularly creative, and conceptual conflations ever more bizarre. The Soviets were labeled "revisionists," "socialist imperialists," "nationalist imperialists," and other politically charged names. "Revisionism" came to be associated with "rightism" or "right opportunism," and thence with "bourgeois thought" and the restoration of capitalism. As Mao confirmed in September 1962 at the Tenth Plenum, "I think that right-wing opportunism in China should be renamed: it should be called Chinese revisionism."[8] In July 1964, Mao released a pamphlet *On Krushchov's Phoney Communism and Its Historical Lessons for the World*. It was a wholesale attack on Soviet "revisionism." Appearing among the proceedings of the Central Committee meeting of that time, the pamphlet was carried in all the major Chinese newspapers. While the author was always given as the Editorial Committees of the *People's Daily* and *Red Flag* (both mouthpieces of the CCP), it is generally agreed that Mao was the motivator behind this pamphlet and its release to the public. The domestic implications of all this were not immediately evident. They were to become so soon enough.

Liu Shaoqi, Deng Xiaoping, and Restoration

Mao's retreat from the political scene left it open for others. The restoration of the economy in the post–Great Leap years called forth the restoration of the bureaucracy. Laid low by hunger and indifference to politics, the masses seemed only too happy to comply. Rather than "leaping," political predictability and economic stability and efficiency were the new orders of the day. Termed by at least one scholar the "Thermidorean reaction," the 1961–65 period was presided over by Liu Shaoqi and Deng Xiaoping.[9] Liu was a Party insider and Yan'an survivor; he had come to prominence during the War of Resistance, after the New Fourth Army Incident. He had remained in the top echelons of power. For his part, Deng had been a student in France with Zhou Enlai in the 1920s, had joined the CCP early, was a Long March veteran, and also had been in Yan'an. He, too, was an insider.

The CCP under Liu's and Deng's direction moved quickly to put into place emergency measures to stabilize the situation. The resumption of centralized planning along with strict rationing immediately addressed the distribution part of the problem. Reviving agricultural production was a different task. Local rural cadres in charge were largely Maoist and dismayed at the turn of political tide. They were rapidly replaced by cadres sent from the cities. Students, soldiers, and the urban unemployed were also sent to help get agriculture back on its feet. This was a policy intended to forestall any possible urban rebelliousness due to either political change or personal privation. It was also intended to flood the countryside with more sober urbanites so as to stem any potential radical rural tide.

Communes were not abolished, but scaled back in size and function.

The self-reliance programs embodying the communes' socioeconomic and cultural purposes were discontinued, and communes became administrative units under the direction of the central state. Corruption ensued, as urban cadres unfamiliar with local conditions came to rely for administrative assistance on the former village elites—ex-landlords and rich peasants —who had been unhappily dispossessed and now saw an opportunity to make a comeback. Private family plots, abolished during the high tide of communization, were returned to the peasants, and family agricultural production was encouraged with the resurgence of private markets. In an astonishingly short time, rural inequality burgeoned. And yet, there was food. There was also a major baby boom. Later, this was to be called by Mao "the restoration of capitalism in the countryside." For the time being, it was official policy.

In the cities, after first shoring up critical food shortages, industrial production was addressed. Workers designated "excess labor" were sent to the countryside for a temporary period of work with the peasants. Those remaining in the cities were charged with getting the factories back up to speed. Factory floor discipline was reestablished, and experiments in factory democracy were suspended. Managers reoccupied administrative offices, and workers retreated to the assembly lines. Women workers were marginalized; masculine authority was restored. Centralized planning took over. Other old hierarchies also reasserted themselves. Rural-urban disparities widened. The urban economy was unambiguously favored. The cost of industrial goods sold to the peasants was kept high, whereas the cost for agricultural goods sold to the cities was kept artificially low.[10] Even though property was not the measure of wealth (nobody had much of it), geographical location and access to the bureaucracy and power became the equivalents of wealth.

Another restoration was also achieved. Intellectuals were returned to the ranks of "the people." The anti-rightist campaign was discontinued, and the politically mandated isolation endured by many educated people was reversed. Educational institutions in the cities resumed their normal functioning, even as rural educational opportunities, enhanced when schools had been established in the remotest of backwaters, were cut back with the communes. An urban managerial, technocratic class was reinvigorated and set down roots.

Mao, even in his effective exile from the center of government, did not remain silent. He attacked "revisionism" within the Party, and advocated the method of "unity-criticism-unity" to take care of the Party's mistakes.[11] Following Zhou Enlai's insinuation in 1964 about the "new bourgeois elements" in society,[12] Mao abandoned his conciliatory attitude and made very explicit where those bourgeois elements resided. In 1965, he named them and their social function: "the bureaucratic class" was the new bourgeoisie and they were the oppressors of the masses. The implications of such a statement were stark. If socialism's historical mission was the overthrow of the rule of the bourgeoisie, and if the new bourgeoisie had taken over the Communist Party, then true socialism would have to retake the Party from the bourgeoisie. How and by whom this would be accomplished was not yet clear.

Of Paper Tigers and the Atomic Bomb

Meanwhile, through the beginning of the 1960s, international threats on China's borders proliferated. The Soviets to the north were a clear enemy, and although war had not broken out, there were frequent skirmishes across the immense border between the two countries. To the west, the war between China and India had ended, but the boundary issues continued to fester. To the south, the Indonesian coup deposing the leftist nationalist, Sukarno, in favor of the right-wing, American-supported militarist Suharto, had brought a U.S. sycophant to power in a formerly friendly country. The ensuing massacre of Chinese-Indonesians, on suspicion of being a disloyal "fifth column," was part of the larger witch-hunt against Communists—assumed to be of Chinese ethnicity—there, as well as in Malaysia and other Asian states. Millions of Chinese ethnics died. The U.S.-led Southeast Asian Alliance, SEATO, was formed with the Philippines, Thailand, and Suharto's Indonesia as charter members. This was seen by the PRC as a clear indication of U.S. and Soviet collusion to surround China with hostile neighbors

Meanwhile, the American buildup of advisors and troops in Vietnam did not go unnoticed. In an early 1965 interview with the American journalist Edgar Snow, who had spent a good deal of time in Yan'an and was officially designated a "friend of China," Mao voiced his opinion that Ho Chi Minh and North Vietnam would have the moral and national support to win the fight.[13] Nobody could have known then how long Vietnamese victory would take and at what cost to the Vietnamese people. For the moment, the presence of American advisors and troops on China's southern border was alarming to Mao.

In spite of all these developments nearby, the Algerian revolution and other African anticolonial independence movements gave Mao hope that the world's peoples—particularly in the third world—would no longer stand for imperialist control. In his statement of support for the Congo in 1964, Mao noted the American-directed murder of the Congolese nationalist hero, Patrice Lumumba, which had motivated the Congolese people's resistance to the reassertion of imperialism. He accused Americans— in collusion with Europeans—of wishing to control not only the Congo, but the entire African continent. But American ambitions did not stop there. Mao's list of nefarious U.S. activities included intervention in Vietnam, Laos, and Cambodia; the "strangling" of the Cuban revolution; support for the Indonesian coup; the occupation of South Korea, Taiwan, and the Philippines; and dominance over Latin America. Mao concluded: "U.S. imperialism has over-extended its reach. It adds a new noose around its neck every time it commits aggression anywhere." Calling U.S. imperialism a "paper tiger"—fierce on the exterior but empty on the interior—Mao issued his revolutionary challenge: "People of the world, unite and defeat the U.S. aggressors and all their running dogs! People of the world, be courageous, dare to fight . . . Then the whole world will belong to the people."[14]

Over the years, Mao had consistently underplayed the nuclear capabilities of the United States, the Soviet Union, and other atomic powers. He had nevertheless directed the Chinese scientific community to pursue aggressively the development of atomic and hydrogen bombs. Through the political upheavals of Maoist rule, the nuclear physics research groups had not been disrupted. The withdrawal of Soviet advisors might have been a blow to Chinese atomic research, but since Krushchev had long since reneged on his pledge to help China get the bomb, Soviet advisors had not been involved directly in the endeavor. Chinese scientists cracked the atomic code on their own, and in 1964 China exploded its first atomic bomb at its test site in the northwest desert regions of Xinjiang Province. One year later, China exploded its first hydrogen bomb in the same region. The results of these explosions were nationally televised in a special program celebrating the massive victory of "Mao Zedong Thought," which allegedly had assisted scientists in vanquishing the objective obstacles to atomic progress. A CIA satellite captured this program off Chinese TV and made it available to the American public as proof of the global threat represented by "Red China."

Global threat or not, the extravagant claims made for Mao Zedong Thought on behalf of China's nuclear program were merely the tip of what was becoming an enormous iceberg of the Mao cult.

Mao's Exile and His Cult

Through his years in exile from power, Mao's control over Party and state was lost. But he did wield influence, in part through his enormous personal charisma and in part because of the reverence in which many held him. This reverence was encouraged by the CCP and grew inexorably into a cult of individual personality. Mao continued to participate in Party meetings, where he railed against what he saw as the expansion of social injustices and the wrong policy directions of the CCP. In 1962, he encouraged the Socialist Education Movement, intended to reacquaint people with the goals of socialism as an egalitarian system. Taking particular aim at cadre corruption, bureaucratic malfeasance, and the retreat from collectivism— issues with which a number of Party leaders were also quite concerned— Mao wished to launch another mass movement against the Party.

He temporarily contented himself with reaching out to two major social constituencies, aside from the peasantry: the military and students. With the latter, Mao had been quite concerned with the reappearance of educational elitism in China. After all, one of the major tenets of Maoism from its earliest days at Jinggangshan had been literacy campaigns and increasing the educational opportunities for all people in China, not just privileged urbanites. The reform of the written language—called "simplification"— was introduced into the schools and into text publishing (including news-papers) in the late 1950s. It precisely was intended to boost literacy by facilitating reading. With the dismantling of communes and education for peasants after the Great Leap, the reproduction of the urban elite through educational biases became a reality. Moreover, the bookishness of the educated—indicating, for Mao, their lack of revolutionary experience or practice and their reliance on abstract theory—was now dovetailing with the technocratic tendencies of the bureaucracy to produce an almost per-manent elite based on residence in the cities and access to knowledge and power. Mao appealed to students' idealism in attacking this elitism.

Meanwhile, Mao's protégé, Lin Biao, had managed to insulate the PLA from the bureaucratic tendencies and interference infecting the CCP. This led Mao to identify the army as the sole remaining bearer of revolutionary values lost by the rest of society. He called upon the army to participate in re-educating society about socialism. While the PLA's role at this point was small at best, it was a harbinger of later army involvement in civilian affairs.

Mao's positioning outside the Party—his effective exile from it—allowed him to ally himself directly with the people in critique of Party practice. This contributed to one of the most dramatic developments on the domestic Maoist front in these years: the exponential growth of the Mao cult. Very soon, this was to have disastrous consequences. For the moment, what originally had been an organic reverence for a leader was becoming an orchestrated affair. The Party abetted the growth of the cult, to provide cover for the CCP's extremely un-Maoist policies. Lin Biao, Minister of Defense, did his part to fuel the Mao cult in the army, by extolling the example of a soldier, Lei Feng, who had drowned in the course of his duties. Lei had kept a diary, published after his death, in which he had recorded his absolute devotion to Mao and to Mao's Thought. Lei Feng became a model soldier, and in time, a model Maoist, whom all proper citizens were exhorted to emulate. Aside from promoting Lei Feng, Lin Biao also edited the first edition of what soon became a ubiquitous accessory for all Chinese citizens: the little red book. This contained a selection of Maoist sayings and aphorisms distilling the wisdom of Mao Zedong Thought into digestible nuggets of truth. Statues of Mao were erected everywhere. Mao was omnipresent. His cult was pervasive.

On this note, the last act of Maoism in China was about to begin.

The Cultural Revolution
POLITICS IN COMMAND, 1966–1969

Beginning in 1966, Mao launched a movement to seize back from the Communist Party what he saw as his right to be the master cultural and historical interpreter of the Chinese revolution and Chinese Marxism. Who would speak of and for the Chinese revolution? Who would speak of and for the culture of that revolution, Maoism? These were central issues animating what came to be known as the Great Proletarian Cultural Revolution—a movement as unpredictable and unintended in its scope as it was organic to Mao's revolutionary philosophy and politics.

What was the Cultural Revolution?

It is said, the Cultural Revolution was launched by Mao to seize state power. This interpretation contains a good bit of truth, and the period certainly exhibits power struggles in abundance. Yet for Mao, state power was never a pursuit unto itself; state power was to be used in the waging of revolution. To explain the complexity of the Cultural Revolution, then, it is more appropriate to understand the movement not merely as a bid for state power, but as an attempt to seize politics—the power of mass culture and speech for revolution.

It is also said, the Cultural Revolution was an outgrowth of peculiarities in Mao's personality: his desire to be immortalized, his basic tyrannical nature, and his fear of death. Mao clearly was a forceful and ruthless man; if not for this, he could never have risen to the heights of power amid the historical circumstances of twentieth-century China. In 1966, Mao was seventy-two years old, surely old enough to be thinking of his own demise. Yet, he was in generally good health. He was, it is true, increasingly concerned about a political successor. Whether this bespeaks a fear of death or an irrational desire for immortality is a stretch. What it does indicate is Mao's concern about the potential longevity and future direction of the revolutionary endeavor to which he had devoted his life, and in which he still believed passionately. Since 1960, all signs pointed to the reversal of his revolutionary vision. To the extent that the Cultural Revolution was about ensuring his legacy, then, it was about securing the historical conditions for the continuation of the revolution.

Some say the Cultural Revolution was an expression of religiosity, and certainly much of the devotion it inspired appears very religious. Yet, Mao's belief in the Chinese revolution was not a question of divine faith. It was a belief in the historically situated capacity of mass activity to change the circumstances of life. For Mao, the whole point of the revolution was the practical one of creating the conditions for the masses to transform their own lives. The Cultural Revolution was launched in part to restore to the people the revolutionary momentum seized from them by Party bureaucrats. Mao was intent on cleansing the Party of these usurpers. If this meant destroying the Party to save it, he was prepared to do so.

Many say the mass resonance and response to the Cultural Revolution are what can be expected from an ant-like, or sheep-like people such as the Chinese, who have no tradition of independence and freedom, and are hence easily tyrannized into blind obedience. To be sure, the scope of the popular response is one truly astonishing aspect of the movement, and it contradicts the view of the Chinese people as sheep-like. Rather, it suggests that six years into the post-Leap restoration, a good number of people were dismayed by the direction in which the country and Party were headed. They were apparently ready to do something about it, and, when given the chance, they acted.

The Cultural Revolutionary call to reconnect "culture" to "revolution" through mass politics sometimes was as straightforward as smashing temples to destroy the sites of old superstitious beliefs, deemed unsuited to the new culture of the revolutionary everyday. At other times, the connection between culture and revolution was as labyrinthine as the dizzying number of alleged intrigues, or as incomprehensible as the waxing and waning Red

Guard factions fighting each other over the proper practical interpretation of an utterance.

However one sees it, the Cultural Revolution was a failure. It failed to achieve any of its lofty or base goals. Most prominent, it failed to secure the Maoist-style revolution. The quick reversal of Maoism after Mao's death and the complete repudiation of the Cultural Revolution precisely indicate that Mao's fears of the abandonment of revolutionary practice were in fact correct. The Cultural Revolution's failure to break the back of the Party bureaucracy is also remarkable. All it did was bequeath to the CCP a new lease on life, as the savior of China from chaos. Not only was the Cultural Revolution a failure in its own terms, it was often a cruel and demoralizing movement that ruined the lives of many, took the lives of many others, and permanently altered the trajectories of several generations. Yet, the many memoirs published in retrospect also make clear that, within the cruelty and violence, the Cultural Revolution was at times also an exhilarating, liberating, and optimistic period—so optimistic in fact that its failure produced complete disillusionment.

The Cultural Revolution was not one movement but many, and it does not lend itself to one narrative line. It has many internally complex and overlapping stories. Narrowly defined, it lasted from 1966 to 1969 and, unlike previous peasant-centered movements, it was predominantly an urban phenomenon. The ensuing seven years were its aftermath. It is, however, now conventional to speak of the Cultural Revolution as spanning the decade of 1966–76, ending with Mao's death.

The Prelude: Hai Rui

The prelude to what came to be known as the Cultural Revolution began in November 1965 on a literary note, with a critique of a play written in 1960 regarding Hai Rui. The play had been staged during the post-Leap restoration, although not since 1962; it was taken to be an allegory. Hai Rui was a fifteenth-century Ming dynasty official who was upright, honest, and spoke truth to power; he was for centuries a popular subject for local operas. In one famous episode from his life, Hai Rui was sent into exile after criticizing the emperor for land policies. He had been a favorite historical character of Mao's, until Peng Dehuai had spoken truth to power at the Lushan conference in 1959. After this, Hai Rui's fortunes dipped as quickly as did Peng's.

The critique of the play in November 1965 was written by a Shanghai-based literary critic, Yao Wenyuan. Yao made up for his weak grasp of drama and of Ming dynastic history by his strong grasp of ideology. Yao's critique, featured in a leading Shanghai newspaper, pointed to the counter-revolutionary message supposedly encoded in the Hai Rui play. This critique provoked first confusion (why would this play be a subject of review three years after its last staging?) and then a debate among literary and academic circles in Shanghai for the next six months. The evaluation of most of the participants in the debate was disdainful dismissal of Yao. The Beijing-based cultural oversight group chaired by Politburo member and Beijing mayor Peng Zhen, weighed in on the topic in February 1966, commenting that Yao's political treatment of academic and cultural matters was out of order. It all seemed quite insignificant.

Few knew the article had been commissioned and planted by Jiang Qing, Mao's wife, at his direction. This was an opening salvo against the Party establishment. And, it was fired from outside Beijing; Mao, keeping his distance, was traveling in the provinces.

Mao's Travels

In 1965, Mao was rarely in the capital. After the Chinese New Year in February, he journeyed by train across the country. In May, he went to Jinggangshan, the base area where he had established himself as a revolutionary leader after 1927. In part nostalgic, this trip was also intended to remind everyone of where Mao's revolution had begun. He arrived back in Beijing in June.

At the time, the rural areas were embroiled in a large-scale divisive campaign, called the "four clean-ups," aimed at sweeping out corruption among rural cadres. Mao did not participate directly, but he sent his daughter Li Na, now twenty-four years old, and a student in the history department of Beijing University. Li Na went to the Jiangxi countryside with a group of Mao's assistants from Zhongnanhai on a fact-finding trip. Li Na was not well liked. Reputedly quite temperamental, she was apparently not helpful in the Jiangxi endeavor, complained about the living conditions, and wished to be sent back to Beijing. Willful in her ways, she demanded special privileges. Mao consistently refused to have Li Na, Li Min, or his nephew Mao Yuanxin treated differently from others. In Li Na's case, this provoked tension between Jiang Qing and Mao.

In November 1965, as the Hai Rui critique was getting under way, Mao went south to Hangzhou. Hangzhou is best known for its scenic West Lake (a topic and setting of China's best-known classical poems), its Dragon's Well tea, and its beautiful women. Mao stayed for a month in a retrofitted Qing-dynasty guesthouse on the banks of West Lake set aside for his use. December found him in Nanchang, the Jiangxi capital, where he celebrated his seventy-second birthday. He then moved on to Wuhan, a dusty industrial entrepôt in the center of China, where he stayed in a former tea merchant's estate on the East Lake.

By March 1966, Mao was back in Hangzhou presiding over an expanded meeting of the Party's Central Committee, during which he took Peng Zhen and others to task for their timid cultural policies and failure to deal adequately with the Hai Rui critique. Pressing his charges against Peng Zhen occupied him for some time, and to do so he shuttled the short distance between Shanghai, where meetings were being held, and Hangzhou. Then he visited Shaoshan, his hometown in Hunan; when the heat got too much to bear, he returned to Wuhan. Restless, Mao let the Cultural Revolution develop, in his absence from Beijing.

The May 16th Directive

Literary debate was hardly all Mao had in mind by planting the Hai Rui article. The playwright, Wu Han, Beijing vice-mayor and Beijing University professor, was quickly disposed of. Mao then raised the stakes. As he later put it, he wished for a revolution that "touches people to their very souls."[1] With Lin Biao and the army on his side, Mao used an editorial in the PLA mouthpiece, *Liberation Daily*, to demand a purge of "bourgeois elements" from cultural circles and of "right opportunists" from within the Party. In this unsigned piece of early May 1966, the two major targets of the Cultural Revolution were announced. Intellectuals and Party cadres would have to be on their guard. The major location of the movement—the cities—was also indicated.

On May 16, Mao, still outside Beijing, followed up with a directive. In the name of the Party's Central Committee, the directive attacked the Beijing Mayor, Peng Zhen, for dampening political enthusiasms, promoting bourgeois literary critical standards (art for art's sake, rather than art subordinated to politics), and shielding "anti-socialist element," Wu Han. Peng was removed from power. The Beijing Party structure was quickly reorganized, and the cultural oversight group Peng chaired was dissolved.

Even more dramatic, the directive announced that "representatives of the bourgeoisie" had infiltrated the Party and were preparing to use it to restore bourgeois rule. It accused the Party of harboring a number of minor Krushchevs—revisionists and bourgeois traitors to socialism—under the protection of one big Krushchev, as yet unnamed. Few could guess who it was.

Things proceeded with lightening speed, as did the creation of ever more fanciful political language. Along with the Beijing Party organization, national organs of propaganda and communication were purged, including the editor of the Party mouthpiece, the *People's Daily*. Zhou Yang, the Hu Feng antagonist of 1955 and post-1949 cultural policy leader, was ousted. Mao's secretary, Chen Boda—who had been with him since Yan'an—along with Jiang Qing became the nucleus of a new "Central Cultural Revolution Group" (CCRG) that took over national communication and culture policy. They handpicked a number of like-minded people to assist; among those was Yao Wenyuan, the Hai Rui critic from Shanghai, and his senior supervisor, Zhang Chunqiao, a friend of Jiang Qing's and Party Secretary of Shanghai. Jiang, Yao, and Zhang were the three original members of what later became known as the "Gang of Four."

From early on, Mao and the CCRG framed the movement—formally named the Great Proletarian Cultural Revolution—as a life and death struggle between capitalism and socialism, with capitalism residing in all forms of "bourgeois ideology" and socialism residing in Mao Zedong Thought, as interpreted by Mao and the CCRG. With this struggle on the agenda, Mao was not even close to finished in May, nor was the CCRG and its now-invigorated leader, Jiang Qing.

Jiang Qing's Rise

When Jiang married Mao in Yan'an, she was widely resented by Party leaders as a home wrecker. Unfair as this may have been—Mao's and He Zizhen's marriage was already shaky by then—she had for years bided her time, in enforced leisure and with much bile accumulating against those she considered her or Mao's enemies. Through the years, her relationship to Mao became increasingly attenuated, and they spent more time apart. Jiang's real and imagined illnesses had made her a paranoid hypochondriac, and Mao's dalliances with young women became more frequent and disrupted any possibility of a settled relationship with his wife.

As a former actress, Jiang had remained interested in, and connected to, the cultural world, particularly that in Shanghai, China's cultural capital.

She habitually watched movies in her custom-designed screening room at Zhongnanhai and she was an accomplished photographer. Jiang had long desired to get into the political and cultural fray, but had been forestalled by the opposition of Party leaders. Mao had agreed it was best for Jiang Qing to remain apart from politics.

In 1965, Mao changed his mind and commissioned Jiang Qing to do a number of secret jobs in the cultural sphere he could entrust to no one else. The Hai Rui incident was an example of Jiang's success in implementing Mao's directions. She soon moved into political position, publicly through the CCRG, and privately through a shadowy organization named the Central Case Examination Group. The latter took on the task of digging up damaging gossip against proposed targets of struggle or removal.

Ultimately, Jiang Qing became a scapegoat for the Cultural Revolution and for her role in the Gang of Four. At her public trial in 1981, she was accused of many specific crimes. She also was accused of being the female demon power behind the throne and of demonstrating all of the reasons why a woman with power was a bad woman. In such a context of vilification, it perhaps can never be known just how much she operated on her own, and how much only at the behest of Mao. She remains widely reviled in China.

Big Character Posters

Soon after the May 16th directive, when the Party's alleged infiltration by the bourgeoisie was announced, Mao issued a call to students. "Dare to rebel against authority," he told them. They soon responded in their millions.

On May 25, students at Beijing University (Beida)—the site of the May Fourth Movement in 1919—affixed a "big-character poster" to the campus walls. It denounced the university's highest authority, the president, for suppressing discussion of the Hai Rui play. The poster called for a battle to begin between revolutionary intellectuals and bourgeois school bureaucrats. Big-character posters were an important weapon in the ensuing struggles. They were a tool of popular political communication and warfare. They could be anonymous or signed; they could be posted anywhere on any surface, hence available to anyone with a brush, ink, and paper; they could be dashed off or labored over; they could level accusations without proof, or they could adduce evidence at their leisure; their accusations were almost impossible to refute, other than through reactive posters, which were never as dramatic as the originals; and they were ephemeral: if not read immediately, accusations could change, compounding the difficulty of responding fast enough to forestall the spread of reputation-destroying rumors.

The authors of big-character posters used all of these guerilla tactics to seize the right of speech away from those who normally controlled the organs of mass communication. They turned politics into a mass politics by making political voice available. Students and soon residents all over the urban and rural areas were bombarded with political posters, much as product advertisements now occupy the same walls that used to be public political not privatized space. For most in China, from this time on, there was no life without the posters and politics.

The Beida poster was torn down immediately by Party authorities. A few days later, Mao praised its content. A little later, he went on to note, "youth is the great army of the Great Cultural Revolution! It must be mobilized to the full." And, in a caution to his fellow leaders against dampening youth enthusiasm, he told them, "You must put politics in command, go among the masses and be at one with them, and carry on the Great Proletarian Cultural Revolution even better."[2] A *People's Daily* editorial, assumed to have been written, or at least approved, by Mao, shortly thereafter proclaimed, "Revolutionary Big-Character Posters are 'Magic Mirrors' That Show Up All Monsters."[3] Mao's support fueled the ensuing student revolution.

Attempts by Liu Shaoqi and other Party leaders to keep the students under control failed. The movement spiraled in its own momentum, taking professors, administrators, writers, and others down at will and without logic.

Education, Authority, the Bourgeoisie, and the Red Guards

Teachers, professors, and intellectuals in general were accused of being the primary harborers and spreaders of bourgeois thought. Education—in its guise as rote memory, exam taking, bookish knowledge, and abstract principle—was faulted for being divorced from the practical needs of the revolutionary masses. Schools were identified as the reproducers of the bourgeoisie. The urban and elite bias of institutions and instructors was blamed for producing a generation of apolitical careerist youth, who had no concept of revolutionary sacrifice or practice. Mao was intent on shaking all that up; he mobilized students—who he called "revolutionary successors"—to do it.

Teachers, professors, and school administrators were attacked in big-character posters and then arrested by students. They were detained and forced to write self-criticisms addressing the crimes of which they were accused. Some were harassed or even beaten to death; some committed suicide rather than face the harshness of treatment. Others endured long days, weeks, months, and years of humiliation. They had dunce caps placed on their heads and were paraded around with their alleged crimes presented on sandwich boards hung around their necks. They were forced to attend struggle sessions. They had to stand in painful positions while being accused. They had to admit publicly their crimes. Even if they did all that was asked, they were usually not released. The point was to demonstrate the hollowness of all authority, whether bureaucratic-administrative or knowledge-based instructional. It was to impress physically upon those in positions of authority that they could be humbled. It was to demonstrate the power of the masses over the authority that oppressed them, and to give the masses a voice where it had previously been suppressed. Or that was the idea.

Observing from Wuhan, Mao wrote in a letter to Jiang Qing of July 8, 1966, that he wished to "create great disorder under heaven" so as finally to achieve "great order under heaven."[4]

The revolution spread from universities to senior and junior high schools, with the first Red Guard groups formed by high school students in Beijing. The movement became a tide of attacks, factions, allegations, and punishments. Youths as young as thirteen took their teachers, school principals, and parents to verbal and physical task. None of them dared fight back. Red Guard factions multiplied. Erstwhile friends became enemies; enemies became friends. Dorms were occupied and barricaded. Violence broke out. At ostensible issue were correct politics and interpretations of Mao's thought. The debates became exercises in arcane textual analysis, as big-character posters festooned every available surface.

Summer came, and classes were suspended. Students did not disperse; they continued the struggle. Party work teams were sent into the schools to try to sort things out, but they merely contributed to further factionalizations and were driven away. In July, Mao criticized the work teams for obstructing the revolution. He ridiculed them for being afraid: "You people! If you don't make revolution, the revolution will be directed against you." He went on, "After two months, you still haven't got the slightest perceptual knowledge and you are still bureaucratic. . . . The first thing is struggle, the second is criticism, the third is transformation. Struggle means destruction, and transformation means establishing something new."[5]

Mao Swims the Yangzi

In a celebrated event on July 16, 1966, Mao went swimming in the Yangzi River near Wuhan. He swam many miles. It was claimed the seventy-two-year-old Chairman swam faster and more vigorously than any Olympic swimming champion. Numerous photographs, said to demonstrate Mao's virility and vitality, were published in China and globally.

It seems clear that Mao was aided mightily in his swim by the strong river currents. Yet, since Mao had been out of the public eye for so very long, the photographs of him swimming and in good health served to bring him back to popular attention. Two days later—on July 18—Mao turned up in Beijing.

Received by Mao

By early August 1966, students sporting Red Guard armbands began roaming the streets of every city and town in the country. They chanted slogans and policed revolutionary practice, between themselves and among others. Mao wrote to the Red Guards at various locations to urge them to continue rebelling against "reactionaries"; at the same time, he encouraged them to unite with "all who can be united with." He reminded the Red Guards of what Marx had said: "the proletariat must emancipate not only itself but all mankind." Hence, rather than just destroy individuals, those who made mistakes should be offered a "way out."[6]

Mao received the Red Guards at an ecstatic dawn meeting on August 18 at Beijing's Tian'anmen Square. A million students attended, each waving his or her little red book, now a mandatory revolutionary accessory. (The little red book is the second most published text in the world after the Bible.) As Mao stood on the reviewing stand overlooking the Square, he received a female Red Guard emissary, who offered him a red armband. He placed it on his left arm over his familiar army fatigues, symbolizing his command of, and solidarity with, the Red Guards.

The ubiquitous uniform for Red Guards now became an army outfit, with a red armband attached on the left. The sartorial and gender ideal was masculine and military. Girls dressed to be less identifiably female, wearing clothing as baggy as possible. They cut their hair very short, or had it summarily shorn on the streets. Red Guard patrols routinely stopped those deemed too pretty, accusing them of harboring bourgeois ideas of beauty. The only real beauty, it was said, was revolutionary beauty, not a physical but a political manifestation. Femininity was bourgeois, and all personal adornment became politically suspect.

Sixteen Articles and Four Olds

In mid-August 1966, a Party Central Committee meeting formally proclaimed the Cultural Revolution a movement to overthrow "those within the Party who are in authority and taking the capitalist road." Names were not named. A closely related purpose was the destruction of what was called the "four olds"—old ideas, old culture, old customs, and old habits. These were said to be the tools through which the bourgeoisie ensured its own reproduction as a class.

After the meeting of August 18 on Tian'anmen Square, the Red Guards began the destruction of the "four olds" with breathtaking violence and thoroughness. Obvious targets such as temples were first taken down. The destruction then moved into homes, the spaces where bourgeois reproduction happens at the level of quotidian practice. Flower gardens, planters, and even pet birds in their cages were destroyed as signs of bourgeois thought and habit; classical records, pianos, foreign-language books, and anything smacking of refinement or high culture was dragged out and destroyed, or at least confiscated. Nobody's home was safe from Red Guard inspection and sacking. The residences of Party members were the first targets; soon the homes of former capitalists (whose productive properties had long since been nationalized but who had retained their private residences) became targets, as did former landlords (whose houses and possessions were more lavish than most), and anyone whose life was not the paragon of revolutionary class position. Various leaders tried to rein in the zeal with which the "four olds" were attacked and destroyed. They, in turn, became targets of verbal and physical assault for giving succor to the bourgeoisie.

In previous Maoist practice, if one had revolutionary consciousness and acted upon it, one could overcome background or actual class standing to become part of the "people." This changed during the Cultural Revolution. Now, the only important marker was "bloodline" demonstrating the correct family class position—poor or middling peasant, proletariat, or soldier. All others, no matter what their *current* position, were expelled from "the people" into the "black categories." This had the curious effect of casting suspicion on the vast majority of the old revolutionaries. After all, the nucleus of the CCP back in the 1920s and 1930s had been urban, educated youths along with some offspring of landlord or rich peasant families (for example, Mao himself). They were now suspected of secretly harboring bourgeois thoughts and actions.

The blackest of all categories, aside from counter-revolutionaries and traitors, was intellectuals, the progenitors and promoters par excellence of bourgeois ideas. They were called "the stinking ninth [category]" (of ten), and were specifically marked out for attack, re-education in proximity to the masses, and the confiscation of their belongings, all now tainted with a bourgeois odor. The works of venerable and celebrated leftist and Communist writers—stalwarts of the CCP and the Revolution included—were reinterpreted through new eyes. These writers were now declared "snakes" for hiding so well their bourgeois sympathies in the midst of ostensibly radical texts. They were masters of disguise, it was said, and it was the task of the Red Guards to strip their masks away to reveal the bourgeois essence underneath.

Red Guards carried portraits of Mao, of red suns (Mao was the "reddest sun in our heart"), of Mao peering over the red sun, of Mao as the red sun was rising, of Mao juxtaposed to the rising red sun, and so on. If Mao was depicted looking right instead of left in these portraits, the artist, as well as the person carrying it, could be accused of political crimes. The little red book became an object of devotion, to be memorized and cited by verse and page number. Revolutionary names were concocted for city streets and affixed over old signs (leading to much confusion at the post office). The location of the former American embassy was renamed "Anti-imperialism Street."

Chaos and violence flowed unabated through the end of 1966, when the CCRG—Jiang Qing and her crowd—decided that the utility of the Red Guards was mostly spent. But before the students were dispersed, the "big Krushchev" had to be exposed and deposed.

The Fall of Liu Shaoqi (and Deng Xiaoping)

Liu Shaoqi, who had taken over from Mao after the Great Leap, was ill with tuberculosis. He nevertheless was in power, with loyalists staffing high Party positions. In the beginning of the Cultural Revolution, these loyalists were systematically labeled "little Krushchevs" and removed. It now became clear that the main Chinese Krushchev was Liu himself.

In the summer of 1966, Liu was identified within Party circles as the "leading person in authority taking the capitalist road." Deng Xiaoping was named along with him as a "capitalist roader." Liu vigorously defended himself, counting upon his strong Party alliances to bail him out of trouble. Soon, he found the cards stacked against him, as those loyal to him lost their own positions. He disappeared after November 1966 and was publicly identified and formally dismissed in disgrace in 1967. He was expelled from the Party in 1968, and died of pneumonia in 1969. This was the result of pure neglect, as he was denied medical treatment. His wife, Wang Guangmei, a veteran revolutionary, now under the same political cloud as her husband, had been sent to be re-educated in prison; she had not seen Liu since 1967 and was not present for his final illness. Liu was left to die in obscurity. He was posthumously rehabilitated in 1980, whereupon his ashes, carefully preserved, were handed over to his wife.

By contrast, Deng Xiaoping wrote a self-criticism and was sent to repair tractors in rural Jiangxi. Through labor, he rehabilitated himself. Mao brought Deng back to Beijing in 1973.

"Bombard the Headquarters!" and the Shanghai Commune

On August 5, 1966, Mao wrote a big-character poster with the message, "bombard the headquarters." It called upon the masses to dismantle the very Party of which he was Chairman, and to which he had devoted his life. This not only meant struggling against individuals, it also meant destroying the structures of power through which the Party oppressed the people. It meant replacing those structures with new ones.

As the Party was pervasive through all levels of society, the movement now expanded beyond students. Mass organizations were formed. Likened to those of the Paris Commune of 1871—the short-lived paragon of Marxist revolutionary practice—these new structures took over Party headquarters and functions. The CCP reeled from attacks and the gutting of its membership.

Meanwhile, the revolution was taken up in the factories. In the late autumn of 1966, the Shanghai Municipal Party Committee came under attack from a newly formed alliance, named the Headquarters of the Revolutionary Revolt of Shanghai Workers. The purpose of this organization, led by Wang Hongwen, a young textile worker, was to reintroduce the factory floor democracy discontinued after the Great Leap experiments. What the workers envisioned was a cooperative relationship between themselves and managers, to help transform the relations of production from commandism (bureaucratic rule) to genuine proletarian democracy.

The Shanghai Party Committee refused the Workers' Headquarters demands. To press their case, workers commandeered a train to Beijing intending to go directly to Mao. The train was stopped by Party authorities not far from the Shanghai station. A siege ensued. From Beijing, Mao's longtime secretary, Chen Boda, in his capacity as CCRG leader, ordered the workers back to work; a fellow member of the CCRG, Zhang Chunqiao, former Party Secretary in Shanghai, remanded the order. In Beijing, this spelled the demise of Chen Boda's career. In Shanghai, it meant temporary victory for the proletariat.

The Shanghai Party Committee disintegrated. Red Guards along with worker groups proceeded to organize students and workers in the city. A number of different workers' groups sprang up, most radical among them, the Workers' Second Regiment, and most conservative, the Workers' Scarlet Guards, comprised of technicians and skilled workers. By the end of 1966, the majority of the workers of Shanghai—the most industrialized of all Chinese cities, responsible for over half of all industrial production in the nation—were organized into one of these groups.

In December, the conservative Scarlet Guards provoked a violent competition with the Workers' Headquarters for leadership of the proletariat. The remnants of the Shanghai Party Committee attempted to gain covert control of the Scarlet Guards, by buying off workers' support. This was duly discovered by the Workers' Headquarters, who managed to rally remaining workers to their side. The now compromised Scarlet Guards, along with the financially exhausted and politically disgraced Party, were overthrown.

In this "January Revolution" (1967) workers took over the major newspapers of Shanghai and immediately published a "Message to All the People of Shanghai." It condemned the Scarlet Guards and the Party, while calling for all workers to return to their factories to resume production. In a mass meeting on January 6 sponsored by the Workers' Headquarters, the Shanghai mayor, Party leaders, and Party functionaries were publicly excoriated, physically and verbally humiliated, and then summarily dismissed from their posts. On January 9, Mao affirmed what had happened in Shanghai, calling it a "great revolution" and confirming that the "upsurge of revolutionary power in Shanghai has brought hope to the whole country." He was especially pleased by the workers' seizure of the organs of mass communication.[7]

Suddenly, former Shanghai denizens Zhang Chunqiao and Yao Wenyuan, now leaders of the CCRG, arrived on the scene from Beijing. They struck an agreement with Wang Hongwen, the textile worker leader of the Workers' Headquarters (who became the fourth member of the "Gang of Four") and attempted to bring Shanghai to order. The triumvirate of Zhang, Yao, and Wen proclaimed the founding of the "Shanghai Commune." Radical worker groups—such as the Second Regiment—contested this alliance for being imposed by Beijing rather than voted in by Shanghai workers. Violence broke out between the groups and lasted through the end of January. Zhang and Yao were recalled to Beijing in February to give an account to Mao. While Mao agreed with their overall approach, he suggested it was time to deepen the movement and rather than merely chanting slogans, "students should make a deeper study of things and choose a few passages to write some critical articles about."[8]

By this point, not only in Shanghai, but all over China's cities, Red Guards were roaming streets perpetrating violence against one another; schools were out of session, as the teachers had been deposed and children were at loose ends; many parents were involved in political struggles in their places of work or residence, and were unable to look after their children; workers were organizing, contesting each other, management, and Beijing's authority; and the Party was all but destroyed as a functioning administrative body.

Linking Up

As students were freed from study and as school and parental control weakened or disappeared altogether, many of them took to the roads and railways to travel the country and see the revolution unfolding. Non-Beijing residents seized the opportunity to travel to Beijing, in hopes of being received by Mao on Tian'anmen Square, as he had done in August 1966. (He did in fact receive Red Guards a total of eight times.) Meanwhile, many from Beijing took the opportunity to travel elsewhere. Some decided to make pilgrimages to hallowed revolutionary sites, such as Shaoshan (Mao's hometown), Jinggangshan and Ruijin (the pre-Yan'an base areas), and Yan'an. Several particularly intrepid groups decided to retrace the steps of the Long March.

A huge movement of youth got under way, "linking up," in the language of the time, the various revolutionary movements in different parts of the country. Railroads suspended the need for tickets, as did buses and other modes of public transportation. Students crowded onto trains with little more than a toothbrush in their hands. Food was distributed free, and students stayed with Red Guard groups at university dorms or public spaces. Travelers overwhelmed the capacities of smaller sites, and larger places overflowed.

These experiences were perhaps the most exhilarating aspect of the Cultural Revolution for many. Never before given so much freedom of movement—pressures and poverty served to keep most youths rooted to their places of residence—this was the first time most had ever traveled anywhere; and it was the first time most were away from home. They got their first glimpses of their huge and diverse nation. For a few, travel confirmed what they thought they already knew; for the majority, travel was extraordinarily eye-opening.

The continued poverty of the rural areas was a shock to those from the cities, who had never seen or dreamed of such conditions. The difficulties peasant women continued to face, due to gender inequality, was astonishing to city girls, who took their equality for granted. The unevenness of socialism, or perhaps, the unevenness *caused by* socialism, came as a revelation. Urban privilege and rural disadvantage became clear. Some formed the desire to lock this unevenness in place in order to protect their positions; many formed the desire to do what they could to change it.

The People's Liberation Army

Through the beginning of 1967, Mao became increasingly dismayed at the lack of unity among rebel groups. He was staring at the specter of complete chaos in the country. There was only one ideologically trustworthy organization left intact that could bring order to the situation: the army.

In late January 1967, the PLA was called on to intervene in the internecine battles on the streets, campuses, and factories of the cities. Lin Biao, on Mao's orders, moved the army into Beijing, Shanghai, Wuhan, and other areas in chaos. While the PLA remained under civilian control—Mao's control—its intervention nevertheless tipped the balance toward certain outcomes. In the interests of restoring order and stability, from February to March 1967, the army forcibly disarmed rebel student groups and radical worker organizations, killing thousands and arresting many more. Much of the vast violence of early 1967—often attributed to "radical Maoist" students and workers—was perpetrated by the army. This had an obvious dampening effect.

The next step came as the army redefined the Cultural Revolution as a movement to study Mao Zedong Thought, rather than to use Mao Zedong Thought as a guide to action. By discouraging activism and encouraging study, this, too, tamped down some of the passions.[9] And the tamping down of passion was precisely what Mao desired at this point. He began calling some of the more radical manifestations of the previous six months "anarchistic," and was insistent that these tendencies be staunched. In particular, he called for the cessation of the physical assaults on Party cadres and state leaders, and for the revival of certain functions of the state and Party apparatus.

Through the early spring of 1967, the PLA took over the mass organizations formed in the Party's stead. By May, mass resentment was high— against the PLA and its restoration of deposed Party cadres. Beijing, Shanghai, and especially Wuhan exploded in mass activism all over again. In a series of bloody and Byzantine intrigues, these rebellions were quelled, although in the process, the specter of civil war and of PLA factionalism was raised. In August, these possibilities came to the fore, as the mass movement broke down and different sectors attempted to ally with the PLA.

Mao remained silent. Jiang Qing goaded the Red Guards on, advising them to "defend themselves with weapons." And yet, the Party was regrouping under the protection of the military. It was preparing to re-seize command, now with Mao and Lin Biao on its side and at its head, rather than in opposition.

"Normalcy"

In the summer of 1967, Mao embarked on an inspection tour of the provinces. He was evidently appalled at what he witnessed. In September 1967, the PLA again was sent to crush opposition, to disarm civilian groups, and to restore "normalcy." The order was signed by Mao, the Central Committee, the CCRG, the Central Military Affairs Committee of the PLA—in short, by all conceivable branches of the government, to demonstrate its definitive nature and its seriousness. Jiang Qing was tasked with announcing the order and in the process renouncing her previous views that students and mass organizations were justified in taking up weapons against the army. The about-face was total, and the suppression of mass initiative all but complete. The process was long and difficult, and in the provinces quite bloody. Yet, by October 1, 1967, the PLA's generals, reviled as covert capitalists just a short few months before, now stood atop the Gate of Heavenly Peace alongside Mao for the National Day celebrations. By mid-October, the Red Guards were ordered to disband, and students were instructed to return to their classrooms.

In an attempt to explain the chaos, Mao "revealed" that Liu Shaoqi had been at the root of the anarchy. With the toppling of Liu, now publicly named the "big Krushchev" and dismissed in disgrace, the poison could cease to flow through the veins of the Chinese body politic. However, the ferocity with which mass organizations in many places fought against the PLA to retain their hard-won political gains is testament to how unsuccessful the propaganda campaign against Liu was in convincing anyone that a covert puppeteer controlled the movement. Indeed, it was quite clear to workers and rebel students that the promise of the Cultural Revolution— mass politics in command—was being betrayed.

By the end of 1967, while the CCP staged its revival, Zhou Enlai presided over the rebuilding of the state apparatus. The forces of order were readying their comeback.

"Down to the Countryside"

The summer of 1968 saw the last-gasp attempts of the mass organizations and student groups to recapture the political energies of the year before. Anger over the restoration of those who had been mercilessly critiqued and so very recently deposed boiled over in many places. Before it could become a renewal of mass activism, a ruthless military crackdown was launched to suppress, once and for all, the challenges to "normalcy." University campuses were the sites of this last-ditch struggle, and they turned into bloodbaths.

The only way to diffuse, finally and completely, student passions and organizational densities, Mao decided, was to disperse them. Starting in 1968, university and senior and junior high school students were systematically invited to volunteer to go down to the countryside and into the factories to work with the peasants and proletariat. A very large number of idealistic students did go of their own free will to "rusticate" themselves. Piling into railway cars, buses, trucks, and tractors, students were shipped out of the cities, batch by batch, to places both close to and far from their hometowns to learn from the peasants, humble themselves before the nation's workers, and cleanse themselves of bourgeois tendencies, thoughts, and habits.

Once those who volunteered departed, a huge number of remaining students were forced out of the cities by urban authorities. They were placed in small factories and collective farms in remote areas, where they were expected to produce for their living. Originally designed as a short-term solution to the rebelliousness and violence of Red Guard organizations, the voluntary "down to the countryside" movement became a coercive measure of being "sent down," so as to empty the cities of potential challengers to the restoration of Party power.

The students who went early and voluntarily often recall the idealism with which they began their sojourns among peasants or workers. The dreams of growing their own food, relying on their own labor, and learning from the hard-working class leaders of the revolution (peasants and proletariat) sustained many a teenager through very tough transitions to unfamiliar terrain far from familiar faces.

These idealisms and dreams were followed by progressive disillusionment with the circumstances. Some of this had to do with the incredible poverty and straitened conditions in which they found themselves, for which the socialist propaganda about ever-improving standards of living had ill prepared them. Some of it was related to the relative hostility with which the students were received by unsuspecting villagers, forced by local Party leaders to accommodate youths who had never seen a rice shoot, never carried a shoulder pole, and never done manual labor of any sort. Much of the disillusionment was due to the cultural conditions of the rural areas and what urbanized educated students understood to be the "feudal" unschooled and traditional thoughts of peasants. Mostly, forbearance turned to despair as paths back to the city were closed off and rusticated youths realized they were now expected to stay forever in their new locations.

Students with powerful and politically intact families were able to maneuver their way around the regulations to get back to the cities after a few years. Students, whose families had been politically active, now destroyed, but who still had good contacts within the system, were stuck for a while longer yet had an escape route. Students who had never had powerful or politically connected families gave up all hope of escaping their circumstances; they reconciled themselves with resignation or extreme anger to their dashed expectations. Power, it turned out, was eminently corruptible by those who could work the system.

The emptying of cities removed the student elements from mass organizing, helping calm the urban areas and restore order. Workers went back to work, with only some of the democratic factory floor gains they had sought. Spaces were opened at the universities and urban learning institutions for peasant and proletarian children, who had never had a chance at college-level education or maybe even at urban life. When schools reopened in the early 1970s, it was with the favored "worker, peasant, soldier" student as the major constituency. Curricula were redesigned to serve these students and the goals of the Cultural Revolution, to render culture into something useful for the revolutionary everyday lives of the masses. Bookishness, abstract research, learning for the sake of learning—all this "bourgeois" dross was discarded in favor of practical education. The teachers allowed back into the classrooms took instruction from the students by enhancing their own practical skills, and students spent only a fraction of the day in the classrooms, with the rest of it spent in practical training. Campus life was thoroughly revolutionized and politicized. *This* was approaching Mao's vision of education for the masses.

The Ninth National Congress of the Chinese Communist Party

In 1969, the CCP convened its ninth national Congress. In his opening address on April 1, Mao reviewed the long and torturous history of the CCP—from its twelve-delegate founding in 1921, through the lean years and Yan'an, to the present. He lauded the Party for having rid itself of its internal enemies, primarily Liu Shaoqi and Peng Zhen, and expressed the hope that after all the divisiveness resulting from exposing enemies, the Congress would be one of unity and victory.

Mao had reason to feel confident. He had marginalized his enemies. The Party, state, and cultural apparatuses were now preponderantly staffed by Maoists. The country was relatively quiescent, having come through a cataclysmic set of events kindled by Mao himself, and taken up by millions of students and workers. He had reoriented the course of development, education, and cultural policy toward revolutionary goals. Institutions had been remolded around Maoist ideals, and bureaucratic Party cadres had been sent in droves to cadre schools in remote areas for re-education through labor. Industrial and agricultural production was stable and growing. China increasingly was hailed, in many places around the globe, as a leader in a type of Communism appropriate for the nonindustrialized third world. The PRC in fact had become a pilgrimage site for left-leaning people from all over the world. Mao met with as many as he could, including African, Asian, and Latin American leaders, as well as writers, cultural figures, and Communists from Japan, Europe, and the United States.

However, there were still a few things bothering Mao. In his speech of April 28 at the First Plenum of the Ninth Congress, he vented. First, Mao complained about Soviet verbal attacks that labeled the CCP as a "petit bourgeois party" rather than a party of the proletariat. These attacks loomed particularly large in the wake of the airing of the "Brezhnev doctrine." Proclaimed in 1968, just as Soviet troops were violently quelling the Prague Spring in Czechoslovakia, this doctrine held that Moscow had the right to depose those in the socialist bloc posing a challenge to Communist principles. As with Hungary in 1956, there was no Chinese support for the Prague Spring. But there was considerable discomfort about Soviet troops marching into other people's territories, and about the "revisionist" USSR as the self-proclaimed leader of correct Communist doctrine and practice.

Second, Mao complained that factories were still being run along old Liu Shaoqi rules of material incentives and profits in command. The point, Mao noted, was to make the factories bastions of proletarian politics in command. "Economism," or rewarding productivity with money, in Mao's view, demonstrated the wrong values; production should be led by (revolutionary) politics, not cash. Third, Mao complained that rusticated youths and those in cadre schools had become divorced from the world and the life of the nation. He urged that they should be brought back in through study classes organized to "talk about history . . . about the course of the Great Cultural Revolution during the past two years."[10]

Mao also warned that China was still not sufficiently prepared for war. With the Americans in Vietnam and the hostile Soviets on the northern border, Mao cautioned that it was probably only a matter of time before "imperialists and revisionists" (Americans and Soviets) attacked. Lastly, Mao complained about the continuing signs of disunity in the country, from small-scale petty quarrels to larger matters of policy. In this regard Mao proposed "the answer to the problem of the localities lies in the army; the answer to the problem of the army lies in political work."[11]

The corollary to relying on the army for domestic solutions, in the context of potential war, was the naming of Lin Biao—the PLA commander and one of the most respected generals of the anti-Japanese and civil wars—as Mao's successor. Nobody could have predicted that a short year later, Lin was to be accused of sedition and "exposed" as the biggest CCP snake of all.

9

The Cultural Revolution

DENOUEMENT AND DEATH OF MAO, 1969–1976

As the Cultural Revolution was unfolding in China, the 1960s were unfolding across the rest of the world. From Africa, Latin America, and Asia, to the United States and Europe, domestic radicalism and anti-colonial revolutionary nationalism were shaking up the global establishment. These upsurges were met, sooner or later, by forces of national and international order. Corresponding to attempts to beat back the transformative tide was a rise in revolutionary internationalism. This internationalism—in its domestic and global forms—spun a vision of a new world without domination or exploitation.

Revolutionary Internationalism and the Global 1960s

The Chinese Cultural Revolution was an inspiration for many in envisioning this new world. This was not because the movement was well understood. Far from it. The idea and image of a people, apparently set free from constraint to practice mass politics, appealed to those, who were increasingly disaffected from the routines of life. They were tired of political quiescence, and impatient with grinding exploitative, sexist, and racist views and practices. The perceived imaginative and creative exuberance of the Cultural Revolution—particularly in its early days—tapped into burgeoning desires everywhere for common people to seize politics from the dead hands of faraway bureaucrats, technocratic social engineers, and militaristic warmongers and turn it into something of culturally enduring and everyday significance.

INTERLUDE: MAO AND THE CULTURAL REVOLUTION IN JAPAN

The following excerpts are from my interview with the Japanese-born, New York–based independent writer Sabu Kohso. Growing up in postwar Japan, Sabu entered high school in the early 1970s, and there came into contact with student radicals and experienced political struggles. It was then that he became aware of the Cultural Revolution, Maoism, and China.[1]

Q: When and how did you become aware of Mao and China's Cultural Revolution?

A: The late 1960s and early 1970s in Japan were exciting; it was an entire decade: you walked the streets of Tokyo, and there were student demonstrations, struggles with the police, cultural experimentations, politics in the streets. Those of us who were just coming of age at that time were excited. . . . I happened to have a friend, whose tutor was one of the founders of DIC— Destruction is Construction—one of the leftist sects at the time. This guy was really critical of the previous New Left line in Japan. . . . He found the real core of revolution in China's Cultural Revolution: . . . to change the values of everyday life, to undertake social revolution. This was a big deal for us, because, even though we were affected by the atmosphere of revolution all around us, we were after all the children of Americanization—John Ford movies, Coca-Cola—and so to find some new values for everyday life in Chinese things was really different!

. . . My generation faced severe entrance exams; to be socially successful, you had to go to great schools, and our work was to study constantly. Today, students face a more complicated situation; but in our time, climbing the ladder of social success—reproducing ourselves as a class—was accomplished directly through education. We focused, therefore, on "stop the examinations" campaigns, using propaganda and discussions with students and teachers. We formed networks against education as a class reproduction system. . . . I was probably fifteen or so, and was the youngest. Other students participating in this campaign had more experience. . . . We believed in the Maoist line based upon the Cultural Revolutionary idea, which was to transvalue our everyday life through cultural rebellion.

Q: Did you base your actions on Maoist writings?

A: . . . We read Mao's works every day. We were intent on shifting the values of Japanese society from being based on the United States to China. We were not officially connected to China, not like the Sino-Japanese Friendship Society, but we were convinced that we were the more serious ones and thought *we* were the ones who should be in Tian'anmen Square meeting with Mao Zedong and Lin Biao.

Our focus was really on the Japanese underclass, the ones who had been left out of the postwar middle-class centered society. . . . We believed Mao's words that the revolution should start from the countryside; of course, in Japan, this was very unrealistic, as Japan was already mostly one big metropolitan region! But, Okinawa was the last place we could organize. . . . By 1972 or 1973, the core members of DIC became determined; they went to Okinawa to build a revolutionary base. They asked us to choose whether to go with them or not. I didn't quit high school to go; I couldn't . . .

. . . There were lots of events, films from China, even a good bookshop, which still exists, called *Toho Shoten* [Oriental Books]. Our fashion was different. Back then, most leftists looked like American hippies, with long hair, jeans, and so on. We sought to be different, more humble like Chinese students. The majority of the New Left groups focused on street fights, from militant ones to nonviolent actions; but we thought we needed revolutionary acts in day to day life, so as to depose the educational machine.

Q: What Maoist texts interested you most at the time?

A: It was mostly the short citations from the *Little Red Book*, as well as the philosophical texts like "On Contradiction" and "On Practice." . . . We also read Mao's writings on the war against Japan—"On Protracted War." My favorite was always his addresses to students, his encouragement to students to rebel and to speak their minds. . . . The Cultural Revolution . . . was encouraging to us; it helped us dare to think we could *do* something. [Here, Sabu showed me his marked up copies of the *Little Red Book* and Mao's *Exhortation to Students*. On one page, in the margins of the text, Sabu had traced out in Chinese characters: *"zaofan you li"*—"It is right to rebel"—Mao's most famous slogan calling students into being as a revolutionary force in 1966.] . . . This was really the beginning of thinking about the world for me; . . . the Cultural Revolution helped me think on my own terms. I couldn't follow my mother's hopes for me to become a banker; the Cultural Revolution gave me an imagination of what might be possible.

Q: What did you think when Nixon visited China?

A: We didn't know what to make of it. Some insisted it was necessary for China to confront the USSR. But it was a shock. . . . It was a big disappointment: I even stopped listening to the daily radio broadcasts, "Peking Hoso" [Peking News]; at the beginning of those broadcasts they would sing "The East is Red" [here, Sabu hummed the first few bars of the tune, which was ubiquitous in China at the time]. When Nixon went to China, I stopped listening to those broadcasts.

The potential of the Cultural Revolution was not fulfilled, either in China or elsewhere. Various forces of order and "normalcy" were able to quash, while co-opting, parts of the 1960s movements. In China, as Mao was declaring victory for the Cultural Revolution in April 1969, it had already become clear to those who had engaged in it with passion and conviction that the promise of mass politics in command had been betrayed. The "victory" turned out to be for the Party alone; it was not a triumph for the masses, who had embraced the movement as theirs to shape and claim.

Laying "China Cards" on the Table

At the same time that Maoism was being promoted by many as an exciting alternative to the moribund Soviet variety of socialism, the Chinese were engaging in a showdown with the Soviets on their border. In March 1969, after many minor incidents and wars of words, outright hostilities broke out at the Ussuri River, the boundary between Soviet Siberia and Chinese Manchuria. Whether the Chinese instigated the events or were provoked is the subject of heated historical debate. Whatever the onset, one upshot was the manifest spectacle of the two socialist "fraternal allies" engaged in a hot war. American spy satellites operated by the CIA captured the results, noting "the Chinese side of the [Ussuri] river was so pockmarked by Soviet artillery that it looked like a 'moonscape.' "[2] The PLA was put on high alert. In China, warnings about full-scale war were issued to great patriotic effect.

Meanwhile, the Soviets attempted to play their "China card" by sounding out Washington about the potential of a surgical strike against Chinese nuclear weapons installations. President Nixon and his National Security Advisor, Henry Kissinger, had by then given up pressuring the Soviets to influence North Vietnam. They decided to play their own "China card" and warned the Soviets not to escalate attacks on China.

The momentous Nixon opening to China germinated. It was now clear that the Cold War bogeyman of a Communist monolith was a postwar fantasy, invented and sustained to whip up American patriotic fervor. Yet, in 1969–70, Chinese newspapers were in full-scale vitriol against American escalations in Vietnam and the "secret" bombing of Cambodia. Editorial after editorial called for "the people of the whole world [to] unite, [to] defeat the U.S. aggressors and all their lackeys." As Mao wrote in May 1970 for the *People's Daily*, "U.S. imperialism not only massacres foreigners, it also massacres white and black people in its own country. Nixon's fascist atrocities have enkindled the raging flames of the revolutionary mass movement in the United States."[3] In a different venue, Mao went on to proclaim that "imperialism [i.e., the United States] is afraid of the third world," a category to which China belonged, in Mao's view.[4] It was hard to imagine two more firm foes than the PRC and the USA in rapprochement.

Throughout 1969 and 1970, the prospect of full-scale war with the Soviets was a major Chinese preoccupation. The Soviets moved battlefield nuclear weapons to the border, even as Mao pressed on with bilateral negotiations. Zhou Enlai was sent to Hanoi for Ho Chi Minh's funeral, where he met with Soviet Premier Kosygin; a delegation went to the border to hold talks. At the same time, China prepared for extended hostilities. Key economic and research installations, located in large urban areas, were dismantled and concealed inland, to protect them from potential Soviet strikes. Tens of millions of people were moved to rural areas, in anticipation of an urban nuclear holocaust. In mid-October 1969, the CCP leaders —including Mao—were evacuated from Beijing, each to a different location. Mao went to Wuhan.

Mao in 1970

In the autumn of 1969, central China experienced unusually cold weather. In Wuhan, Mao refused, as he normally did, to turn on the heat in his residence so early in the season. Now in his late seventies, Mao still believed that enhanced exercise would help him withstand the climate. He was wrong. No matter how much squatting and swimming in the indoor pool he accomplished, he caught cold. It soon turned into severe bronchitis.

In mid-1970, from his base in Wuhan, Mao journeyed to Lushan for a Party conference. It was here that many insiders began to have an inkling of a conflict between Mao and his designated successor, Lin Biao. At Lushan, Lin tried to reinstate the post of head of state, as the office had remained empty since Liu Shaoqi's fall from power. Lin argued it was time to fill it. Mao argued it was best to abolish the post altogether. Lin's argument seems to have led Mao to conclude that Lin was attempting to seize state power, in addition to his military command—thus to isolate Mao as Party chairman in an end-run maneuver around him. Things were not resolved.

Mao left Lushan and returned to Wuhan in poor health, experiencing shortness of breath. It turned out that he had contracted pneumonia. Treated for that on top of the recent bronchitis, Mao was physically weakened through the end of 1970. His battle with Lin Biao was to further affect his physical condition. Despite his illnesses, Mao managed to attend the National Day celebrations in Beijing on October 1, when, as usual, he stood atop the Gate of Heavenly Peace.

In December, Mao was well enough to meet his old friend, Edgar Snow, the American journalist who had spent time in Yan'an and written a best-selling account of Chinese Communism in the 1940s for an American audience. Snow had long since been named a "friend of China," a label used by the Chinese to indicate foreigners not hostile to the PRC. Considered a suspicious figure in the United States because of his "commie" sympathies, Snow nevertheless was used by Mao in late 1970 as a conduit to the American government. In their meeting of December 18, Mao informed Snow he would be delighted to meet with Nixon or any high-level American official willing to come to China. Indeed, Mao stated that it would be best to allow Americans—rightists along with leftists—to visit the PRC, since "right now we must straighten things out with Nixon." Mao's urgency was, in part, informed by the festering Taiwan situation, in part, by the American escalations in Vietnam and the fear they would spill over into China, and in part, by Soviet hostilities. His urgency was also spurred by his eagerness to maneuver around his Ministry of Foreign Affairs, which he accused of ideological rigidity in formulating foreign policy. Mao was confident that the United States, would sooner or later welcome his initiative; after all, he noted, "*we* haven't occupied your Long Island!"[5]

The Fall of Lin Biao

The Party unity proclaimed at the Ninth Congress in April 1969, proved to be short lived. Division seized hold of the CCP's inner circles, and struggles were re-animated over issues of personnel and policy. The most spectacular of these was the split between Mao and the PLA commander Lin Biao.

One of the more extraordinary developments, the Lin Biao affair remains shrouded in mystery. The ending is mostly known: a little after midnight on September 13, 1971, a Trident jet carrying Lin Biao, his wife, and his son (the commander of the air force) took off from an airfield near Beidaihe, the summer retreat for CCP leaders. Lin Doudou, his daughter, was left behind, and it was she who alerted Zhou Enlai to the event. The jet was headed toward the Soviet Union. After a flight of an hour or so, it crashed in Outer Mongolia, either because of a shortage of fuel (most plausible), or because it was shot down by the Soviets or the Chinese (for which no evidence was ever found). All on board were killed. Lin Biao's presence on the plane was soon confirmed through his dental records.

What prompted Lin Biao to flee is in dispute. It is said, Lin was preparing to launch a coup against Mao involving the assassination of the Chairman. The coup was discovered by Mao loyalists, but Lin was tipped off in time to flee. It is also said, the alleged coup was a Maoist invention to depose Lin Biao, whose power within and over the PLA had grown too fast and great for Mao to countenance. Rather than a successor, Lin had become a rival. Or it is said, Lin Biao was always a stooge of the Soviets, through an alleged longtime secret connection to Chiang Kaishek. He had bided his time until he could deliver China to the USSR and thence to the GMD. This, it is said, explains why Lin fled toward the Soviet Union just as the Soviets and China were still engaged in a border war. Recently it has been suggested Lin was not power hungry, was indeed a Mao loyalist, and had not hatched a coup conspiracy, but was somehow induced to board the plane and flee by Ye Qun—his power-mongering wife—and his son, both of whom perceived doom on the horizon and wanted to save themselves, and their father, for another day.[6]

While this dispute cannot be resolved, it is quite clear from the Lushan conference in mid-1970 onward that Mao was increasingly uneasy about the role of the military in civilian life. Of course, it had been Mao himself who had called the PLA in to quell the mass movements. Yet, since the Ninth Congress in April 1969, Mao had been trying to rebuild the CCP. The PLA now stood in the way, as it had stepped into the vacuum created by the gutting of the Party. The PLA's ubiquitous presence now appeared suspicious.

Throughout late 1970 and into 1971, Lin Biao increasingly came under verbal attack. Nevertheless, he continued to be the biggest spokesperson for the Mao cult. In 1970, Lin advocated Mao be proclaimed a "genius" in the state constitution (Mao refused); Lin promoted the little red book and the ritual devotions it inspired (Mao acquiesced); Lin pronounced Mao above the Party and above the State (Mao objected). All of this has been taken as evidence of Lin's loyalty, as proof that Lin's fall was due to Mao's alleged perversities. It seems more plausible, as a few argue, that Lin's promotion of the Mao cult and the adulation it demanded made Mao extremely suspicious of Lin's motives.[7]

The final days are impossible to pin down. The coup plot is said to have included an attack with artillery and bazookas on Mao's special train, returning to Beijing on September 12 with Mao aboard; in the event of failure, there was to be a frontal assault by a specially trained commando squad. The subsequent purge of military commanders and, in the Politburo, of military members, speaks to the suspicions harbored about the PLA's loyalty. Yet, details of the coup planning have never been substantiated.

In the two years of intrigue before Lin Biao's death, Mao moved to ensure that the troops, whose loyalty Lin commanded, would obey Mao's orders. Immediately before Lin's demise, Mao had embarked on a tour of the provinces to shore up PLA support. In his talks to military commanders, Mao, as usual, gave a narrative history of the CCP's founding and its improbable rise to power. In this particular version of the story, Mao emphasized various subtle signs (retrospectively discovered) of Lin's treachery, stretching back to 1928, when Lin joined Mao at Jinggangshan. What Mao emphasized were "questions of principle" with which, he implied, Lin fundamentally disagreed. This version of the past demanded that Lin be removed in the present.[8]

In the early morning of September 13, on Mao's return from the provinces to Beijing, Zhou Enlai informed him of Lin's flight and death; Mao was both shocked and relieved. Explaining this development to the people —who knew Lin as Mao's "closest comrade in arms"—was going to be another story altogether; it would take more than a year before Mao coordinated a minimally plausible line through which to denounce Lin publicly. Ultimately, Lin's supposed disagreements on matters of principle became the building blocks of the denunciation. The thoroughness with which Lin's reputation was tarnished at this time has prevented Lin's status as traitor from ever being overturned or rethought. However, it appears his role in the successes of the pre-1949 rise of the CCP is now being recognized in China. This represents a major reversal of the post-1971 airbrushing of Lin from history.[9]

Model Revolutionary Culture

Through all the political upheaval, the impetus to create a revolutionary culture proceeded, and once the destruction of the "four olds" had abated, construction of this new culture began in earnest. The Maoist theory of the relationship between revolution and art, elaborated in Yan'an in 1942, was vigorously promoted. This resulted in "model" dramas, soon adapted to Beijing opera and ballet. These were eight well-honed and well-vetted works, whose combination of revolutionary aesthetics and artistic practice exemplified a Maoist revolutionary cultural ideal.

In propaganda posters and dramatic performances, the new revolutionary aesthetic was formulated out of a socialist realism of the Soviet type (in which all representations were outsized) and transformed into a socialist realism brought to the level of the everyday life of the masses. Idealized as they were, representations of socialism as a quotidian politics proved to be emotionally powerful and attractive (as advertising subsequently has been). For in various venues—in print or on stage—art did not just mimic (idealized) life; rather, life was transmuted into aesthetically politicized theatre.

In the 1970s, print art sought to combine realism with folk art in a rediscovery, as it were, of the authentic mass origins of native Chinese drawing. (Many artists by this time had been sent down to the countryside, facilitating this "rediscovery.") The accustomed sharp outlines of revolutionary heroes, rendered in bold primary colors, were blunted with new softer color schemes and less abrupt brush- and pen strokes. In ballet, an obviously imported art, fluid classicism was combined with revolutionary gestures and rigid body postures to produce a recognizable, but defamiliarized form, drawing from apparently opposed traditions of physical movement. New musically hybrid scores were composed for the purpose. In Beijing opera, the accustomed trilling atonality was slightly blunted into more melodic albeit still shrill enunciative form. Lyrics were adapted from revolutionary narratives to accompany new scores, combining Western and Chinese classical traditions with Chinese folk music. Movements—formerly meticulously calibrated—were broadened into gestural revolutionary positions to suggest collective strength alongside individual fortitude.

Revolution was art; art was revolutionary. Artistic creation was to bring to light what was already beautiful in the revolutionary masses, and by stimulating the masses through aesthetics, the artist was to bring his or her capacity and energy into play in the revolution. For Mao, revolution was in some sense a drama filled with exhilarating spectacle. As he once said to the French writer André Malraux, revolution is "a drama of passion; we did not win the people over by appealing to reason, but by developing hope, trust, and fraternity."[10] These innovations, before they were dogmatized, initially provided creative space for artists, even if the topics were proscribed to a few acceptable ones.

The revolution as a drama of (platonic) passion was perfectly, if rigidly, exemplified in the eight models of revolutionary culture. These models played ceaselessly in China over many years and were practically the only cultural products available to a mass audience. They seeped inexorably into people's consciousness, penetrating their feelings and shaping their judgments. Yet, these were neither dramas to be contemplated from a distance, nor were they commodities to be consumed. (Nobody even had to pay to see them.) These were dramas exhorting audiences to participate, emotionally and physically, in the revolutionary activities they staged and encouraged.

A majority of these model dramas had women as their title characters. Rather than being sexualized objects, these female protagonists generally begin the narratives as victims of class, gender, and imperialist oppression. The stories then revolve around their liberation through a simultaneous discovery of hitherto unsuspected internal strength and of the Communist Party. While the formula was predictable—this predictability in fact had been adapted from 1940s and 1950s Hollywood melodramatic templates— the stories nevertheless packed a punch. However, their depictions of female liberation always hinged upon an enlightened male Party leader, who guided the woman to revolutionary consciousness and action. The frequency with which women had to await liberation by men (in the guise of the Party), and the denial of sexuality and romantic possibilities to these unions (always confined to revolutionary Puritanism), promoted the CCP's version of state feminism, while undercutting any possibility for the development of autonomous feminist principles.

Whatever the dogmatic and formalistic elements—repudiated in the 1980s—parts of this revolutionary cultural ethos persisted long after the demise of the revolution itself.

The Gang of Four

As political infighting proceeded, the "gang of four" flexed its muscles in the cultural and media spheres. They attempted more. The gang label was affixed by Mao only in 1975, in condemnation of their conspiratorial methods. But the four who comprised the gang emerged in 1970 from the dissolution of the Central Cultural Revolution Group, after Mao's longtime secretary and group leader, Chen Boda, was deposed. Left standing from this dissolution were Mao's wife, Jiang Qing, and the three radicals from Shanghai: the literary critic Yao Wenyuan, the former Shanghai Party chief Zhang Chunqiao, and the textile worker and Shanghai Commune leader Wang Hongwen. By 1973, all four were in the Politburo, while Zhang and Wang were named members of the Standing Committee (the highest ruling body in the land).

The Gang's political constituency was not comprised of the old-time revolutionaries, with whom they were locked in constant battle. Indeed, the older revolutionaries—Long March and Yan'an veterans—despised Jiang Qing and had contempt for the Shanghai upstarts who, in their view, understood nothing of true sacrifice and revolutionary practice, and only knew how to manipulate intrigue. By the 1970s, though, newer Party members had emerged from the struggles of the late 1960s and joined the leadership ranks. These were not the mass organization activists (students or workers), long since banished from the urban areas and from any hint of power positions. Rather, these were members, who had opportunistically risen with the rebuilding of the Party after the cataclysmic events. Outnumbering the old revolutionaries by a good proportion, the newer members threw their support behind the Gang, in an attempt to seize control of the Party and state apparatus from old-timers. The battles were epic in proportion, Byzantine in nature, and vile in underhandedness. They proceeded behind the scenes until Mao's death and slightly beyond.

Of Ping Pong and Kissinger

Meanwhile, throughout late 1970 and into 1971, contacts between China and the United States flourished through the intermediary of the Pakistani president Yahya Khan. These were kept as secret from the U.S. State Department as they were from China's Ministry of Foreign Affairs. Zhou Enlai was the point person for Mao on this initiative; Kissinger was Nixon's man. The secrecy was mandated, in part, by Mao's distrust of his foreign policy crew and Nixon's own secretive nature; in part, because a USA-PRC rapprochement would have extraordinary global impact.

The first public breakthrough occurred in mid-April 1971. The U.S. Ping-Pong team, competing in the thirty-first world table tennis championships in Japan, received an invitation to play friendly matches with the

Chinese team in China. Unenthusiastic when the idea first was presented, Mao became convinced that sports were a great way to push forward diplomacy. On April 10, after a flurry of bewildered communication with the State Department, the U.S. team went to Hong Kong and proceeded across a footbridge to the PRC. From April 11–17, the Americans played ping pong, toured the Great Wall, and attended a performance of a model ballet. Zhou Enlai received them formally, lauding the visit as a harbinger of a new era in China's relations with the United States.

Meanwhile, the top-secret Pakistani-mediated negotiations continued. In July 1971, Kissinger, pleading illness on a trip to Pakistan, slipped away to fly to Beijing to finalize details about the Nixon visit. Several days later, on July 15, it was publicly announced in China and the United States that Nixon would visit China in February 1972.

Joining the United Nations

As the world was digesting this news—and as several western European governments were stewing about it—the groundwork the PRC had laid since the Bandung Conference in 1955 finally bore fruit at the United Nations in late 1971.

At the end of the Second World War, the GMD-controlled Republic of China (ROC) had assumed the China seat in the United Nations. One of the five war victors, the ROC also had a seat on the UN's Permanent Council. After the GMD's removal to Taiwan, the ROC continued to hold the China seat, since the CCP was not recognized as the legitimate government of China by the United States and its allies. Every year since, the PRC had petitioned to be seated in the UN in place of the ROC. Every year, the petition had been defeated. Through the 1960s, the defeats had become narrower, as former colonies gained their independence and were seated as sovereign nation-states in the UN. Since Bandung, the PRC had promoted itself vigorously as a "third world" nation. Particularly in the Cultural Revolutionary years, but even well before, the PRC had been one of the loudest global stalwarts rhetorically to support anti-colonial movements around the world (particularly in Africa) and had competed with the United States and the Soviet Union for influence in these countries.

At the annual vote on the PRC's petition to join the UN on October 25, 1971, for the first time, countries sympathetic to the PRC outnumbered those that the United States and the GMD could line up in support of the ROC on Taiwan. The PRC was voted in, and the ROC was banished. This began the long fall from international influence of the GMD and the ROC and the long rise of the PRC from revolutionary internationalist icon to bulwark of the established global order.

Mao Receives Nixon

Richard Nixon was to arrive in Beijing on February 21, 1972. Preparations for his visit to Zhongnanhai—Mao's residence and workspace—were feverish. Mao had long since ceded the courtyard house to Jiang Qing and others, whom he no longer wished to see on a daily basis; he had removed himself to the indoor pool area, where a bedroom and a study were installed.

After Lin Biao's flight and death in September 1971, Mao's health had taken a plunge for the worse. Always susceptible, his lung infections accumulated, his breathing became labored, and his heart started to fail. As always, Mao refused treatment until the ailments had become acute. Three weeks before Nixon's arrival, Mao finally agreed to take action. He did, after all, want to be in shape for the triumphal reception in Beijing of the firmest anti-Communist ever to be American president. A good deal of hospital equipment was moved into the indoor pool area and Mao concentrated on regaining strength. Prior to Nixon's visit, the oxygen tanks and other paraphernalia were disassembled or hidden from view. The hospital bed was moved into a corridor, and the pool was covered over. The area was turned into a reception hall, albeit one that could be transformed instantaneously into an emergency room, if required.

The day of Nixon's arrival, Zhou Enlai met his plane and escorted him to the villa where he would stay. A luncheon was held. After a rest, Nixon boarded a Red Flag limousine to Zhongnanhai and was whisked through the streets of Beijing, which were closed to all bicycle and bus traffic (the only kind of vehicular traffic at the time). Nixon entered the "reception area" with Kissinger and Winston Lord (later ambassador to the PRC). The Secretary of State was excluded by design. As Nixon entered, the tin roof of the pool-cum-reception hall blocked Secret Service radio contact, and panic among the Americans ensued. Chinese security forces assured them Nixon was safe with Mao. The visit proceeded without the American Secret Service.

Mao was not able to talk well, because of his illnesses. He was also quite bloated because of medication and congestive heart failure. Nixon had been alerted to Mao's difficulties, although not in detail. Originally scheduled for fifteen minutes, the encounter lasted for sixty-five. A number of photographs were taken by the assembled press, the most famous being one of Mao and Nixon locked in an historic handshake.

Aside from his visit with Mao, Nixon was accompanied in Beijing by Jiang Qing to the model opera, *The Red Detachment of Women*. Nixon liked the opera well enough, although he apparently did not at all like Jiang—whom he described as "unpleasantly abrasive and aggressive."[11] Then again, Jiang did not like Nixon either, finding him arrogant and insufferable. Moreover, she saw his visit as undermining her position as an unrelenting foe of "American imperialism." Indeed, Nixon's visit was Zhou Enlai's coup, and Jiang Qing was at this point already conceiving a plan to sideline Zhou. After leaving Beijing, Nixon was escorted south, to the famous scenic city of Hangzhou, where over the years Mao had spent much time near West Lake. Nixon ended his trip in Shanghai.

Shanghai Communiqué

Negotiations on the content of the joint statement about Nixon's visit consumed a good deal of Kissinger's time in China. Again, the State Department was shut out of these discussions. The document was finalized in a series of late-night moves during the last days of the visit. Issued in Shanghai, historians generally have seen the Communiqué as a huge coup for the PRC.

After courteous preliminaries, the Communiqué first contains two separate statements. The American side notes, "No country should claim infallibility and each country should be prepared to reexamine its own attitudes for the common good." But then, the United States goes on to aver an unwavering belief in "individual freedom and social progress for the peoples of the world." Further, the United States pledges to find a solution to the Vietnam War, to continue its alliance with South Korea and Japan, and to support the recently negotiated Pakistani-Indian cease-fire. The Chinese statement begins with China's basic principles: "Wherever there is oppression, there is resistance. Countries want independence, nations want liberation and the people want revolution—this has become the irresistible trend of history." The Chinese go on to reaffirm their support for the peoples of Indochina, for the peaceful reunification of Korea, and for UN supervision of the Pakistani-Indian cease-fire.

The arenas of agreement include a reworded affirmation of Zhou's and Mao's foreign policy doctrine of "peaceful co-existence," first offered at

Bandung in 1955, as a principle of nonalignment in the Cold War. Both sides then pledge to work toward normalization of relations, to reduce the danger of international conflict, not to seek hegemony in Asia, and not to collude with others. Disagreement revolves around Taiwan. While both the USA and the PRC agree that there is only one China, the PRC claims that the Taiwan question is an internal domestic dispute in which the United States has no legitimate interest. By contrast, the United States claims an ongoing, albeit diminishing, interest in the problem. The United States then pledges to withdraw its troops and installations from Taiwan as soon as feasible.

This latter was the poison pill the GMD was forced to swallow, without warning or consultation, so eager was Kissinger to conclude a statement with the PRC. The Chiang Kaishek–aligned "China Lobby" in the United States screamed bloody murder, and it took until 1979 for the United States Congress to overcome its strength and formally establish diplomatic relations under President Carter. Yet, immediately after the Nixon visit, U.S. allies—including Japan, Great Britain, and West Germany—stampeded toward China. Within a year, all had broken relations with Taiwan in order to establish relations with the PRC. By the 1990s, the Taiwan government—now no longer even under GMD rule—was recognized diplomatically by only five nations.

The Fading of Mao and the Old Revolutionary Generation

The public appearance with Nixon was one of the last in Mao's life. His health was quite precarious, and his powers of speech were all but gone by early 1973. His heart was failing, his eyesight hazing, and his extremities trembling. His distrust of medicine continued, however, and he refused treatment, or even proper diagnosis, for all but the most obvious of his symptoms. Because he could no longer see well enough to read, Mao occupied himself with watching movies. He loved the martial arts films from Hong Kong best of all.

With his mind absolutely clear even as his body failed him, Mao continued to attend Party meetings, albeit now surrounded by medical staff and nurses. He also met with a few foreign visitors, including the president of Zambia, with whom he discussed the theory of the "three worlds," and the former British prime minister, Edward Heath, with whom he discussed the ongoing issue of Hong Kong. His "talks" with them were conducted in writing.

Many of Mao's generation of revolutionaries were also in poor health. In late 1972, Zhou Enlai was diagnosed with lung cancer; the despised chief of the secret service, Kang Sheng, a staunch Mao loyalist and the object of much distrust among everyone else, learned he had bladder cancer. Others were just too old to work effectively. And yet others had been banished to the countryside, where they languished away from intrigue and far from top-notch medical care.

Deng Xiaoping Returns

It is in these circumstances that Mao decided to pluck Deng Xiaoping from the tractor repair factory in Jiangxi and restore him to power. Zhou was slowed due to illness, and by May 1974, hospitalized. The day-to-day administration, over which he normally presided, was grinding to a halt, as the State and Party apparatus were staffed with relative newcomers. If not incompetent, they were untrustworthy. Mao wanted an older-generation revolutionary by his side and in charge. Deng—a decade younger than Mao and a veteran of the Long March and Yan'an—was the man.

Despite Deng's association with the now-disgraced and deceased Liu Shaoqi, he had never been the object of Mao's distrust in the same way as Liu. An accomplished administrator, Deng's restoration through 1973, after an absence of seven years from the halls of power, became the major political story in China. Mao's and Zhou's respective declines left the field open. His only rival—and she was a huge one—was Jiang Qing, who regarded Deng as a "rightist" not to be trusted to continue the revolution. As 1973 proceeded, Mao also restored to power a number of formerly disgraced "rightists," all of whom were associated in some way with the early 1960s economic restoration after the Great Leap disaster. This confirmed to Jiang Qing that the fate of the revolution hung in the balance.

By 1975 and the Fourth National People's Congress, Deng was elevated to the Politburo's Standing Committee. He was also appointed the chief of staff of the PLA. He was widely recognized as the hand-picked successor to Zhou Enlai. Zhou's final appearance was at this same National People's Congress, held in Beijing in mid-January 1975. Zhou's speech to the 2,800 delegates reaffirmed the goals named at the 1949 founding of the PRC. China was to be a "powerful country with a high degree of socialist industrialization," and would pursue the modernization "of agriculture, industry, national defense, science and technology" in a context of global peace and stability. This policy—soon honed and championed in the post-Mao period by Deng Xiaoping—came to be called the "four modernizations."[12]

Mao's Final Trip

With increasingly intractable health issues making it hard for him to speak, eat, or breathe, Mao wanted to go on one last trip, to visit Wuhan and his home province, Hunan. Jiang Qing, whom he could no longer bear to be around, stayed in Beijing. While in Wuhan and in good spirits, Mao received Imelda Marcos from the Philippines.

In September, once the summer heat had abated, Mao, his doctors, nurses, and others in his personal retinue went to Changsha, capital of Hunan, where Mao had begun his political education so many years earlier. In a nostalgic mood, Mao wished to go swimming, for it was in the Xiang River at Changsha, where he had spent so many pleasurable afternoons as a young man. His doctors were alarmed and dissuaded him from swimming in the river; he attempted to swim in a pool instead but his breathing problems made it impossible for him to continue. At eighty-two, Mao finally faced up to the fact that he would never be able to engage in his favorite activity again.

Mao stayed in Changsha through his birthday in December 1974 and into the beginning of 1975. Zhou Enlai traveled to Changsha to see Mao in late December. From afar, Mao helped tip the balance at January's Fourth National People's Congress, when he supported Deng Xiaoping's appointment over any of Jiang Qing's candidates.

"Criticize Lin, Criticize Confucius"

Jiang Qing and her gang's last effort to re-appropriate the mantle of revolution came in the launching of the most improbable "criticize Lin [Biao], criticize Confucius" campaign. This was an attempt to rally support against the restoration of the bureaucracy represented by Deng Xiaoping's rise to power.

Begun in August 1973, this campaign attempted to link Lin Biao's perfidy and treachery to his alleged love of Confucius and Confucianism. Lin was depicted as the heir to a 2,500-year-old tradition of Confucian reaction, as someone who represented himself as a Marxist in order to smuggle the poison of Confucianism into the unsuspecting Chinese body politic. This assault on Lin and Confucius was waged by respected historians and literary scholars—many of whom were fished back to Beijing from exile in the countryside and shut into a building at Beijing University. There, they were to do the "research" required to substantiate these charges. Many of the arguments adduced for this campaign were abstruse close textual readings, which took passages of Confucius and of Lin Biao out of context, in order to establish an ostensible family resemblance between them.

These charges filled the newspapers from mid-1973 through 1974. They were recognized by almost all readers as total nonsense. Indeed, many students and intellectuals stuck in the countryside correctly read them as the signs of the death throes of the Cultural Revolution (albeit without any knowledge of what would come next). As most correctly surmised, the ultimate target was neither Lin Biao—already dead for two years—nor Confucius—already dead for more than two millennia. The target was Zhou Enlai, and through him, Deng Xiaoping.

By 1974, the "criticize Lin, criticize Confucius" campaign had abated. In its stead were raging ideological debates within the Party over the relationship between revolution and development. These were, of course, old issues that had bedeviled post-1949 Chinese economic and social policy. They were restaged in 1975 as a debate between the "bourgeois right" (Deng et al.) and the Maoist left (Jiang Qing et al.). In keeping with Mao's late-1950s reinterpretations of Marxism for Chinese historical circumstances, Maoists maintained that the transformation of social relations was the only way to properly achieve socialist development. In contrast, Deng and the "rightists" maintained that the building of productive forces (industrial capacity and efficiency) was the only way to achieve development. These were vital issues, and Deng Xiaoping eventually came out on top after Mao's death and the arrest of the Gang. But the 1975 debate was conducted under the threat of political terror. Factional politics quite overshadowed the actual issues.

Zhou Enlai's Death and the April 5th Movement

On January 8, 1976, Zhou Enlai died in a Beijing hospital at the age of seventy-eight. His funeral was held on January 15, with a eulogy delivered by Deng Xiaoping. Mao was too ill to attend. Jiang Qing took the opportunity to press her attack on Deng, whom she accused of being "China's new Krushchev" (an old label) and, in a new twist, "an international capitalist agent." Her chance to push Deng off the political stage only came in April 1976.

A few days before the traditional tomb sweeping festival, which in 1976 fell on April 5, students, workers, cadres, and common Beijingers from all walks of life began laying wreaths in Tian'anmen Square, at the base of the Monument of People's Heroes, in honor of Zhou Enlai. This was in clear opposition to ongoing attempts to wipe out old customs now labeled as superstitious. The wreaths accumulated, and soon, so did wall posters, poems, and speeches eulogizing Zhou. Trucks were sent by the Beijing government on April 4 to cart the wreaths and posters away. On April 5, large numbers of people arrived on the Square to protest. They came in the tens of thousands. While most were soon persuaded to leave the Square, some were violently removed.

Deng Xiaoping was blamed for this "counter-revolutionary" mass protest, soon commemorated as the "April 5th Movement." He was the subject of vitriolic attack, crowned with every political label of which editorialists could avail themselves. In May 1976, he was banished, this time to a pig farm in the south. Meanwhile, workers engaged in deliberate slowdowns, absenteeism, and strikes to protest. Social struggle broke out all over again, this time without even the veneer of ideological substance. People were weary of these struggles, and once again intellectuals were their main target.

Mao lay dying and did not witness the final disintegration of his dreams and lifework.

Mao's Death

Perhaps the final piece of good news Mao received, before his own death, was that Chiang Kaishek had died in Taiwan on April 5. Mao could take comfort in the knowledge that he had outlived his bitter enemy and Chiang had never been able to take back China, as had been his dream. Bad news overshadowed this, however. For, also in April, one of the oldest revolutionary cadres still living, Dong Biwu, passed away; by December, the reviled secret service chief, Kang Sheng, succumbed to illness. Zhou was dead in early 1976, and by July 1976, Zhu De, the founder of the Red Army and PLA, had also died. A generation was passing on. Their dreams of making China both modern and socialist were dying with them.

On July 28, 1976, a massive earthquake shook northern China. Its epicenter was one hundred miles from Beijing. It flattened the coal and steel city of Tangshan and killed over two hundred and fifty thousand inhabitants. The area's survivors were left bereft. International assistance was rejected, and the PLA was mobilized—quite effectively—to assist survivors and the cleanup. As the social world seemed to be falling apart, the earthquake came to be interpreted by many as an omen of worse to come, as a sign from the natural world that the human world was in great disorder. Much as the CCP tried to tamp down such "superstitious" belief, such an interpretation was nevertheless quite rampant.

Several weeks later, on September 9, 1976, a somber announcement blared over the numerous public loudspeakers in urban and rural areas alike. The announcement stopped the nation in its tracks. Mao was dead. However people had felt about him and his era, the uncertainty of what would come next filled them with both grief and dread.

10 Reform, Restoration, and the Repudiation of Maoism, 1976–Present

On his deathbed, Mao apparently passed the mantle of leadership to a fellow Hunan native, the colorless vice premier, Hua Guofeng. Hua had been elevated to his position during Deng Xiaoping's second fall from power in early 1976 but had no independent national-level base of support. In a bid to shore up his position as Mao's successor, Hua reported Mao had written a note to him just prior to death reputedly saying: "With you in charge, I am at ease." Despite wide play in the newspapers, few were convinced; indeed, most believed the note to be apocryphal.

The Arrest of the Gang of Four and the Two Whatevers

With Mao lying in state at the Great Hall of the People in Beijing, the reaction against Jiang Qing began. Formerly shown much deference, she was now all but ignored. She tried to arm supporters in Shanghai and Beijing and also made an alliance with Mao Yuanxin, Mao's nephew, the political commissar of the Shenyang Military Region in Manchuria. It appears that Jiang Qing was hoping to seize power through a military coup.

Mao's funeral was held at 3:00 P.M. on September 18, 1976. Over a million people attended. Early in the morning, they began gathering on Tian'anmen Square to mourn or at least mark the passing of a leader and an era. The Square was filled to capacity with workers, students, cadres, and urban dwellers. There was grief as well as ambivalence. Domestic and international leaders filed past the casket in the Great Hall of the People, abutting the

Square. Nobody there or on the Square itself quite knew what to expect next.

A heated discussion took place about what to do with Mao's body. Some leaders wanted him buried. Others argued that Mao should be embalmed for display in a mausoleum to be built on Tian'anmen Square, just as Lenin was on Moscow's Red Square. Even though Mao had always objected to the handling of Lenin, the embalming faction won. A magnificent structure was built in the middle of the Square to house Mao's body. Viewing the body attracts a large number of visitors to this day.

Immediately following the mourning period for Chairman Mao, Hua Guofeng was persuaded to move against Jiang Qing. He presided over the "smashing" of the Gang of Four on October 6, 1976. Jiang and her three Shanghai associates were arrested one by one by military guards loyal to CCP old-timers. None resisted arrest. Along with these four, Mao Yuanxin and many other suspected Gang supporters were also taken into custody. In 1980–81, the four were given a public trial in a sensational media event intended to close the era of the Cultural Revolution with finality and a whiff of legality. While some advocated a "gang of five" label (with Mao as the fifth), this was firmly resisted by the leadership. All talk of Mao's "guilt" was deferred to a formal Party assessment.

With the Gang sidelined and their major supporters in jail, CCP veterans wasted no time in purging all levels of the Party of the Cultural Revolutionary upstarts, whose rise to power and credentials rested on their loyal implementation of Gang policies. The majority of these were worker and peasant cadres, elevated into the Party as the intelligentsia and old Party cadres had been removed. The post–Cultural Revolutionary order was restoring old prerogatives: CCP bureaucrats rose from the ashes stronger and more vigorous than before.

Hua's brief leadership was marked by rhetorical loyalty to Mao, sarcastically dubbed the "two whatevers" position: "to support whatever policy decisions were made by Chairman Mao" and "unswervingly to follow whatever instructions were given by Chairman Mao." With little autonomy, Hua did what he could to stabilize the country. His most important task was to regain the confidence and loyalty of intellectuals and Party cadres, the two major casualties of the Cultural Revolution, whose restoration would lead to stability and the rebuilding of Party strength.

Revitalizing Economy, Culture, and Education

Despite the "whatever" rhetorics, Hua endeavored to return China to the pre–Great Leap economic policies of tolerance toward a marketplace in agricultural goods, centralized planning, and economic incentives for industrial productivity. Removing what was called the "ultra-leftism" of the Cultural Revolution, Hua encouraged a revival of local-level economies that combined planning with limited market freedoms. This is what Maoists derisively had labeled "economism." Hua also moved quickly to erase the control the Gang had asserted over cultural and educational policy. Movies, plays, and books long suppressed now appeared for public consumption; scholarly journals began to solicit academic articles; and new periodicals and magazines sprang up, and the literary sphere was much enlivened by the publication of a flood of short stories and poems narrating the wounds of the Cultural Revolution. Soon called "scar literature," these works set China onto a path away from mass revolutionary culture and the culture of revolution toward an introspective and individualist market-driven and market-dependent literary practice and style.

Educational institutions were shored up with the reintroduction of the entrance exam system, designed as of old to offer admissions into high schools and universities only to the academically qualified. The years of urban educational opportunity for poorly prepared but motivated peasant, worker, and soldier students were over. Rusticated youths whose education had been interrupted flocked to exam sites, in an attempt to escape their marginalized rural or factory locations. Those who had remained defiantly engaged in reading and intellectual practices during their years of rural or industrial labor generally fared well in the exams and were able to vault out of remote areas into urban educational institutions. A generation of older students returned from rustication to take up their studies where they had left off. Their teachers, rusty in their specialties and chastened by political exile, were usually happy to resume their work. Those former students who had given up hope or had gotten married and started families in their new locations either failed or were barred from taking the exams. They were stuck where they had been sent down as youths, victims of personal choices, whose historical implications they could hardly have fathomed.

The elitist bias of top-notch educational opportunity was quickly restored as a birthright of the urban intellectual class. Practical and vocational education at the tertiary level was cut back drastically, as universities emphasizing research regained the financial and academic upper hand they had hitherto possessed. The roots of the post-Mao technocratic ascendance were being sown, as a new elite was recruited, trained, and affirmed as masters of society.

The Cultural Revolution–era constitution was rewritten, and leftist policies were deleted. In their stead, the "four modernizations" were enshrined. Harking back to 1949, but most recently to Zhou Enlai's rearticulation of them in 1975, the four modernizations called for emphasis on science and technology (for which elite education was necessary); mechanization of agriculture and the freeing of rural labor for local industry; material incentives in urban industrial production along with the return to an efficient management style; and a streamlining of the military through the resumption of hierarchical ranks abandoned during the latter phases of the Cultural Revolution. Economic growth was to trump revolution, and the Maoist attempt to make modernization serve social revolution was discarded.

Hua Guofeng presided over the beginnings of this anti-Maoist program, all the while wrapping it in the most Maoist of rhetorics. Yet Hua's essential weakness among Party leaders and his lack of any national-level constituency made him an easy mark. As Deng Xiaoping regathered his political resources, Hua was slated to fall. It took Deng two years to internally maneuver this event. He did so without fomenting a mass movement, a strategy he had learned to hate. Deng's rise was ironically facilitated by the fact that he had been repairing tractors or shoveling pig dung for most of the Cultural Revolution. He had relatively clean political hands and could present himself as the representative of a new beginning for China. He was, of course, one of the last of the May Fourth generation of CCP members, a veteran allied but also in tension with Maoism and Mao himself. The newness and cleanliness were hence quite relative.

By December 1978 at the Third Plenum of the Eleventh Central Committee meeting, Deng was able to take over most of the reins of power. Aided by old-timer CCP members, who had risen again since Mao's death, Deng triumphed over the "whateverists" with a new ideology stating: "Practice is the sole criterion of truth." In other words, Maoist text was not where truth was to be sought; rather, truth resided only in "practice." What the measure of "practice" was to be—e.g., the accumulation of individual wealth or the foundations for collectivist socialism—remained an open question. For the time being, it was clear Deng believed in the Party's centrality as the dominant ruler of China. Much of his early effort was spent on strengthening the role of the Party at the center of Chinese politics and the Chinese state.

In January 1979, Hua was effectively shoved aside when it was Deng Xiaoping who traveled to the United States to celebrate with President Carter the official normalization of PRC-USA relations. By early 1980, Hua was completely isolated when his supporters were purged from the Central Committee. In 1981, Deng's practical ascendance was affirmed by the transfer of all the titles—Party Chair, Military Commission Chair, etc.—to himself. Hua faded into retirement.

Democracy Wall and the Fifth Modernization

One factor assisting Deng in his return to power was the popular support he gained in urban areas from intellectuals and workers, who saw in him the successor to the revered Zhou Enlai. Big-character posters started to appear in late 1978 on the square behind the Gate of Heavenly Peace in central Beijing supporting Deng, mistakenly identifying his desire to normalize society for a desire to democratize it. This mistake became apparent very quickly.

The posters were mostly written by workers and ex–Red Guards, whose desires for mass democracy during the Cultural Revolution had been betrayed. They saw the denunciation of the Cultural Revolution as an opportunity to press for a "fifth modernization" in addition to the other four. It was to be called democracy. Rather than an institutional or procedural concept, democracy connoted for them a popular voice and role in the implementation of policy; it was an anti-bureaucratic mass-line concept of political and social relations.

Through late 1978 and into 1979, the posters multiplied in number as did gatherings of those reading the posters. Enthusiasm grew for the political possibilities that seemed to be on the horizon. The "April 5th Movement" commemorating Zhou Enlai, declared by Jiang Qing a counterrevolutionary action, was reclassified in late 1978 by the Party as revolutionary and patriotic. This gave impetus to more gatherings, more posters, more narrative outpouring of Cultural Revolutionary suffering. The big-character poster, whose original purpose precisely had been the creation of a mass political voice, seemed to come into its own as a mode of genuine mass democratic participation.

This was not to last. The repression began in the spring of 1979, with the arrest of Wei Jingsheng, an ex–Red Guard factory worker and editor of an unofficial journal entitled *Explorations*. He was the author of the original "fifth modernization" poster, and thus became the initial scapegoat for the whole democracy wall movement. Accused of multiple crimes, Wei was sentenced to fifteen years in prison. (He eventually immigrated to the United States.) Many others followed Wei into jail, where they languished for years (and some continue to languish still).

The suppression of the democracy wall movement—completed by 1980—signaled the intention of Deng and the CCP to monopolize political power. No voices other than those sanctioned would be raised in political participation. Democracy—mass or otherwise—emphatically was not on any Dengist agenda. Big-character posters were outlawed, and a regime of "socialist legality" was promoted. In practice, this mostly meant the suppression of views deemed antagonistic to whatever "socialism" was proclaimed to be at any given time. The depoliticization of society was under way.

INTERLUDE: WANG HUI INTERVIEW

In May 2007, I interviewed Prof. Wang Hui in Beijing on issues pertaining to Mao and his reassessment after 1976. In his late-forties, Professor Wang is a literary and historical scholar, currently teaching at Tsinghua University. He served as the longtime editor and intellectual architect of two of the most influential post-Mao journals of academic and scholarly inquiry: Xueren [The Scholar] *and* Dushu [Readings]. *Long attacked by liberals and neo-liberals in China for his critical attitude toward the social consequences of the Dengist reforms and toward global capitalism in general—indeed, labeled a "new leftist," a label intended to tarnish him with the now-repudiated "leftism" of the Maoist period—Wang Hui's analyses of political, economic, historical, cultural, and literary currents in classical, modern, and post-Mao China nevertheless command broad respect and a huge readership. Some of his seminal work has been translated into English.*[1]

Q: How has the definition of "politics" changed since Mao's time?

A: This question deserves attention. . . . Politics in Mao's time had two characteristics. . . . First, Mao's politics was informed by the Marxist theory of class struggle. Yet, Mao's class struggle was very complicated. . . . Although it was about struggles over production, politics, and everyday life, it was more about cultural struggle. Thus, second, Mao's political concepts were related to his understandings of changes in social contradictions at the level of society. . . . Politics in the Mao period was a broad concept. . . . It was widely mobilizable and depended upon everyone's participation. In one word, Mao's politics is the universalization of class struggle on the one hand; and on the other hand, politics is universalized. . . . Politics in Mao's time is everybody's concern . . .

Today's politics is about who is seizing power and who is in the dominant position; there is no consideration of political value. The deepest change in politics is the change of politics itself. . . . After Deng Xiaoping came to power, he denounced the principle of class struggle and shifted the central task to economic construction, which indicated that the previous emphasis on revolutionary politics was withdrawn and the new politics was all about economic development. For Mao, politics and economy were united; under Deng, they were split from one another. . . . This process started from the middle of the 1980s and continued in accelerated form after 1989.

War with Vietnam

In 1979, a border war between the erstwhile socialist allies, Vietnam and the PRC, broke out. If any further proof were needed that China was charting a new course, this war sealed the verdict. The war was provoked by two things. Of lesser importance were policies in Vietnam that had an adverse impact on the Chinese ethnic population of Saigon. In the wake of the American defeat and the Communist unification of the country, the Vietnamese capitalist class was dispossessed. It so happened that most small-level capitalists in Vietnam were Chinese ethnics. Politically persecuted and economically ruined, many fled over the border to China. At the same time and much more significant, Vietnam moved to depose Pol Pot in Cambodia, whose genocidal policies and incursions across the Vietnamese border had proven to be destabilizing to Vietnam. Pol Pot was a PRC ally. The Vietnamese invasion sparked a Chinese reaction. Deng Xiaoping promised to "teach Vietnam a lesson."

After his February 1979 return from normalizing relations with the United States—symbolically enough—Deng sent the PLA into Vietnam. The Chinese were singularly unsuccessful in teaching any lesson. Rather, the PLA learned one: that it was unprepared to fight against such battle-hardened troops as the Vietnamese. The cost in lives and property was enormous, despite the short duration of the war (a few very bloody weeks). One of the only vocal protests in China against the PRC invasion of Vietnam was Wei Jingsheng's. This dissent, along with his democracy wall advocacies, hastened his arrest and silencing.

Assessing Mao

By 1981, Deng Xiaoping was enough in control to embark on a very delicate task. The Party needed to account for the Cultural Revolution, and to assess Mao in the process. This was of both historical and contemporary urgency. It was urgent for the present, because the Party's legitimacy had to be affirmed. If the Party were responsible for the "catastrophe" of the Cultural Revolution, why should it be entrusted with the current and future rule of the country? The issue was urgent for history, because any state power knows that the national past and the national present are intimately intertwined. That intertwining needs to be captured and narrated by the state.

The conundrum, simply and functionally put, was: In the process of narrating modern Chinese history, it was impossible to denounce Mao simply as a tyrant, because Mao stood at the origins of the legitimacy of CCP rule. All veteran CCP leaders were in fact tightly connected to Mao. However, Maoist policies now were being dismantled and repudiated. They had to be put in proper historical perspective. In the apt characterization of one historian, Mao, the revolutionary, had to be rescued *for* history by separating him from the worst of his revolutionary policies.[2]

To deal with these problems, a document was commissioned and heavily discussed. Its formal name is "Resolution on Certain Questions in the History of Our Party since the Founding of the People's Republic of China;" it was adopted by the Central Committee of the CCP on June 27, 1981. Its verdict: Mao was 70 percent correct and 30 percent wrong. This ratio provided the necessary ideological sanction for continued CCP rule, albeit with a radical departure from Maoism.

The document's first section is a historical review. It affirms pre-1949 Mao as first among equals in the promulgation of "Mao Zedong Thought" and revolutionary practice. Mao is demoted to be one among a collective leadership successfully guiding China to the revolution. Yet, the successful revolution is proof of the correctness of Mao Zedong Thought, itself a product of the collective, with Mao in the lead. The second section takes up an assessment of the Maoist period. The basic successes are stated as the achievement of national independence and unity; a centralized government and strong army; the transformation of social classes; industrial and agricultural advances as expressed in China's economic self-sufficiency; the expansion of basic education and medical care; and PRC leadership of the third world, exemplified by the seat at the UN. However, the document notes, errors of concept and practice were made. These, it is said, were due to "subjectivism." Hence, to the extent Mao stayed within the collective leadership, he was correct. To the extent he insisted on "subjectivist"—or, individualist—tendencies and departed from collectivism, he made errors. The roots of "subjectivism" are traced back to the onset of the Great Leap in 1957, even as the hundred flowers is affirmed and sweeping antirightism repudiated.

In this view, the years from 1957 to 1964 saw "setbacks," but in general, the period is affirmed. (The twenty to thirty million dead during the famine are not mentioned, other than obliquely as a setback.) The document explicitly notes, "Although Comrade Mao Zedong must be held chiefly responsible, we cannot lay the blame for all those errors on him alone." Sharing the guilt are none other than Jiang Qing, his reviled wife; Kang Sheng, the loathed secret service chief; and Lin Biao, the PLA commander turned traitor. It is such "careerists" who, "harboring ulterior motives, made use of these errors and inflated them. This led to the onset of the 'cultural revolution.'"[3]

Grave mistakes begin in 1965 and continue afterward. The attack on intellectuals is repudiated, and the dismantling of the Party condemned. Liu Shaoqi and Deng Xiaoping, among others, are formally rehabilitated and praised. As the document notes, "Chief responsibility for the grave 'Left' error . . . does indeed lie with Comrade Mao Zedong. But after all it was the error of a great proletarian revolutionary."[4] In fact, the measure of Mao's greatness is said to be that the system he designed survived him. It has emerged stronger than before. (This was the very system he had tried to destroy!) Mao, therefore, remains a "respected and beloved great leader and teacher."[5] The worst mistakes are laid at the door of the "counterrevolutionaries," Jiang Qing and Lin Biao. The document pledges the mistakes of the Cultural Revolution would be overturned. Leaders and common intellectuals would be rehabilitated, reputations restored, jobs given back. The definition of "the people" was re-expanded to be as inclusive as possible, and the strengthening of all levels of the Party was stated as basic policy.

The end of the document attempts to draw a line from the past to the present of 1981 through to the envisioned future. The three major precepts of Maoism to be extended are said to be, "seeking truth from facts; the mass line; and national independence." National independence is clear. The first two precepts required ideological somersaults. For Mao, the relationship between facts and truth was never self-evident; it was always a political problem attached to the analysis of a specific historical circumstance. Thus, what is a fact and what is truth is dependent on a political-historical analysis and determination. Similarly, the mass line had a revolutionary connotation in Maoism; it was not a mere bureaucratic technique of dictating policy to the people. However, under Deng, enshrined in the 1981 document, these two principles are ostensibly derived from Maoism, yet they are shorn of all political and revolutionary meaning. They are ripped from context, and set back down as principles of centralized Party rule. In Dengist policy, a fact was an empirical (not a political) problem of measurement; truth was what the Party said it was; and the mass line was there to foster an obedient populace. If ever there was a use of Maoist theory to sanction extremely un-Maoist policy, this was it.

The document's penultimate section includes a restatement of basic issues for the present. In addition to the four modernizations and reunification with Taiwan, there are four "cardinal principles" to which all must adhere. These are named as 1) upholding the socialist road; 2) upholding the people's democratic dictatorship; 3) upholding the leadership of the CCP; and 4) upholding the guidance of Mao Zedong Thought and Marxism-Leninism. As the document ominously warns in rigid legalistic language, "Any word or deed which deviates from these four principles is wrong. Any word or deed which denies or undermines these four principles cannot be tolerated."[6] Finally, the document states, the direction China will travel in the next historical period will be based on the building of the productive forces (industrial capacity) rather than the transformation of social relations. Forces are elevated above relations in a complete reversal of Maoism. With revolution not desirable, people are exhorted to work hard and listen to and follow the Party's lead.

Rural Reform

More complete de-Maoification now could proceed. In terms of social structure, one of the first priorities was the undoing of the agricultural communes, whose form had become quite elaborate during the Cultural Revolution. They were to be scaled back. The collective rural economy—not yet abolished—was to be supplemented by contracts peasants would sign, as individual families, with the state. This contract system called for peasant families to turn over a certain proportion of their yield to the state for a fixed price; all surplus beyond that, peasants could market for profit. This ensured that inflation did not get out of control and that the state had enough staples for distribution in the urban areas at a predictable price (thus protecting urban consumers without too completely sacrificing the rural population). It also permitted peasants to earn extra money from marketing surpluses.

Through the early 1980s, state prices for grain, cotton, and other staples were set quite high, helping to stimulate growth in peasant household income. Villages, still the unit of a reduced collective rural economy, could tap into state funds to establish (or, really, reestablish) small-scale industries as collectively owned resources to employ village residents and from which the villagers could derive a share of the profit. This dual system—of collective economy supplemented by the market economy—had the immediate effect of accelerating rural productivity and raising living standards among the vast peasant population. This boom lasted through the mid-1980s.

Yet, these measures soon had the effect of accelerating regional inequalities. Those in fertile soil regions or in locations close to transportation routes and big cities were able to take advantage of market opportunities much more readily than were those who lived in more remote places. Local inequalities also developed apace. Differences in ability and capacity to tap labor resources produced disparities between families. But the largest polarizations occurred as collective property was seized by those in positions of power—mostly village Party secretaries—who had access to bank funding because of superior contacts outside of the locality. Before most villagers even knew what had happened, collective property became the private property of Party leaders. When objections were raised, Party secretaries used every means at their disposal to silence them.

While the original design of the household contract system was not market dependent, state prices for staples soon fell so far below market price that peasants stopped growing state-mandated crops or began hiding crops from the state in order to market them directly for higher profit. Inflationary pressures became huge, and, as these grew, the threat of urban unrest became manifest as the price of food rose precipitously. By the mid-1980s, the state was forced to retreat; most commodities were by then directly marketed by peasants themselves. The collective economy was soon dismantled completely, and with the removal of that social safety net, the poor, old, sick, or honest were on their way to getting poorer while the rich, young, healthy, and unscrupulous, were becoming richer.

Rural entrepreneurialism grew quickly. The first experiments in entrepreneurship were engaged by peasant women—the first "millionaire" in post-Mao China was a woman who ran a small-scale duck farm for profit. The assumption was that if such activity was found illegal (too capitalist), women would be dealt with less harshly than men. When it became clear rural entrepreneurship was here to stay, women were shoved aside, and men took over.

As the educational and medical advances of the Maoist period were erased with the end of collective funding, the free-for-all of primitive accumulation by any means possible began. This coincided precisely with the late-1980s fiscal austerity measures initiated by the state, which blunted the ability of the central government to intervene forcefully or adequately in the snowballing local problems. Since the late-1980s, rural productivity has declined in absolute terms as well as in relation to urban productivity. Rural polarization is enormous, while rural-urban disparity, in economic, cultural, and social terms, has grown exponentially.[7]

Illicit privatization of public property—including, most recently, land seizures retrospectively legalized through manipulation of political connections and hastily passed laws—became endemic in the rural areas by the 1990s. This is an ongoing story. Corruption is entrenched, fueling a socially destabilizing dynamic comprised of grasping officials and wealthy locals versus victimized peasants. Village and local leadership focused only on short-term profits have become exceedingly rapacious. Longer-term considerations—environmental, social, cultural, and educational—are sacrificed for immediate gain. Unrest grows, but it remains local and thus containable for the time being. Yet, the accession of the PRC to the World Trade Organization in 2001, opening the doors to agricultural imports, dealt a heavy blow to China's rural economy. Soon thereafter, the Chinese state announced self-sufficiency in food—a cornerstone of the Maoist vision of independence—was no longer a national goal. Most recently, a new property law has been passed, that legalizes the re-concentration of land into private hands through purchase. This law is an attempt to undercut the illegal appropriation of lands and to ensure that peasants are properly compensated for their land; in addition, it is an attempt to achieve rural economies of scale, without relying on the discredited collectivization of agriculture. This law was suspended in 2008 due to the financial crisis and fears of social unrest.

The One-Child Policy

Two things converged in the early 1980s to produce the urgency for a draconian one-child policy. One was purely demographic and harked back to the post–Great Leap baby boom. The other was a result of the socio-economic restructurings of the rural economy. As for the demographics: by the early 1980s, the post-Leap baby boom generation was just entering its marriage and childbearing years. This presented a demographic time bomb, whose multiplier effects would ripple into the next several generations. With the abandonment of the Maoist policies of labor-intensiveness and the turn to mechanized modernization, a large population was now a liability rather than an exploitable resource. This large population was now relabeled "redundant." The potential for the baby boom generation to triple or even quadruple itself appeared as a nightmare. Demographers and sociologists—academic disciplines abolished during the Maoist period (as un-Marxist) but now resurgent—argued for the implementation of a stringent population policy to contain the potential explosion. The unfortunate generation on whom this was visited were those in their twenties and thirties in the 1980s and early 1990s. And the burden of this policy fell directly on the massive rural population, whose rampant reproduction was most feared.

The demographics coincided with socioeconomic restructurings breaking apart the collective economy. Previously dominated by the collective, where labor was pooled, the rural economic unit was returned to the family. Production was now to be accounted for within the family. It thus became imperative for peasants to concentrate labor within the family, for which more children (particularly boys) was a better strategy. The economics of more children for individual peasant families butted up against the national policy calling for fewer children overall. The convergence triggered unrest and massive coercion in the countryside.

On the sexist assumption that birth control is a women's issue, and thus with women's fertility as the overriding target of population policy, the Women's Federation was put in charge of the draconian implementation, permanently tarnishing its reputation as an advocacy group for women. Soon, the policy triggered a rise in female infanticide, as girl children became disposable because the only labor that counted within the family was male labor. (Girls marry out of the family.) A socioeconomic predisposition favoring boys quickly was translated into a revived cultural prejudice against girls, with the two aspects reinforcing one another completely.

In the mid-1990s, the one-child policy was partially, if selectively, relaxed, as the life cycles of the baby boom generation advanced beyond childbearing years. While all population controls are contested in the rural areas—where intrusive monitoring and coercive abortions were (and to some extent continue to be) frequent—the one-child advocacies took root in urban areas and became the norm by the end of the 1980s. Boys and girls in urban families are equally spoiled. In the countryside, two decades of female infanticide has led to a shortage of girls. Aside from the infants thereby killed or not born, the gender imbalance has become an enormous social problem leading, among other things, to entrenched criminality (involving kidnapping of women for marriage, now often crossing into Vietnam, Cambodia, North Korea, and Laos).

In addition, age-based population imbalance is on the horizon and now urgently debated. While the health of the population has declined, primarily due to the withdrawal of medical care in the rural areas since the breakup of communes and the vast pollution of the water supplies, nevertheless, an aging population with fewer young people to support it is a growing problem. The demographics, economics, and social impact of this skewing continue as problems into the present.

Urban and Industrial Reform

Reform of the urban economy proceeded on the heels of the initial restructuring of the rural economy. Industry had long been structured on socialist principles, with job security (known as the "iron rice bowl"), housing, education, and medical care provided for workers and their families. This was all accommodated within the "work unit." The socialist economy was not based on the compiling of private profit, but on the leading role of the proletariat in furthering the revolution.

With urban reform and de-Maoification, profit became more important. As profit became the measure of success, the cradle-to-grave social programs became liabilities, and workers became expendable and exploitable. The whole state-owned structure first was transformed in the 1980s through a series of reforms in management, profit-making, and responsibility systems loosely modeled on the rural contract system. Yet, as the increasingly porous patchwork of the state-owned economy confronted a new vibrant private economy growing alongside it (with none of the social responsibilities attached to the state sector), it became very apparent that state-run factories could not compete. They were then more or less wiped out. As a result, as one sociologist has recently analyzed, China currently has two main industrial types, the "rustbelt" and the "sunbelt."[8]

In the state-owned sector, over the course of the 1980s and into the 1990s, in the name of efficiency and streamlining, the first to be laid off or encouraged to leave were women workers. They were instructed, in private and public rhetoric, to return to the home, where life was more comfortable and supposedly more suited to the female psyche and physical condition. Decades of state feminism exhorting women to participate fully in production as a right and obligation of socialist citizenry screeched to a halt. Next to go were the older (male) workers, who could not or would not adapt to the economistic measures of productivity now being promoted. Accustomed to working in the context of at least some factory floor democracy, members of this generation felt the new regime of profit-driven managerialism was improper, unsocialist, and unseemly. It didn't matter, as they soon lost their jobs. Finally, many state-owned industries, now with skeletal staffs and production teams, were allowed to go bankrupt, of which workers were usually not informed until they found themselves locked out and the assets being sold out from under them. By the time they could organize a protest, the industrial plant was no more, and the leadership had fled. Left was the housing—now maintained by no one—and the crumbling schools and medical clinics, abandoned once state and industry funding had dried up. Massive numbers of state employees were left to fend for themselves.

This is the situation comprising the rustbelt: old state-owned industries, with pensioned and laid-off employees cut off from their sources of income and medical care. With properties privatized, several generations of workers, who grew up and worked under the socialist system, accepting lower wages in return for state benefits and a stake in the products of their labor, are bereft. The leading role of the proletariat in the revolution has devolved completely. There is little recourse for the workers, as local leaders often are in cahoots with the plant managers and leaders. These workers have seen an absolute decline in their standards of living, have no medical care, and have no future in the new economy.

By contrast, there are the "sunbelt" enterprises, mostly foreign-invested sweatshops or manufacturing plants located in the fast-developing southern regions close to Hong Kong or Taiwan. The city of Shenzhen adjacent to Hong Kong is exemplary. Declared a "Special Economic Zone" in the late 1980s, Shenzhen and its environs were exempted from the socialist legal system pertaining to the rest of the country, and promoted as a developmental zone with completely different rules. This encouraged foreign investment—primarily from Hong Kong, Taiwan, the United States, and Japan—whose rates of profit repatriation could skyrocket with no fuss. Wages were set very low, labor regulations were relaxed, taxes were nonexistent, and land was given away (after being expropriated through eminent domain from those living on it). A small village, Shenzhen became within a decade a veritable boomtown, as lawless as it is exciting, as astoundingly rapacious as it is architecturally stunning in its disorganized growth.

Shenzhen and its environs now draw millions of young women from interior China to work in the sweatshops and plants for low wages. In exchange, these girls escape at least temporarily the stifling atmosphere of a dying rural China. Leaving parents and siblings behind, the mostly unmarried young women (their average age ranges from fifteen to twenty-three) flock to the factories, sending part of their wages home to help support their natal families. Remaining wages in hand, they join the ranks of urban consumers at the lowest end of that totem pole. With some education, no access to medical care, and the "freedom" of job mobility (that is, no job security), these girls work in the midst of a globalized economic system, whose practices post-Mao Chinese policy enthusiastically helps elaborate. For, the inexhaustability of the Chinese labor force contributes enormously to the enhancement of the global labor regime, in which labor is disposable and capital moves at will.

The financial meltdown and global economic crisis begun in 2008 and continuing apace is now threatening this model of development. It remains to be seen how China will respond. Signs of intensified police action, to rein in potential unrest, do not bode well for China's workers.

The Household Registration System and Internal Migrant Labor

The Chinese household registration system facilitates the pliability of this new labor regime. From the late 1950s Great Leap period onward, China promoted a household registration system to designate each person's hometown and right of residence. Originally conceived as a way to restrict rural-to-urban migration and the overcrowding of cities, the system forced peasants to remain on the land. As such, it functioned to lock into place a fundamentally uneven distribution of collectively produced social wealth. (By the same token, the slums that ringed cities in the undeveloped world were completely avoided in China at the time.)

An urban residence registration confers on urban citizens the right to public education for their children and public medical care in local hospitals and clinics. Rural citizens have the right to a state-allotted plot of land—now increasingly jeopardized by illegal seizures and expropriations as well as by the new property law—and nothing more. With the breakup of the communes, which used to fund village schools and clinics, access to educational and medical facilities has all but disappeared in many rural areas, particularly those in the interior farther from the coastal boomtowns. The central and provincial governments have not picked up the slack.

In the 1980s, as the labor needs of booming cities grew, internal migration also grew. With the final dissolution of state rationing and the floating of all commodities on the market, it became possible for peasants to reside on the margins of the cities without worrying about access to goods (they could use money to purchase, whereas previously, urban residents had access to many things only through residence-issued ration tickets). By the 1990s, as regulations for urban housing and labor mobility also gave way, more rural migrants arrived to take up service, construction, and other work at unregulated and thus very low wages in the cities. Up to two hundred million people—equivalent to two-thirds of the American population—move around every year. Women became nannies (formerly seen as a bourgeois practice, now common in most urban intellectual and entrepreneurial homes) or joined the sweatshop labor force; men joined the urban workforce in manual and other sorts of undesirable labor, such as trash collecting, recycling, and rag picking.

While this employment provides a better income than could be earned on the land, without the right to urban residence, these migrant laborers live a most precarious existence. They can be deported to their hometowns at any time of the government's choosing; they have no recourse to medical care, other than through exorbitant fees; they work under unregulated conditions, with few safety or other guarantees; and they discover that the legal system does not usually work for them. Wages can be depressed to the lowest possible rate—and sometimes, wages are not even paid for work done—and migrant laborers have had little leverage over the situation.

With people unmoored and portions of the rural population rendered destitute, gangs and criminality have made a roaring comeback, as have drug use, prostitution, and all manner of social ills previously stamped out. Everything from internal labor recruitment and overseas labor smuggling to child bride kidnapping, from drug cartels to prostitution are now parts of criminal gang activities stretching across the nation and its borders. An overextended, underfinanced, and often corrupted police force cannot keep up or is bought off by the gang system to keep the peace.

1989: The Demise of Communism and the Tian'anmen Social Movement and Massacre

As China's marketization and de-Maoificiation were proceeding under the firm guidance of the CCP, and as China normalized trade and diplomatic relations with the Western world, the socialist bloc of which China had always been a notional part crumbled. The specter of the overthrow of communist states from Poland, East Germany, and Romania to the Soviet Union, Albania, and beyond struck fear in the hearts of CCP leaders. It hardened among many of them a resolve that no such thing would happen in China.

Although Deng Xiaoping had been consistently critical of the Soviet leader Mikhail Gorbachev's political reforms—encapsulated in the concept of *glasnost*—he had sought to normalize PRC-USSR relations, to mute the two decades of mutual vitriol. In the midst of this initiative, Gorbachev indicated that the Soviet Union would no longer enforce communism in Eastern Europe. Each of those countries had burgeoning political movements, and the removal of the threat of Soviet intervention immediately led to the fall one by one of the governments of Eastern bloc states in violent and jubilant mass activity. Wang Hui, the Tsinghua University scholar, wrote about this spectacle from the vantage of China, "The year 1989 was a historical watershed; nearly a century of socialist practice came to an end. Two worlds became one: a global capitalist world."[9]

As these events were unfolding on China's ideological doorstep, as it were, a remarkable event was getting under way in China. In the midst of internal economic transformations and the global collapse of the socialist world, a post–Cultural Revolution generation of university students was coming through the newly revitalized educational system. Caught in the interstices of a crumbling socialist regime and a developing capitalist one, this new generation was particularly concerned to secure their post-educational lives in a manner of their own choosing. And yet, economic instability and social insecurity were making this quite difficult.

Most important to many students was the rampant systemic corruption they experienced as a part of their everyday lives. To get anything done required a "backdoor" of connections to power. The gathering crisis of the planned economy thus met the reality of market and power monopolization through corruption, all of which led to snowballing injustice and inequality. This spurred huge demand for an increased tempo of reform, which could possibly clear away the obstacles to social justice, as conceived by students. It soon appeared to students—and to many others—that a transformation of political structure was necessary to accompany the rapid economic transformation. In this light, Gorbachev's glasnost was attractive.

Again, it was the death of a leader that provided a spark to action. Hu Yaobang, who had risen and fallen in the 1980s, died on April 15, 1989. Hu was lionized by many students as a Party spokesperson for the political openings they hoped for. While this was a vast misreading of Hu's overall position, that is not the point. For, Hu had been deposed by Deng Xiaoping in 1986 precisely on suspicion of his sympathies for some form or degree of democratization. The deposing allowed students to identify Hu with their political cause and social malaise. On the evening of Hu's death, students went to Tian'anmen Square to lay wreaths at the Monument to the Heroes of the Revolution. This was no innocent act; it was meant as a provocation in emulation of the April 5th (1976) Movement to honor Zhou Enlai. Students spontaneously gathered not only to mourn Hu, but also to press the Party and the state for dialogue and reforms. At first a completely amorphous event, student activities gathered momentum and soon took on organizational form. Daily demonstrations with increasing numbers of participants followed, with "long marches" through the city streets accompanied by the spirited singing of revolutionary songs of defiance. International media quickly focused on the events.

Hu Yaobang's funeral was held on April 22, and more than a hundred thousand people stood on the Square outside the Great Hall of the People in defiance of a government decree banning the public from the Square. Deng Xiaoping lashed out in an editorial of April 26, declaring the students and others part of a conspiracy to overthrow the Communist Party. Deng's elevation of the movement to an anti-Party conspiracy inflamed the situation, as students had been quite careful to avoid any suggestion of anti-Party rhetoric or activity. The editorial, rather than tamp down and frighten the students, stimulated their anger and activism.

The seventieth anniversary of the May 4th (1919) Movement was the occasion for a new spurt in activities. More than three hundred thousand people filled city streets for marches culminating in Tian'anmen Square. Soon, under the watchful eyes of the enormous Mao portrait hanging on the Gate of Heavenly Peace, the Square was occupied: tent cities sprang up, student guards took on the responsibility for security and sanitation, and food deliveries were arranged. Classes were boycotted, and high school and junior high students joined in. The Party and state leadership were paralyzed. The specter of the Red Guards appeared. On May 15, Gorbachev arrived for a historic visit to China—the first since the Sino-Soviet split in 1960; Chinese authorities were unable to bring him to downtown Beijing because of the student occupation of the space.

By this time, urban dwellers from all walks of life had joined the students, in sympathy and in protest against government corruption, inaction, and stalling. Workers organized and staked out a presence on the Square. Journalists and editors of the Party mouthpieces, such as *People's Daily* and the Central Television Station, began publishing and broadcasting pieces sympathetic to the students. They marched behind banners to make their own voices heard. The movement spread to urban centers across China. While peasants remained mostly uninvolved, most cities were turned upside down by student, worker, and common people's activism. No single voice in all of this prevailed, although Beijing remained the center of the movement, and a small group of elected students from Beijing-area Universities represented the whole.

Divisions within the Party and state became evident. Behind closed doors, there was a great debate about how to handle the movement. It took Deng Xiaoping several weeks to assert his will and leadership. As the student occupation of central Beijing stretched into its third and fourth weeks, martial law was declared. This indicated a factional victory for Deng. Some students embarked on a hunger strike to protest and to press Party and state leaders into a dialogue with student leaders. Deng Xiaoping was induced to agree. In a dramatic encounter at the Great Hall of the People, hunger-wracked students hooked up to IV drips lectured Deng on democracy and freedom. The performance was magnificent, the spectacle more dramatic than any reality TV could possibly dream up. Enraged and upstaged, Deng's resolve to crack down was enhanced.

Meanwhile, Zhao Ziyang, the then–Party General Secretary, having lost the intra-Party struggle, decided to make his oppositional stance public. Zhao went to the Square to meet with students in a quiet but powerful midnight encounter. Deng was incensed. The PLA was immediately called in to restore order. Stopped on the outskirts of Beijing by citizens who gathered to talk the troops out of advancing, the PLA's progress into the center initially stalled. Local commanders and troops were quite hesitant about shooting at unarmed civilians. New troop contingents were called in from the provinces; these had no connection to Beijing or to the movement. They could be counted upon to obey orders without question. By the end of May, Beijing was surrounded.

A last-ditch effort was made by workers and common urbanites to defend the city against the PLA. It failed. On the night of June 3, 1989, troops moved into central Beijing, shooting their way through crowds of workers, onlookers, and regular Beijingers. Hundreds, if not thousands, were killed in the glare of media coverage. At the edge of the Square itself, the PLA stopped to give the remaining students there an opportunity to vacate the space. Those who refused to leave were shot down or run over on June 4. No accurate numbers of the dead are available.

Different cities dealt with activists differently. For example, Shanghai, under the leadership of its Party secretary Jiang Zemin, refused to use violence. After witnessing and protesting the events in Beijing, Shanghai crowds dispersed on June 5 and 6. Jiang ordered the arrest of student and intellectual leaders of the Shanghai movement, but defied Beijing and would not engage in mass arrests or violence.

Once again, silence fell in China, other than the shrill denunciations of the "counter-revolutionary" student movement and the self-congratulations about the correctness of the Party's decision to suppress the threat. The forces of law and order swept into schools, factories, and media outlets across the nation to arrest those held responsible in addition to anyone who had participated. Over forty thousand people were swept up in the dragnet; the vast majority of those imprisoned and executed were workers or other ordinary citizens. Student leaders ran for their lives, many making it across borders before being caught. Others were trapped and hauled back for court hearings and punishments. Students remaining on campuses were sent home. Workers resumed production under a vise of surveillance. New news anchors and editorialists obedient to the Party line appeared as if by magic. Zhao Ziyang was formally purged from his posts. (He died under house arrest of illness in 2007.) Other leaders were promoted or demoted, depending on the positions taken in the final weeks of the events. Shanghai Party chief, Jiang Zemin, was promoted and eventually replaced Deng Xiaoping, when the latter's health failed.

The Southern Tour and the Retreat of Politics

The global reaction to the Tian'anmen massacre was a temporary retreat from investment in China. Yet Chinese leaders worked hard to normalize the situation, by proceeding with economic measures intended to encourage individual consumerism and enrichment. The temporary downturn in foreign investment proved to be easily overcome by the return to economic activity and the almost immediate dissipation of political passions in the wake of the vast repressions. With critics silenced—either through emigration, imprisonment, or self-imposed censorship—economic programs could proceed away from the glare of public scrutiny.

By 1992, Deng Xiaoping had formally given up his titles to handpicked successors, primarily Jiang Zemin, the erstwhile Shanghai Party chief. Deng nevertheless remained extremely influential and kept his hands in politics and policy until his death. In January, in part to escape the winter chill in the North, Deng embarked on a long tour of the south, including the Special Economic Zone of Shenzhen, Guangzhou, and Shanghai. Much as when Mao had toured the people's communes and pronounced them "good" in the mid-1950s, Deng's January 1992 pronouncement that economic development was "good" and should be deepened stimulated an all-out market-based race for personal wealth and economic power all over China.

This new round of accumulation and expropriation, in turn, inaugurated a new spurt in foreign investment, with multinational corporations and banks, as well as smaller-scale investors from Taiwan and Hong Kong, now assured that economics would trump all and profit-killing political instability would be crushed. China's extraordinary decade and a half of double-digit growth began and has only recently begun to abate. With economic growth proclaimed the highest good, politics of any sort retreated to a position of marginality bordering on invisibility. Intellectual life was revitalized after two years of silence, and it now proceeds on the premise of a "professionalization" explicitly precluding politics. This is as much a development of self-censorship as of new conviction in the superiority of depoliticized scholarship and objective empiricism, of the catastrophic consequences of "radicalism" and political engagement.

INTERLUDE: WANG HUI INTERVIEW, CONTINUED

Q: How is "new left" defined, and what do you, its supposed leader, think of this label?

A: . . . I am reluctant to be labeled as such. It is my opponents who label me a leader of the (Chinese) New Left. After the Cultural Revolution, "left" became a notorious word. It means sympathetic to the "Gang of Four." To be labeled "new left" is to be deprived of the right to speech. In addition, in the 1990s, when depoliticization, marketization, professionalization, and neoliberalism came to prevail, "new left" became a dirty label. I was attacked by different people . . .

Q: What are the questions for scholarship in the post-Mao period?

A: . . . Marxism has been completely replaced by modernization theories. This is the shift from one type of deterministic narrative to another—from revolutionary teleology to depoliticized economic developmental teleology. This shift got under way in the mid-1980s and has continued strongly ever since. In the mid-1990s, under the impact of extensive marketization and globalization, this trend was reinforced. . . . In historical research, emphasis is now on a normative and typical nationalism; this is the direct result of a de-emphasis on revolution and radical ideas or movements.

In perhaps the most un-Maoist of all developments in post-Mao China, as an analytical and philosophical matter, economics and social development are now thoroughly divorced from politics. The definition of politics now is monopolized by state and Party procedures, while economics and social development are monopolized by market-defined success.

Deng Xiaoping died in 1997 at the age of 92 with the post-Mao reforms as his major legacy. He was the last of Mao's revolutionary generation.

Consuming Mao

With the marketization of everything, it was only a matter of time before Mao too became an item of consumption. In the early 1980s, people threw away many Mao items: the aluminum badges embossed with Mao's image and sayings (by 1969, 4.8 billion of these with 100,000 different motifs had been printed[10]), the little red books, the Red Guard armbands, the clocks and vases and pencil holders and paperweights sporting Mao in all conceivable dignified poses, the propaganda posters, . . . the detritus of a revolutionary dream and desire now repudiated. With the passage of years, however, all of these items, and more, have become valuable, as collectibles, as museum items, or merely as one commodified historical curiosity among others. This has fueled a huge market in reproductions, as well as enormous domestic and global collectors markets in genuine pieces of the period. Mao is for sale, and he sells.

Beginning in the early 1990s, several other faces of Mao also emerged. One is Mao, the publishing sensation. Everybody who had ever been close to him, had touched him, had had anything, even peripherally, to do with him, personally wrote a memoir claiming to reveal the "true" Mao. From salacious gossip to character assassination to hagiography: all of this is represented in the flood of published material featuring stories of Mao. Such materials continue to pour forth.

Another face of Mao is his representation in art. During Maoist times, Mao's image was everywhere, his portrait hanging in every office, and his statues dotting the landscapes of every city and town in the nation. His portrait continues to hang at the center of the nation, in Tian'anmen Square, even as most of his statues have long since been hauled away. In the early 1990s, Chinese artists, such as Zhang Hongtu, began to play with Mao images. Zhang's most famous painting of Mao depicts him in a loincloth as acupuncture art. Parts of his body are indicated as acupressure points, but the labels are political and ideological, not medical. Taking Mao's image a step further were international fashion designers, such as the Hong Kong native Vivienne Tam, who used Andy Warhol–like Mao images in her fabric designs.

A popular version of Mao is as talisman. In the 1990s, taxi drivers all over China began to hang portraits of Mao on their rearview mirrors. When questioned about the meaning, most replied that he functioned as protection against accidents and misfortune. In temples in the south, Mao was seated among various Buddhas, as one god among others. The religious and superstitious appropriation of Mao is particularly ironic, in light of Mao's lifelong hostility to the divine and belief in fate.

Hong Kong

Hong Kong's retrocession to Chinese sovereignty was scheduled for June 1997. As the last symbol of China's weakness during the imperialist period,

Hong Kong's continued domination by a British colonial government was a constant thorn in the sides of Chinese leaders. Its return was desired as final proof, if any were needed, of China's elevation by the Western powers into the ranks of what used to be called the "civilized" nations.

Unfortunately for Deng Xiaoping, he did not live to experience the event itself. However, it was under his negotiating instructions and with his handpicked team that Britain was induced to hand Hong Kong back to China on essentially Chinese terms. The defeat of imperialism had been one of Mao's central quests; with Hong Kong's return, this at least was fulfilled.

The 2008 Beijing Olympics and Beyond

After its bid for the 2004 Olympics was rejected, China made absolutely certain that its 2008 bid would be unbeatable. The Beijing Committee assembled a team comprising the award-winning filmmaker Zhang Yimou, well-known actors, spokespeople whose linguistic skills were impeccable: the most worldly and cosmopolitan group it could find. With dour Party officials and state bureaucrats taking a decidedly backseat in public to these beautiful people, the Beijing bid won in the second round of voting in 2001. Celebrations in Beijing were wild. Tian'anmen Square was filled with joyous urbanites; a magnificent fireworks display was unleashed; jubilant crowds bursting with nationalistic pride roamed the city, congratulating friends and strangers alike. In the provinces, the mood was less giddy. Most knew the national budget would be bled dry by Olympics-related construction; this could only be detrimental to those locations not designated part of the Olympics bonanza. Even Beijingers soon became skeptical, as financial and architectural boondoggles mounted, huge migrant labor construction crews camped out all over the city in makeshift housing, and the massive expropriations of property and personal enrichments proceeded under the cover of Olympics preparations. Many now wish the Olympics had been held anywhere but in Beijing.

The reduction of Mao's dream of socialist modernization to a crass fulfillment of nationalist pride was completed with the successful running of the 2008 Olympics in Beijing. With the Olympic slogan "One world, one dream," Mao's dream is clearly not the one being dreamt in today's Beijing! Rather, it is the nightmare overcome. Even the opening ceremonies—spectacular and comprehensive as they were in ranging over five thousand years of Chinese civilization—had no room for even a mention of Mao.

Thirty years after the death of Mao and Deng Xiaoping's rise to power, China under CCP rule is a global cultural hotspot as well as an economic powerhouse. Chinese language learning is booming across the world. China's influence and attraction is manifest from Africa and Latin America to the United States, Europe, and Asia. Despite a spate of terrible publicity —most recently tied to lead paint in toys, toxic toothpaste, environmental disasters, slave labor, repression in Tibet, Olympic torch protests, poison milk powder that kills children, and so on—China's cachet seems quite firm. The breathlessness generated by a country growing at breakneck speed seems to appeal to practically everyone.

Modernization certainly is happening in China today. It is ugly, uneven, and unjust, even as it can also appear exhilarating, exciting, and extraordinary. How Mao is connected to this process actually is tangential to what Mao himself represented as a historical actor and as a philosopher of revolution and modernization. Only in repudiating Maoism and everything Mao stood for is it possible for current Communist Party leaders to retain Mao as their fig leaf of legitimacy. The current Party slogan of building a "harmonious society" is just about as far from Mao's vision of revolutionary leaping as one can get! Whether the current extraordinary pace of China's growth can be sustained, therefore, has very much less to do with Mao and his legacy than with the current and future configurations of the global economy, politics, and society and with China's place therein. In this sense, while China certainly is a question for the Chinese to resolve, that resolution poses questions for the rest of us as well.

Notes

1. China in the World in Mao's Youth

1. Edgar Snow, *Red Star over China*, 112–24.
2. "Mao Zedong's Funeral Oration in Honor of His Mother" (October 8, 1919), in Stuart Schram, ed., *Mao's Road to Power: Revolutionary Writings*, Vol. 1, 417–18.
3. Snow, *Red Star over China*, 115.

2. From Liberal to Communist

1. "A Study of Physical Education," 113, 119, in Schram, ed., *Mao's Road to Power* 1:113.
2. "Commentary on the Suicide of Miss Zhao," in Schram, ed., *Mao's Road to Power*, 1:421. All citations from Mao's writings on Miss Zhao are taken from 421–49.

3. Toward the Peasant Revolution

1. Lu Xun, "In Memory of Miss Liu Hezhen," in Hua R. Lan and Vanessa L. Fong, eds. *Women in Republican China: A Sourcebook*, 110–15.
2. Schram, ed., *Mao's Road to Power*, 2:430.
3. Ibid., 433, 434, 452–53.

4. Establishing Revolutionary Bases

1. Schram, ed., *Mao's Road to Power*, 3:61. For a description of Huangyangjie, see Stephen C. Averill, *Revolution in the Highlands: China's Jinggangshan Base Area*, 1.
2. Averill, *Revolution in the Highlands*, 310.
3. Cited in Maurice Meisner, *Mao Zedong*, 60.
4. "Oppose Bookism," in Schram, ed., *Mao's Road to Power*, 3:419.
5. Schram, ed., *Mao's Road to Power*, 5:8.

5. Ya'an, War of Resistance, and Civil War

1. Mao, "Declaration Opposing Japan's Annexation of North China and Chiang Kaishek's Treason" (June 15, 1935), in Schram, ed., *Mao's Road to Power*, 5:12.
2. "Telegram from Mao Zedong and Zhou Enlai to Zhang Xueliang" (December 13, 1936, at noon), ibid., 539.
3. "Two Principles in Negotiating with Nanjing" (April 1, 1937, 2:00 A.M.), ibid., 632.
4. Mao, "On Protracted War," in *Selected Works of Mao Tse-tung*, Vol. 2, 121, 125.
5. Ibid., 133.
6. Cited in Mark Selden, *The Yenan Way*, 125.
7. Ibid., 260–61.
8. I was assisted in this interview by my student Ms. Zhu Qian and my longtime friend Mr. Wu Hongsen. The interview was conducted by me in Chinese; Qian did the taping and transcribing, as well as the preliminary translations of the interview into English.
9. Ding Ling, "Thoughts on March 8th," in Tani E. Barlow, ed., *I Myself Am a Woman: Selected Writings of Ding Ling*, 317.
10. Ibid., 319.
11. Zhou Enlai, "Zenyang zuo yige hao lingdaozhe" [How to be a good leader], *Selected Works of Zhou Enlai*, Vol. 1, 132.
12. "Circular to Zhou Enlai and Others from Mao Zedong, Zhu De, and Wang Jiaxiang . . . ," in Schram, ed., *Mao's Road to Power*, 7:633.
13. "To Zhou Enlai and Ye Jianying Concerning Political and Military Preparations for an Overall Counterattack," ibid., 637.
14. "Dispatch to Liu Shaoqi Regarding the Estimate of the Situation after the 'January 17' Order," ibid., 654.
15. "Directive of Mao Zedong, Zhu De, and Wang Jianxiang on Guidelines for the Action of the New Fourth Army after the Southern Anhui Incident," ibid., 660.
16. "To Mao Anying and Mao Anqing," ibid., 665.

6. Stabilizing Society and Socialist Transition

1. Mao, "The Chinese People Have Stood Up," *Selected Works of Mao Tse-tung*, 5:15.
2. Ibid.
3. Li Zhisui, *The Private Life of Chairman Mao*, 51.
4. Mao, "Always Keep to the Style of Plain Living and Hard Struggle" (October 26, 1949), *Selected Works of Mao Tse-tung*, 5:23.
5. Mao, "Speech on Arrival at Moscow Train Station" (December 16, 1949), Kau and Leung, eds., *The Writings of Mao Zedong*, 1:51.
6. Mao, "Speech on Departure from Moscow" (February 17, 1950), ibid., 61.

7. "Chinese bid farewell to Mao Zedong's second son," *People's Daily Online*, April 2, 2007, at http://english.people.com.cn/20070402_363016.html (accessed July 2008).

8. Mao, "Soliciting Suggestions on the Question of Strategy for Dealing with Rich Peasants," *Selected Works of Mao Tse-tung*, 5:24–25.

9. Meisner, *Mao's China and After*, 98–99.

10. Mao, "Orders for the Chinese People's Volunteers" (October 8, 1950), in Kau and Leung, eds., *The Writings of Mao Zedong*, 1:139–40.

11. Mao, "Comment on Hearing of Mao Anying's Death" (November 1950), ibid., 148.

12. Mao, "Oppose the Bourgeois Ideology in the Party" (August 12, 1953), ibid., 367–68, 369, 365.

13. Mao, "Preface and Editor's Notes to Material on the Hu Feng Counterrevolutionary Clique" (May–June 1955), ibid., 1:562–63.

14. Meisner, *Mao's China and After*, 141.

15. Mao, "On the Cooperativization of Agriculture" (July 31, 1955), Kau and Leung, eds., *The Writings of Mao Zedong*, 1:591.

7. Great Leap and Restoration

1. Mao, "Situation in the Summer of 1957," *Selected Works of Mao Tse-tung*, 5:475.

2. Li Zhisui, *The Private Life of Chairman Mao*, 269.

3. Mao, "The United States Must Withdraw Its Troops from Taiwan" (May 10, 1959), *On Diplomacy*, 294.

4. Li Zhisui, *The Private Life of Chairman Mao*, 259.

5. Mao, "Speech at the Lushan Conference," in Schram, ed., *Chairman Mao Talks to the People*, 141–42.

6. Mao, "Speech at the Lushan Conference," ibid., 139.

7. Mao, "Speech at the Enlarged Session of the Military Affairs Committee and the External Affairs Conference" (September 11, 1959), ibid., 145.

8. Mao, "Speech at the Tenth Plenum of the Eighth Central Committee" (the morning of September 24, 1962 in the Huai-jen Hall), ibid., 192.

9. Meisner, *Mao's China and After*, 255.

10. Ibid., 267.

11. Mao, "Speech at the Tenth Plenum of the Eighth Central Committee," in Schram, ed., *Chairman Mao Talks to the People*, 193.

12. Zhou Enlai, "Report on the Work of the Government" (December 1964), cited in Meisner, *Mao's China and After*, 267.

13. Mao, "Talk with Edgar Snow on International Issues" (January 9, 1965), in *On Diplomacy*, 416.

14. "American Imperialism is Closely Surrounded by the Peoples of the World" (1964), in Timothy Cheek, ed., *Mao Zedong and China's Revolution*, 167–68.

8. Cultural Revolution: Politics in Command

1. *Peking Review* 9, no. 24 (June 10, 1966): 8–9.
2. Mao, "Talk to the Leaders of the Centre" (July 21, 1966), in Schram, ed., *Chairman Mao Talks to the People*, 255.
3. K. H. Fan, ed., *The Chinese Cultural Revolution: Selected Documents*, 308.
4. Cited in Roderick MacFarquhar and Michael Schoenhals, *Mao's Last Revolution*, 52.
5. Mao, "Speech at a Meeting with Regional Secretaries and Members of the Cultural Revolutionary Group of the Central Committee" (July 22, 1966), in Schram, ed., *Chairman Mao Talks to the People*, 257, 258.
6. Mao, "A Letter to the Red Guards of Tsinghua University Middle School" (August 1, 1966), ibid., 260–1.
7. Mao, "Talk at a Meeting of the Central Cultural Revolution Group" (January 9, 1967), ibid., 276.
8. Mao, "Talks at Three Meetings with Comrades Chang Ch'un-ch'iao [Zhang Chunqiao] and Yao Wen-yüan [Yao Wenyuan]" (February 1967), ibid., 279.
9. Meisner, *Mao's China and After*, 334.
10. Mao, "Talk at the First Plenum of the Ninth Central Committee of the Chinese Communist Party" (April 28, 1969), in Schram, ed., *Chairman Mao Talks to the People*, 282, 284, 289
11. Ibid., 287.

9. Cultural Revolution: Denouement and Death

1. I interviewed Mr. Kohso at my New York University office in February 2009.
2. Cited in MacFarquhar and Schoenhals, *Mao's Last Revolution*, 309.
3. Mao, "The People of the Whole World Unite, Defeat the US Aggressors and All Their Lackeys" (May 20, 1970), in Mao, *On Diplomacy*, 444.
4. Mao, "Imperialism is Afraid of the Third World" (July 11, 1970), ibid., 446.
5. Mao, "If Nixon Is Willing to Come, I am Ready to Hold Talks with Him" (December 18, 1970), ibid., 449–50.
6. See Jin Qiu, *The Culture of Power: The Lin Biao Incident in the Cultural Revolution*, 11–12.
7. Meisner, *Mao Zedong*, 187.
8. "Summary of Chairman Mao's Talks with Responsible Comrades at Various Places during his Provincial Tour" (mid-August to September 12, 1971), in Schram, ed., *Chairman Mao Talks to the People*, 290–99.
9. "Lin Biao's Return," *International Herald Tribune*, July 16, 2007.
10. Cited in Wang Ban, *The Sublime Figure of History*, 212.
11. Cited in MacFarquhar and Shoenhals, *Mao's Last Revolution*, 348.
12. Meisner, *Mao's China and After*, 395.

10. Reform, Restoration, and Repudiation

1. This interview was conducted with the assistance of my student Ms. Zhu Qian, who transcribed and prepared a preliminary translation of the text. Below are excerpts from a three-hour-long discussion.
2. Meisner, *Mao's China and After*, 443.
3. *Resolution on Certain Questions in the History of Our Party since the Founding of the People's Republic of China*, 31–32.
4. Ibid., 41.
5. Ibid., 42.
6. Ibid., 44.
7. Lin Chun, *The Transformation of Chinese Socialism*, 94–98.
8. Ching Kwan Lee, *Against the Law: Labor Protests in China's Rustbelt and Sunbelt*.
9. Wang Hui, "Contemporary Chinese Thought and the Question of Modernity," 45.
10. Michael Dutton, *Streetlife China*, 240.

Bibliography

Averill, Stephen C. *Revolution in the Highlands: China's Jinggangshan Base Area.* New York: Rowman & Littlefield, 2006.

Barlow, Tani E. *I Myself Am a Woman: Selected Writings of Ding Ling.* Boston: Beacon Press, 1989.

Cheek, Timothy, ed. *Mao Zedong and China's Revolution: A Brief History with Documents.* New York: Bedford/St. Martin's Press, 2002.

Dirlik, Arif, Paul Healy, and Nick Knight, eds. *Critical Perspectives on Mao Zedong's Thought.* Amherst, N.Y.: Humanity Books, 1997.

Dirlik, Arif, and Maurice Meisner, eds. *Marxism and the Chinese Experience.* New York: M. E. Sharpe, 1989.

Dutton, Michael. *Streetlife China.* Cambridge: Cambridge University Press, 1998.

Dutton, Michael, Hsiu-ju Stacy Lo, and Dong Dong Wu. *Beijing Time.* Cambridge, Mass.: Harvard University Press, 2008.

Fan, K. H., ed. *The Chinese Cultural Revolution: Selected Documents.* New York: Monthly Review Press, 1968.

International Herald Tribune. Online edition.

Jin Qiu. *The Culture of Power: The Lin Biao Incident in the Cultural Revolution.* Palo Alto, Calif.: Stanford University Press, 1999.

Knight, Nick. *Rethinking Mao: Explorations in Mao Zedong's Thought.* Lanham, Md.: Lexington Books, 2007.

Kraus, Richard Curt. *The Party and the Arty in China: The New Politics of Culture.* Lanham, Md.: Rowman & Littlefield, 2004.

Lan, Hua R., and Vanessa L. Fong, eds. *Women in Republican China: A Sourcebook.* New York: M. E. Sharpe, 1999.

Lee, Ching-Kwan. *Against the Law: Labor Protests in China's Rustbelt and Sunbelt.* Berkeley: University of California Press, 2007.

Li, Zhisui. *The Private Life of Chairman Mao.* New York: Random House, 1994.

Lin, Chun. *The Transformation of Chinese Socialism.* Durham, N.C.: Duke University Press, 2006.

MacFarquhar, Roderick, and Michael Schoenhals. *Mao's Last Revolution*. Cambridge, Mass.: Harvard University Press, 2006.

Mao Zedong. *Chairman Mao Talks to the People: Talks and Letters, 1956–1971*. Edited by Stuart Schram. New York: Pantheon, 1974.

———. *On Diplomacy*. Beijing: Foreign Language Press, 1998.

———. *Mao's Road to Power: Revolutionary Writings*. 7 vols. Edited by Stuart Schram. New York: M. E. Sharpe, 1992–2005.

———. *Selected Works of Mao Tse-tung*. 5 vols. Peking: Peking Foreign Language Press, 1965.

———. *The Writings of Mao Zedong: 1949–1976*. 2 vols. Edited by Michael Y. M. Kau and John K. Leung. New York: M. E. Sharpe, 1986.

Meisner, Maurice. *Mao's China and After*. 3rd. ed. New York: Free Press, 1999.

———. *Mao Zedong*. Malden, Mass.: Polity Press, 2007.

Peking Review 9, no. 24 (June 10, 1966): 8–9.

People's Online Daily. Http://english.people.com.cn.

Resolution on Certain Questions in the History of Our Party since the Founding of the People's Republic of China. Adopted by the Sixth Plenary Session of the Eleventh Central Committee of the Communist Party of China. June 27, 1981.

Saich, Tony. *The Rise to Power of the Chinese Communist Party*. New York: M. E. Sharpe, 1996.

Selden, Mark. *The Yenan Way*. Cambridge, Mass.: Harvard University Press, 1971.

Siao-yu. *Mao Tse-tung and I Were Beggars*. New York: Colliers Books, 1959.

Snow, Edgar. *Red Star over China*. New York: Bantam Books, 1978.

Wang, Ban. *The Sublime Figure of History: Aesthetics and Politics in Twentieth-Century China*. Palo Alto, Calif.: Stanford University Press, 1997.

Wang, Hui. "Contemporary Chinese Thought and the Question of Modernity." Translated by Rebecca E. Karl. *Social Text*, 12:1 (Summer 1998): 45–66.

Zhou, Enlai. *Zhou Enlai Xuanji* [Selected Works of Zhou Enlai]. 2 Vols. Beijing: Renmin chubanshe, 1980.

Žižek, Slavoj. *Repeating Lenin*. Zagreb: Bastard Books, 2001.

Index

Rebecca E. Karl is an associate professor of history and
East Asian studies at New York University. She is the
author of *Staging the World: Chinese Nationalism at the
Turn of the Twentieth Century* (Duke, 2002). She edited
(with Peter Zarrow) *Rethinking the 1898 Reform Period:
Political and Cultural Change in Late Qing China* (2002)
and (with Saree Makdisi and Cesare Casarino) *Marxism
beyond Marxism* (1996).

Library of Congress Cataloging-in-Publication Data
Karl, Rebecca E.
Mao Zedong and China in the twentieth-century world :
a concise history / Rebecca E. Karl.
p. cm. — (Asia-pacific : culture, politics, and society)
Includes bibliographical references and index.
ISBN 978-0-8223-4780-4 (cloth : alk. paper)
ISBN 978-0-8223-4795-8 (pbk. : alk. paper)
1. Mao, Zedong, 1893–1976. 2. Heads of state—China—
Biography. 3. China—History—1949–1976. 4. China—
History—Republic, 1912–1949. I. Title. II. Series: Asia-
Pacific.
DS778.M3K359 2010
951.05092—dc22
[B]
2010005250

Made in the USA
Monee, IL
12 September 2023

42621906R00125